W9-BPK-503

Czeching In

Adventures Beyond Prague

Lenka Glassner

Lenka Glassner (signature)

Czeching In: Adventures Beyond Prague by Lenka Glassner
©2017 Lenka Glassner

All rights reserved. No portion of this book may be reproduced in any form without permission from the author, except as permitted by U.S. copyright law.

Library of Congress Cataloging-in-Publication-Data
Application in process

Cover art and design by Luboš Groch, Czech Republic
Book design by Margaret Copeland, Terragrafix.com, Berkeley, CA
Map and interior art by Luboš Groch, Czech Republic
Author's photo by Larry Glassner, Clayton, CA
Edited by Jannie Dresser and Fiona Hughes

ISBN Number: 978-0-9991731-0-7

The author wishes to thank the following publication in which one of the stories, in a slightly different form, has already appeared: *Fungi Magazine*, Volume 3 — Number 3.

For Linda and Peter

"No matter how we look at it, reality is always more interesting then whatever we can create."

— MILOŠ FORMAN

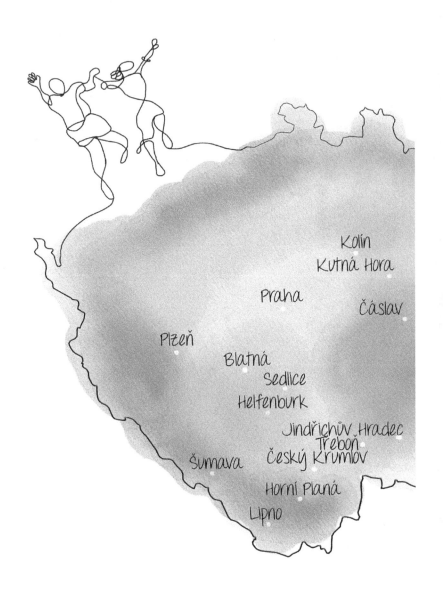

Kolín

Kutná Hora

Praha

Čáslav

Plzeň

Blatná

Sedlice

Helfenburk

Jindřichův Hradec

Třeboň

Šumava   Český Krumlov

Horní Planá

Lipno

Contents

Prologue

Mom packed a bag of potatoes and yellow onions. With the checkered kitchen towel, she set aside a glass jar of strawberry preserves, home-rendered lard, and four jars of preserved pork from my grandparents' slaughtered pig. The usual things one would pack for family vacation. She crammed pots and pans between pillows and sleeping bags. Dad strapped the provisions under the plastic cover on the roof of our brand new 1968 East German-made Trabant. My family's most valued possession looked like that smiling car in the American cartoon "Cars," only ours was weighed down by a load twice its size.

Just a few days before, Dad had shaken his fist at the news reporter on TV, the vein on his neck popping, "Communist bastards!" In the evening, through the thin bedroom wall, I heard his fiery whispering, "They hardly let us exchange any currency. We'll be like beggars. Maybe we should stay home." But the next day, the Trabant's blue toxins puffed happily into the atmosphere. In the back seat, my sister and I, two pigtailed girls in identical yellow t-shirts with pictures of anchors, pinched each other in excitement. Our family's first vacation outside Czechoslovakia had begun.

In the Hungarian deli, my sister and I salivated over the display of their famous sausages. To our surprise, Dad gestured for the clerk to slice a piece, but at the register, he couldn't scrape together enough money to pay for it. When the lady in line behind us opened up her wallet and placed some coins on the counter to make up the difference, Dad's face bloomed red as the paprika sausage.

At the overcrowded campground on the shores of Bulgaria's Black Sea coastline, our fellow Eastern European campers — mostly Poles, East Germans, and Bulgarians — asked where we were from. In a slow, clear voice Dad said, "My jsme Čechoslováci." In every syllable of that last word, I felt his pride take hold: Czech from the west, Slovak to the east. His reverence made a lasting impression on me, yet it didn't make sense. What was so special about being penniless underdogs?

I was born into a country diseased with Communism. Grayness and peeling stucco were visible symptoms of the sickness, but the contamination went deeper. The general apathy consumed my countrymen from within. Like sheep in meager pastures, we kept our eyes on the ground, searching for something special, like toilet paper, Castro's pineapple, or maybe even a morsel of some forgotten, hidden truth.

The school textbooks had all been rewritten to support Communist ideology. My history teachers simply deleted lessons about the early days of Czechoslovakia. Could American kids learn who they are if they were deprived of information about George Washington, the Fourth of July or the Civil War? I couldn't.

In the late 70s I emigrated to the United States. People often stared blankly when I said I was Czechoslovakian. The strange word tangled their tongues. Some asked if Tito was our president. Most thought we spoke Russian, although my Vietnamese hairdresser asked if we spoke "Germanese."

I wished that I was Swiss.

The world has changed much since my early days in America. In 1989, the heat from the collapsing Berlin Wall melted the Iron Curtain into the history books, and democratically elected governments replaced the decaying Communist regimes across the Eastern Bloc: Poland, Hungary, East Germany, Bulgaria, Romania, Czechoslovakia. A newfound democracy opened the door to the outside world. I no longer had to jab my index finger in the middle of my open palm pointing to where my little country, the heart of Europe, is hiding. Through amicable divorce, Czechs and Slovaks became two nations.

"Oh, you're Czech! We love Prague!" American acquaintances announced. With triumph, they added, "We stayed there for three days." In one breath, they named their favorites — the Charles Bridge and the Czech beer. My list wasn't much longer. A mysterious sentence from *National Geographic* magazine kept resurfacing in my mind. *Czechs and Slovaks have some 2,500 noble landmarks listed — enough for a different visit each day for seven years!* A seed of curiosity began to sprout.

My bewildering country — a history book with missing pages. During the 33 years I lived in America, my country's name, size, currency, and politics had dramatically changed. The whole social structure was transformed; even the language went through an inevitable evolution.

Can I still call it home?

The persistent beat of my heart drummed. It's time to know. It's time to go. It's time to understand why my father suddenly looked taller around the campfire at that Bulgarian campground. It's time to find out. Perhaps even to stop wishing to be Swiss.

1. Lerrry Is Coming

Sharing even good news with my parents could be drudgery. In our phone conversations, my role had always been to play defense.

"Why can't you stay longer?" Mom moaned. "Seven weeks is hardly worth the fortune you spend on the flight. And why can't the kids come?"

"The kids are over 30 now," I replied. "Linda is a married woman with a demanding job, and Peter — " I left out the part where their grandson's passion for skateboarding fills his world.

"How about Lerrry? Is Lerrry coming?"

"Which one is Lerrry?" Dad butted in on the second phone.

"Larry is coming," I said, and Mom was finally happy. "Lerrry is coming!" she repeated. I always suspected she favored my American husband over me.

And now the hard part. How to explain that we were not going to stay with them the entire time? In previous visits, my parents claimed the right to our every hour. Mom cooked up a storm, leaving Larry swearing he still has heartburn from all that sauerkraut. Mom and Dad were trying to make up for the years the Iron Curtain blocked the flow of their love. We had not been allowed to see each other for over a decade. I couldn't blame them for wanting to gulp up every last morsel of the rare moments we had together.

This time was different, though. Larry and I were on a mission to explore the country. I took a deep breath, "We're not coming to your house right away. We're going to be doing some traveling. I want to ... umm... I want to write a book

1

about the Czech Republic," I explained sheepishly, hoping my parents would be stunned into silence for a moment.

"Write whatever you like, just don't carry all your money in one place," was Dad's counsel. The stunned silence came from my end. No customary guilt trip? I cleared my throat and said, "About the traveling. When you're touring a castle, do you understand what the docent is talking about?"

"Czech history is too long and too complicated," Mom offered. "I just look around at all the pretty things and try not to lose those felt booties they make you wear over your shoes."

To learn more about my country, Larry and I had searched the library in our California hometown for old *National Geographic* magazines mentioning the Austro-Hungarian Empire, Bohemia, Moravia, Silesia, Czechoslovakia, and the Czech Republic — for me, they are all the same. They are the home of my ancestors and my birth place. There was so much I needed to know before the trip. Some articles had catchy names like "Czechoslovaks, Yankees of Europe" or "Hospitality of the Czechs" written in 1927 before the Czechs and Slovaks even merged, before my parents' time. The oldest story we found was from 1912.

"It's impossible to learn about the Czech history in only seven weeks. You should stay at least seven months," Mom said. She was right. I'd need more than a few *National Geographics* to grasp 20 centuries tempered by many hard fought battles and conflicts in order to forge the Czech nation. One can visit Prague for three days and be in awe over the vast cathedrals and tall towers, but I wanted to untangle the yarns woven into the tapestry of my people. Besides trying to keep the felt booties on, I wanted to understand what the tour guides are talking about.

After our conversation ended, I poured myself a glass of wine, kicked up my feet and said, "At least Lerrry is coming."

2. The Celts

The UPS driver hopped into his brown van in front of our house just as I turned into the cul-de-sac. I saw the box at the top of the stairs, and my heart skipped.

In the living room, I freed the 12 beautiful hardbound history books from the package. They felt wonderful. Heavy and new, they made that crackling resistant sound only pages separated for the very first time make. I could not have dreamed of such a delivery before the borders opened, before the 1989 Velvet Revolution. Even if the government had allowed these books to be published then, in that totalitarian chaos of the Soviet era, one would have had trouble locating sanitary napkins, let alone magisterial books.

During Communism, new books arrived in bookstores on Thursdays. People began to line up at six in the morning, waiting for the store to open at eight. When I was a teenager, I often joined the line along the eaves of the building where I chatted with familiar faces, getting tips on rare, good reads. My "Under the Ledge Book Club" was educational and entertaining. "Sir, sir... a pigeon just shit on you," someone would yell, and the whole line burst out laughing. About half an hour before the store opened, the sales lady came out, announcing, "We got ten Hrabals!" The fortunate first ten people stayed while others hurried to test their luck at another bookstore. It was common knowledge that the sales personnel divided new releases among themselves. Sometimes only one or two new books made it to the regular customers.

How simple things are now: a few Internet keystrokes and less than a week later... *voilà!* Now, I held a complete historical account of my people — the same as God might have in his heavenly encyclopedia.

One by one, I leafed through the books, studying the illustrations of old artifacts, battle scenes, and people dressed in wonderfully impractical clothing. All 12 volumes were titled *Wanderings through Czech History (Toulky Českou Minulostí)*, all written by Petr Hora.

His opening prologue sounded like a poem:

> *"Accept the invitation for a journey against time to places where we live today, to a beautiful land in the center of Europe. We'll walk through a world, for which our mother tongue gave us a lovely name: Domov." (Home)*

I could not have asked for a more passionate guide to hold my hand as I prepared for my journey. Like everything else during the Communist era, the birth of Hora's books didn't come easily. A nonconformist, the historian wasn't allowed to publish. In 1979, when he began his historical *magnum opus,* his formal occupation was a laborer. Hora finished the first two volumes in a wooden trailer he shared with several other workers. Amazingly, under the pseudonym Petr Hořejš, parts of his books showed up weekly in the popular Czech magazine, *The Young World (Mladý Svět).* It became the longest-running series in the history of all Czech magazines. By 2017, over 2,000 thirty-minute episodes were broadcasted on major Czech radio stations.

On previous visits home, I joined my parents on the couch after Sunday lunch of pork, dumplings, and sauerkraut. The three of us propped ourselves with pillows, ready to listen to the "Wanderings." Mom cried, "It's too loud!" Dad shouted in George Costanza's parents' style, "I can barely hear it!" They went back and forth, arguing over the volume until I pointed out that the show had already started. In rare harmony, the three of us leaned back to listen.

Sitting on the floor in my California living room, surrounded by Mr. Hora's books, I didn't even stop to make tea, as I normally would have done. I was eager to let Mr. Hora take me to the distant world of my ancestors.

In 400 BC, according to the first written chronicles, the Celtic tribes who lived in what is now Czech territory, called themselves Boii, from which the name Bohemia derived. In Webster's Dictionary, the definitions for a 'bohemian' is one who follows a countercultural lifestyle — a hippie, hipster, vagabond, but also an artist. I would have liked to imagine the Czechs as free spirits, but I haven't come across many such souls. The Czechs I know are thrifty, industrious, resourceful, and wholesome types, not at all like liberal hipsters or rough, fearless Celtic fighters.

I studied the drawings of Celtic glass, and silver and gold jewelry. The timeless designs were familiar: silver-wired necklaces twisted into Celtic knots. The tools we use today, such as rakes, hammers, files, picks or shovels were the same as the Celts used over 2,400 years ago. No need to improve on perfect designs.

Celts were warriors. Women fought alongside men employing psychological war strategies, making subhuman noises that brought terror to the Greek and Roman soldiers. Because Celts believed the head was where the soul dwells, they displayed their war trophies — enemies' heads — on spikes placed at the front of their houses. To own an enemy head meant to own an opponent completely. In religious rituals, Celts used skulls as chalices to drink from.

As a child, I had leafed tirelessly through my favorite fairy tale book, admiring every detail of the full-page colored drawings. I was especially fascinated with Baba Yaga's house nestled in a thick dark forest. Baba Yaga was a witch who impaled human heads on wooden fence posts around her rustic dwelling. I used to study the listless expressions on the purplish gray faces, savoring the delicious gruesomeness. Now I understand that the illustration was inspired by the ancient Celtic practice.

I was surprised to learn that Celtic warriors had established an advanced monetary system. Not only did they mint the first gold coins, the skull collectors paid taxes.

The Celts copied new skills and inventions they encountered during assaults on more advanced civilizations. Celtic pottery masters began spinning the ceramic wheel, refining crude thick-walled earthenware into fine thin-walled ceramics. Four hundred years later, the Celts were pushed out of Czech lands by northern invaders from Scandinavia. With the obliteration and displacement of the Celts, many of their inventions disappeared as well. Centuries passed until the potter's wheel was reinvented and used again.

The doorbell interrupted my studies. My son Peter beamed at the front door, pulling up his sleeve. In a reverent whisper, he announced, "Check out my new tattoo." I stared at the toothy skull, wondering if this descendant of Bohemians knew of his Celtic ancestor's fetish for skulls. I turned toward the kitchen, but before I could offer Peter something to eat, my little barbarian was already assaulting the refrigerator. He took a huge bite out of a juicy apple and then pointed to the explosion of books on the floor. "What are these?"

"Celts. The people who built the first Czech bridges and roads that Larry and I will soon travel. We're taking a trip to the Czech Republic."

"Cool," said Peter, sitting down cross-legged, reaching for the book closest to him.

"Check out this dude." He pointed to a drawing of a Hun warrior from 400 A.D. "He looks Mongolian, not Slavic."

I scanned the text, so I could translate for my son, feeling guilty for not having taught my children the Czech language. I summarized, "Huns, who came from the Asian steppes, swarmed over Europe and pushed out the Germanic tribes that previously drove away the Celts. Huns ripped the world to shreds wherever their horses took them. Horrified people ran from the bloodthirsty, beastly Huns, causing massive population movement. During those wild years, the first Slavic settlers relocated from somewhere north-east of the Tatra Mountains to today's Czech land."

Peter pointed to the picture of the Hun warrior, "So thanks to this good-looker, today we visit our gramps in the

Czech land instead of Siberia." His cell phone rang. "Got to go." Kiss, hug, and I was left alone with the Huns.

The afternoon faded while I pored over more fascinating details. Huns were cruel even toward their children. As soon as their sons were born, Huns cut up their faces, forcing the infants to withstand the pain before their mothers could nurse them. The Huns were ugly, mean, and dirty; they didn't bathe, nor did they change their clothing. The Huns were described by the Roman historian Jordanes as the offspring of witches and evil spirits from the swamps.

The sound of the opening garage door made me jump. "Hi, Larry!" I yelled, remembering I didn't have supper ready. In the kitchen I threw some leftovers into a frying pan.

After dinner, Larry and I relaxed in our weathered Adirondack chairs at the far corner of our garden. The last afternoon sunlight reached us through the branches of a massive redwood tree. I recapped for Larry what I had learned about Czech history.

"The first recorded people on Czech territory, the Celts, were pushed away by Germanic tribes from Northern Europe and Scandinavia, who were in turn pushed out by Huns. Even though the Huns' episode in central Europe lasted only eight decades — a mere drop in the historical bucket — their presence caused a massive migration. The Huns disappeared after their leader Attila died in the year 453 A.D., which finally made room for my people, the Slavs."

Larry refilled my wine glass, and we sipped in silence for a while, enjoying one of the last warm evenings of the year.

"Huns is spell H-u-n-s," I said.

"Yup, except when talking about the children, they called them honeys," Larry grinned.

"Not from affection, though," I said, "Huns deformed their little girls' heads by bandaging them, forcing their young skulls into sort of a honeycomb shape."

"Lovely," appraised Larry, and then added with his customary sparkle: "Are you ready to accompany your warrior up to his cot?"

3. Shopping for the Trip

Regarding fashion, I was concerned since I had never gotten it right on previous visits to my country. In the late 90s, at my high-school reunion, I was mindful not to come across looking like the American show-off. Instead, I succeeded in coming across like a hillbilly as I entered a room full of the latest styles and fads. Clearly, the days when Czech girls wore high heels with socks, wishfully eyeballing Western tourists, were gone. The jacket I wore to the reunion I later discovered on a discount rack in the newly opened Czech K-Mart. On a tag dangling from its sleeve, the column of prices was crossed in red pen. The final cost was so low that it was a shame not to purchase it, if only for rags. Yet, it sat there. Czech women turned up their noses at my jacket.

With an uneasiness lingering over the reunion jacket memory, Larry and I entered our local sporting and travel-goods store. Our Christmas shopping would focus on our upcoming trip. On a discount rack, we marveled over the fishnet lining underneath the back crease of a shirt. "For a private back scratch on a crowded bus," Larry assessed and unzipped a pocket on the sleeve. "For stashing extra airline peanuts."

An elastic blouse with loops on the sleeves for hooking over the thumbs reminded me of the thumb-loops Mom knitted on sweaters to keep my knuckles warm on winter days. I wouldn't mind being bundled up in such a motherly fashion once again.

"Check this out!" Larry pointed to a camouflage shirt. "It has unzipping sleeves that can be worn inside-out, converted into a raincoat, a backpack or a sleeping bag." With a grin, he added, "Wouldn't it be great if it would? We could leave the suitcase at home."

My favorite item was a pair of underwear advertising on its package *"Seven countries-seventeen days,"* but from the box dangled a $17 price tag. I returned the underwear to its place and handed Larry the camouflaged shirt to try on.

"Very cool," he said pulling it over his head. "Nice," checking the mirror, he appraised his new look. "How much is this anyway? Forty-seven frickin' dollars? On a 70 percent discount rack?" Energetically he took off that lightweight, breathable shirt made with partially recycled material and proceeded to circle the rack as if trying not to anger an unpredictable animal, flicking the white price tags cautiously, at times exclaiming: "Seventy-nine dollars! For that? Are they nuts? Who dresses like this anyway?"

We left the store empty handed.

On Christmas morning Larry grinned when the poinsettia wrapping paper revealed the camouflage pattern of his new shirt. My eyes got big as I discovered yet another token of Larry's thoughtful love, a thumb-loop blouse, and two pairs of *"Seven countries-seventeen days"* underwear. I slipped on the shirt, looped the sleeves over my thumbs and began fantasizing. After I hand-washed my new travel underwear, I would find them completely dry in about an hour, ready for another day on the town in, let's say Žabovřesky nad Ohří.

That same evening I rinsed them and ran a drying test. I was disappointed to find they were still damp in the morning. Furthermore, hanging on the bathroom rod, they had stretched considerably. And they were already long to begin with. Larry chose the above-the-belly cut, the *mama's bloomers*, as my daughter Linda would say. How high will they stretch? I wondered. They exceeded all my expectations. When I slouched, I could pull them up to my armpits and wear them as one-piece swimwear.

9

Six months later Larry and I were squished in a Boeing 747. I slipped off the thumb-loop blouse and climbed across Larry's legs. I needed to use the lavatory at the back of the plane.

Friendly people, I thought, balancing myself in the aisle, steadying myself on the cushiony seat-backs, returning the smiles. A very friendly bunch indeed. Inside the cubbyhole, I slid the door knob to the occupied position, faced the mirror and froze. My seven countries-seventeen days underwear showed a good four inches above the waistline of my jeans. My t-shirt was tucked in them! I didn't come out until the bell chimed and the sign "return to your seat" lit up. I would have preferred crawling underneath the seats. As far as fashion goes, I'll never get it right.

4. Arriving in *Prague*

Prague's taxi drivers have worked long and hard on their reputation. After charging me 800 *korunas* (more than a day's wage) for the 20 minute ride between the airport and the train station, they weren't going to get another penny out of me. Although new regulations have now forced them to behave, there are wounds time just won't heal. I raised my chin and led Larry past the line of taxis to bus number 119 to the Metro station.

Larry plunked our suitcases down at the middle platform of the bus and went to take a seat at the back, looking out of the window, away from our belongings, away from the yellow bilingual sign — *Watch for the pickpockets.*

What was he thinking?

Yep, we were in Prague. A young couple was sucking face with a passion only Czech public transportation can inspire. Are couples this extroverted elsewhere on the planet? The clouds of blooming lilac along the road sending sweet fragrance through the bus might have something to do with it — as long as your lover doesn't crush the mood by leaving all your belongings unattended in a bus filled with pickpockets.

Trying not to stare at the kissing couple, I looked out of the window. In the middle of a traffic line stood a confused pheasant. No one seemed to care about the beautiful, but common bird.

We got off the bus and followed the crowd to the Metro, Prague's communal lifeline. The long neck of the escalator gulped us down and shoved us deep into the city's hidden gut. The crammed train provided a perfect opportunity for eavesdropping on two girls in their mid-twenties. They were discussing love, claiming they don't believe in it.

"It doesn't last. Love always disappears. What happens to it?" said one.

"Over and over, it's always like that," agreed her friend.

Infidelity, often a part of the plot in too many Czech movies and books, is presented as something glamorous. In my favorite Czech Oscar-winning film "Kolya," the charismatic protagonist had multiple lovers, among them a married woman. When my Czech friend, an educator, found out about her husband's infidelity, to settle the score, she seduced their colleague. "The best meat on the market!" she boasted. These people were pedagogic institute professors, the teachers of the nation's future educators. Do Czechs really put love and sex in separate boxes?

We got off at the Old Town Station (Stanice Staroměstská), the historical center of Prague. In one hand I was clenching a copy of Brother Cyprian's directions to the Dominican monastery, in the other, I was pulling my rattling suitcase, wondering if the wheels would last on these cobblestones. The fairy-tale buildings momentarily took my breath away, but my body's demand for food and sleep brought my focus back to the directions.

Before our trip I had searched the Internet for inexpensive and unusual lodgings, finding remodeled bunkers, old mills, castles, and monasteries. Now we were looking for the Dominican monastery adjacent to the 700-year-old Saint Giles' Church (kostel sv.Jiljí), where a part of the movie "Amadeus" was filmed. Brother Cyprian accompanied his instructions with three photos. Under the final picture he wrote — black, unremarkable metal door — the entrance to the monastery. I looked up from the information and there it was! With renewed energy, trying not to run over too many tourists on this narrow street, I strode toward the expansive, somewhat weathered three-story building. I then rang the doorbell next to Brother Cyprian's name and waited. I rang the bell next to Brother Romuald, then Jordán, Šimon, Ondřej, Benedict, Antonín, Blažej... Nothing. No answer.

A short, shabby man walked up to us, "Hurry! The concert will start in five minutes," he said in Czech.

"We're not here for the concert. We need a key to our room."

"Then hurry," he pointed to the entrance of St. Giles' church, "in the vestry behind the chancel, one of the brothers will help you. But hurry, the concert is about to start."

I thought of our favorite TV show, "The Amazing Race."

*If you make it to the pit stop, you'll receive your next clue.
The last one to arrive may be eliminated.*

Larry and I rushed to the church past the man collecting the tickets but we were too late, the concert had already started; tones of a violin reverberated from the tall ceiling. Careful not to disturb the handful of listeners scattered in the front, we sat down in the last pew. Dim light mixed with cool incensed air soothed our buzzing, jet-lagged heads. Baroque angels reached to us from wooden carvings, marble frescos and gold frames. Aware that the slightest noise would send an echo throughout the church, we sat still.

It was magical, but outside it was getting dark, and we still didn't know where our room was. After the violinist had bowed, and the musician disappeared in a side-door, the sound of an imposing organ filled the church. "I'll go check what is behind that door, maybe I'll find someone," I whispered. Larry's eyes asked, "do you dare?" I crept toward the door. The round metal handle, like a thick oval spoon, felt cold in my hand. I followed the twisting stone stairs, occasionally stopping to return the stares of priests trapped in ornate frames. At the top of the stairs, I poked my head around the corner, finding myself eye-to-eye with the organist. It was as if I wandered right on the stage in the middle of play. I backtracked with an uncertain smile and a feeble wave.

Down in the church, Larry sat focused, enjoying the music. "I'll go look for some Brothers," I whispered and tiptoed toward the exit.

Outside, a gang of teenage boys crowded the monastery door, pulling a prank on the priest.

"Father, you have to help me. Father, I don't know what to do. Oh, Father I need someone to love me tonight," the long-haired pubescent cried into the intercom. His friends rolled in laughter, encouraging him with shoulder slaps. Crap! Surely the person on the other side will hang up now. I pushed my way through the group. "Father! I am not with those kids...sorry about — "

From the intercom came an easy laughter.

"We are used to all kinds of stuff around here."

"Good. I mean — "

"You are Mrs. Glássnerová, correct? I'll be right there to open the door for you."

In a few moments a charismatic young man in a long white robe stretched his hand in greeting.

"Brother Antonín, come on in."

"But... My husband is waiting in the church."

"Let him enjoy the concert."

I wanted to object, but his white robe was already flying up the stairs.

In a small office, he handed me a key with a magnetic chip.

"This will open the doors in our monastery for you. Follow me."

By placing the chip on a rectangular device on the wall, the old door unlocked with a click and we stepped into a lovely courtyard with a pleasantly overgrown garden, a true oasis of peace; the thick monastery walls created a barrier against the drunken street. I heard the low-pitched chirrup.

"We have a blackbird nesting here this year." Brother Antonín sounded like a proud father.

I rushed along the arcade past the weathered limestone statues of saints, trying to catch up with my guide. On the church tower, the large hands of a golden Roman clock pointed quarter-to-eight. Strange music, which I couldn't place in any genre, came from someplace near. "We have two concerts here tonight," Brother Antonín pointed to the row of arched windows, and I caught a glimpse of a ceiling so elaborately painted that I stopped to take a better look. Brother Antonín was already disappearing through another door. In a hallway on the third floor, his chip unlocked door number seven. A well-lit, clean, room with two separate beds, a wooden table, two chairs, a newly remodeled bathroom with a shower. It was all that we needed. I was anxious to let Larry know what was going on. "How about the money?" I asked.

"You can pay sometime during your visit, at your convenience. Now I let you rest." And with that, he was gone.

In the church, the concert continued. I found my weary pilgrim with our four bags at his feet sitting underneath the giant crucifix, Jesus empathetically looking down at him. Without moving, Larry whispered, "It's so beautiful here."

We tiptoed toward the exit. It was during a Bach violin performance that my suitcase caught the wooden "A" board announcing the concert. With a crash, it folded on itself. The same shabby man we had met earlier rushed to help us. God, send us a more competent guardian angel, I silently pleaded.

I was impatient to show Larry what my magnetic chip would reveal. But this time all the lights in the monastery were turned off. We fumbled along the dark walls feeling for a light switch. The same odd music, something like a Pink Floyd soundtrack for "Jaws," accompanied our steps, a fitting sound to our bizarre predicament. Before long we got disoriented. Panting, we climbed the well-worn wooden stairs to the third floor and down again, groping along the hallways, stumbling into strange rooms. The lightweight suitcases I had been so proud of got heavier with every flight of stairs.

"Why don't you wait here with the bags," I said in the hallway. "No point in both of us hauling all the stuff up and down." I imagined Larry looked agreeable, but couldn't tell for sure. Without the luggage, I was able to wander freely throughout the building which had hosted Czech spiritual leaders for hundreds of years.

With my hands stretched in front of me, I stepped into a room and right away saw the outline of a pale face. I almost touched it. A gasp escaped my throat. The face didn't move. We stood watching each other. My heart pounded. My bulging eyes traced his frozen features. Finally, I exhaled. Trying to collect myself, I rubbed my forehead.

Before I found our room, I wandered into the monastery's museum two more times, and two more times I walked into the statue of the first Czech archbishop. That rascal, Ernest of Pardubice (Arnošt z Pardubic) got me every time. In real life, though, Ernest was a good guy. In 1344 he put a stop to the so-called "God's trials," when the way to determining a suspect's innocence or guilt was to throw the individual into a river — and if he floated, his association with the devil was proven. Another time, the accused was forced to hold a hot metal rod in his bare hands. Blistered limbs were evidence of guilt.

I didn't mind sharing lodgings with someone who put a stop to such madness, even though Ernest scared the living daylights out of me every time I walked past him.

5. Hussites

We were tired but too excited to sleep. We threw our bags in the corner and again groped through the dark hallway corridors, down the stairs and into the streets of Prague. The energy in front of the monastery resembled a summer night in Times Square, New York. The doors of souvenir shops were open. Bright lights illuminated Czech crystal, Russian wooden dolls, Charles Bridge refrigerator magnets and heaps and heaps of wonderfully useless stuff, the requirement of any major tourist destination. What a contrast to my visit to Prague in 1976.

Then, I was 17 and wanted to buy something special to remember my first trip to the capital. After searching most of the day among tedious store goods, I found a cigarette lighter. It was slick, so not-behind-the-Iron-Curtain-like. Made from brushed gold metal, the thin lighter ignited with only a gentle touch and sophisticated click. For me, that shiny little gadget represented the forbidden world of plenty. It contrasted my world of decaying buildings and half-empty shops stocked with only common essentials.

At that time, there wasn't much need for souvenirs, as the Czechoslovakian government was denying visas to almost all citizens and non-native travelers alike. Foreign-language speakers caused curious stares, a complete change from today's Prague where I heard many languages all around us, some I didn't recognize. Now, everyone seemed to wear the vacationers' look of glee and expectation, seeking an authentic Czech experience among Ukrainians, Croatians, or Vietnamese shopkeepers. Larry and I held hands, not wanting to get separated in the crowd. People, people everywhere and not a Czech to spare. I was bewildered.

As we made our way, I recalled a TV documentary about invasive water lilies. The dense colorful plants were choking the lakes, creating stagnant areas with little oxygen, making it difficult for paddle boats to pass through. Every year the patches grew larger and larger. The unstoppable foreign specie shaded out native plants. Since Prague opened its gates in 1989, the tourists have swarmed in. They took over the city like those water lilies took over the lakes. Old apartment buildings in the historical core were converted into hotels. The Praguers moved out of the city center to avoid the masses of tourists and inflated prices. The natives revisit in the slow tourist season, during winter months when the city feels once again like the Prague they love.

Larry and I let the crowd sweep us through the streets, suddenly realizing how famished we were. We reached for the first food at hand: pizza and a canned Heineken from a street vendor. Not the traditional dumplings, sauerkraut and roast pork accompanied by Pilsner draft that I had envisioned. Nevertheless, we inhaled the floppy slices like starved dogs. What our first meal lacked in gourmet quality, it made up for in ambiance.

In the Old Town Square, we sat on a bench next to the colossal Jan Hus monument. Chewing our pizza, we looked around the medieval market place, admiring the mythical-looking buildings filled to their chimneys with stories and legends. A dense crowd awaited the world's oldest still-operating astronomical clock, the Orloj, to set in motion its mechanical parade of saints. The clock was built in 1410 by Master Hanuš who was blinded by the city council so he wouldn't duplicate this mechanical wonder elsewhere. The Baroque St. Nicholas Church with the opulent roofs — like flamboyant hairdos of the ladies Mozart and Vivaldi composed playful symphonies for — looked as if it wanted to steal all the attention. What went on at the opposite side of the square behind the small windows with the round arches? Was it a wealthy merchant's home or a secret workshop where an alchemist searched for the elixir of youth for the narcissistic King Rudolf? From the Týn church's soaring towers, my gaze slid down its tall Gothic windows, back to the Hus monument at the center of the square.

"See that guy with the pigeon on his head?" I pointed to the tallest statue, "that's Master Jan Hus, one of the most important thinkers in Czech history. He's facing the Týn church where his followers worshipped from 1419–1620. And that golden Virgin Mary high between its two spires? She used to be a chalice. Hus' Catholic opponents melted it down into the Virgin Mary." Between chewing on the pizza crust, I told Larry the story about the turbulent Hussite era.

"In feudal society, the Catholic Church made people believe that a person belonged to one of three categories: born with a Bible, the person was destined to serve the Roman Catholic Church; born with a sword, he was to protect the church; and born with empty hands, he was to serve those two groups above. Pretty slick formula eh?"

"Only to remind the poor where their place was," Larry said.

"At sacrament, peasants received the communal wafer — the body of Christ, but they couldn't drink the wine — the blood of Christ. Getting both was for the chosen ones, those higher up, closer to God.

"For centuries, the peasants didn't question that arrangement. In 1389 Hus began speaking openly against the corrupt church and its doctrine which he believed contradicted Christ's teachings. Hus was outraged that the fat-bellied priests sworn to celibacy were having children. He criticized the church's ridiculous practice of selling paper indulgences, to negate sins." To highlight the point, I opened my arms and cried out, "Everlasting life in paradise for all. Just buy some coupons!" A man sitting on a bench next to ours looked at me over the black rims of his glasses. I lowered my voice and went on. "At that time, there were two popes, each cursing his opponent, swearing that he was God's true representative on earth. In the atmosphere of these unholy arguments, simple people recognized the truth in Hus' sermons and for the first time began to question the behavior of their religious leaders. The growing numbers of Hus' loyalists made the holy men in Rome pretty nervous."

"And let me guess," Larry interrupted, "They ordered his heretic ass on the carpet."

"In so many words," I said. "Hus welcomed that opportunity, although he must have feared that he was about to enter the lion's den. He hoped to engage in dialogue, but instead, he was thrown into a dungeon where he was chained and starved. As to be expected from a true reformer, Hus would not recant his teachings. So what is the Holy College of Cardinals to do with a misled preacher? How about burning him at the stake? Now there was a saintly solution."

"Was Martin Luther his ally?" Larry asked.

"Hus was killed in 1415; Luther came a hundred years later. By then the Catholic Church knew better than to get rid of Luther in flames. By burning Hus, Rome ignited a fire that couldn't be extinguished for a whole generation. Jan Žižka of Trocnov organized the outraged Protestants into a massive army, starting a chain of bloody Hussite wars. The Hussites got into the nasty habit of burning and devastating Catholic churches and monasteries. In 1419, they threw seven councilmen out of the Town Hall window, and act called The First Defenestration of Prague. To demonstrate their belief of equality, the Hussite's symbol became a chalice. Partaking of bread with the forbidden wine became their practice. The Hussites established their simple churches, often offering mass under the open skies."

Larry and I took the last sip of beer, brushed crumbs off the bench for the appreciative pigeons, and started to walk.

"Was Žižka that one-eyed fighter?" Larry asked.

"Yeah, he was an ingenious strategist and the inventor of revolutionary war tactics. In school, we used to have to memorize the names of the Hussites' military hardware. Why they made us do that is still not clear to me. All kinds of spiked clubs, mace clubs, swords, or war wagons, their medieval AK 47's. Žižka would take on an army of Crusaders that by far outnumbered his own, winning every battle. Only after much bloodshed did the church council realize that the Hussites were unstoppable.

The Hussites showed their religious independence in several ways: by not believing in the curative powers of saints' relics, by drinking wine when receiving Holy Communion, and by performing sermons and singing hymns in Czech instead of Latin. At that time, no other nation had those privileges. As a matter of fact, elsewhere people were routinely put to death for owning a Bible written in any language other than Latin.

"In 1414 the pope condemned the whole city of Prague. The rest of Europe viewed the Czechs as heretics and troublemakers. Trading roads were empty and the economy suffered. However, the Czechs accomplished their main goal. In 1437, the Roman Catholic Council finally granted the Czechs the right to worship their way, presenting them with a written document, "The Compacta of Prague," granting the rights to their distinctive way of worshipping."

These streets witnessed so much upheaval. So much blood was spilled in the name of religion.

...Love each other and wish the truth to everyone ...I believe, that the angry thunders will cease and the governing of your affairs will return to your hands, oh Czech people...

6. Genius King George

Celetná Street led us away from the Old Town Square. Without a map or city guide, Larry and I wandered, high from the excitement that always emanates the first day of a trip. The cast-iron street lamps poured golden light over the antique buildings and onto the cobblestone streets. We tried to take it all in, but it was like standing in front of a lavish Christmas tree, unable to focus on a single decoration. The medieval city seemed surreal, as if even the passers-by played roles in the archaic set.

A massive black tower rose in front of us. Like Gulliver's foot in the land of Lilliputians, it shrank the surrounding buildings. A man dressed in what resembled a Halloween costume of a 13th century gatekeeper was selling tickets at the entrance. When Larry and I approached him, the man checked his watch, "We are about to close." Then, swayed by our long faces, he added, "If you'll be quick, I'll let you in." We ran up the spiral narrow staircase in fear that he might change his mind. Then, out of his scope of vision and out of breath, we climbed the rest of the stairs in our normal knee-aching pace. The stairway opened onto a foyer. An attendant dressed in that same cheesy costume (in real life a laid-off computer programmer), was happy to talk about his domain: "The Powder Tower (Prašná Brána) was one of the 13 gates through which people entered the walled, medieval city. It served as a watchtower. In the Middle Ages, the coronation processions of kings started here and ended at Prague castle. Once, four camels, then a novelty, took part in the procession, causing great excitement and almost stealing the King's show."

I tried to imagine that extravagant sight. Bells ringing, troubadours playing, cannons firing, acrobats dancing...

The guide pointed to a black-and-white poster, a photograph of a woodcarving where the ribbon-like wall hemmed in Old Prague. "In the 14th century, King Charles IV expanded the city beyond its original walls and the Powder Tower was no longer needed. It became a gunpowder storage warehouse. Thus, its name. In 1475 the outside walls were enhanced by Gothic features and statues of the Czech kings. Among them is my favorite, George of Podebrady (Jiří z Poděbrad)."

"He is my favorite king too!" I exclaimed with the enthusiasm Americans save for movie stars. Such was our sudden kinship that the young guide even broke the rule and opened the stained-glass window. The view was like an illustration in a fairytale. Up on the hill, magnificent Prague Castle was bathed in moonlight. It was hard to envision anything besides happy kingdoms, with loyal bonds between its subjects and their righteous kings and queens, their brave sons and beautiful daughters, all living happily-ever-after. Unfortunately, that was far from the truth. The throne-hungry royal candidates were often killed, castrated, blinded, kidnapped or jailed — usually by each other. Some were killed in wars, others crazed from inbreeding.

"George of Podebrady was the only king who didn't descend from imperial blood," the young docent said. "He was just a low-ranking noble, a little fat man with short legs. Now, we would describe him as a self-made man. He was a brilliant thinker who cared about peaceful coexistence among his people. He challenged the two most powerful and influential men who ruled the world from their high pedestals, God's representatives on earth: the Roman Catholic Pope, Pio II, and his successor Pope Paul II."

At the top of the stairway, the guide opened a vaulted door to a narrow balcony. We stepped outside and looked over the city that George of Podebrady, the unprecedented modern thinker, had once ruled. The breeze touched our faces.

George was born in 1420 to a 17-year-old father who had fought in Žižka's Hussite army. At age seven, George was orphaned and was sent to live with his wealthy Hussite relatives. In his later life George's ambitious energy landed him in politics. He proved to be an extremely capable economist, investor and negotiator, and was appointed top advisor to young King Ladislav Pohrobek, who died without leaving an heir. Thirty-eight-year-old George was selected to be the king's successor. In his inauguration speech he promised equal respect for all his people, Catholics and Hussites alike. He was the first European leader whose political doctrine established religious tolerance. The rest of Europe — at that time, under the persuasion of Catholic dogma — shook their heads over George's priorities. Gradually, George began to achieve his goal of social harmony and got both religious groups to tolerate one another. They learned that the liquidation of an opponent doesn't have to be a requirement for either group's survival.

Increasingly peaceful trade routes in Czech lands began attracting foreign business. But in the midst of these promising years, the Pope played his trump card, proclaiming: "The time has come for all the Czechs to follow the Catholic rules again. No more two religions!"

The Roman church's tragic unwillingness to consider other truths once again deprived Czech soil of its key nourishment. Peace could no longer sprout in the newly oppressed Czech land.

George would not comply with Rome's demands, for that would deny all he had come to represent. Instead, he concocted a brilliant plan to create peaceful unity among nations. Even 500 years can't diminish the king's courage for nonviolently standing up for his beliefs. George applied his motto: *"Rather cautiously and thoughtfully than with weapons."*

All the principles on which the United Nation stands today were included in George's proposal. He suggested creating an organization that would enforce peaceful resolution of conflicts. The coalition would respect the equality of all sovereign states, even the small ones. In the case of a violation of the contract, an organized defense would be assembled. Furthermore, George predicted a single European currency and economic regulation across borders.

Thirty years before Europeans discovered America, George sent the prototype of the UN's peaceful project to leaders of neighboring countries, cautioning about Rome's aggressive force in Czech affairs. "They could do the same to you," he warned. But Europe wasn't ready to consider George's plan.

King George didn't want to force his beliefs of religious freedom on the rest of the world. He only asked the world to let Czechs practice their own beliefs. Even that proved too much. The Pope imposed a sanction on the Czech King, and the weakened George attracted vultures. The Hungarian King Matthias Corvinus, George's son-in-law, took this opportunity to enlarge his kingdom by invading the Czech land. George wanted peace for his land, but he understood that applying force in some situations is a necessity.

Unfortunately George wasn't as skillful a fighter as he was a politician. He suffered many losses. The Czechs were outraged by the Hungarians' iniquitous brand of fighting: they used captive soldier's heads as ammunition for their catapults and executed Czechs by impaling bodies on wooden poles.

In desperation King George made his biggest personal sacrifice. He offered his throne to the son of the Polish King in exchange for military help. After George's sudden death at age 51, the Polish King, Vladislav, of the Jagelon family, became the first Czech king of a 55 year Jagelon reign.

"We need to go now," my docent friend whispered, as if apologizing.

I looked one more time in the direction of St. Vitus Cathedral (Catedrála Svatého Víta), towering behind Prague's Castle.

"That's where King George of Podebrady is buried," the docent said.

Back down on the street Larry and I walked around the Powder Tower, searching for the statue of King George, the short pudgy guy, but the king we found was a great thinker and a gentleman.

7. Grocery Gazing

The next day I snuck out of the room at dawn, cautiously opening and closing all the doors leading into the monastery garden. I almost walked into that mischievous Ernest of Pardubice again and was tempted to push him five feet further away from the door to save myself from having a heart attack.

In the monastery's courtyard, all was quiet and still except for the blackbirds' melodic song coming from the fig tree. There wasn't any movement behind the rows of lace-curtained windows. The purple clouds were still unsure if they would share the sky with the sun. It felt like I was the only person awake. I sat down on the cool stone edge of a water fountain and watched daybreak, zooming in on my surroundings. The Dominican Brothers had planted strawberry, parsley, and chives; it was not the neatest garden, but lovely nevertheless. Even the soot-stained yellow walls with their peeling, mildewed stucco corners held charm.

At once the solitude ended. The church bell shook everyone out of bed. Everyone, but Larry. I found him asleep with pillows covering his ears and decided to surprise him with breakfast. Again I left the room, careful not to awaken him. At the courtyard, all was still as before. But no, I heard the squeak of hinges. A priest in a long black habit came into view. "Excuse me, Father," I said in Czech, rushing along the cloister to catch up with him. "I have a question. You would surely know — " The foreign-speaking priest kindly interrupted, "Spanish? German? French? No Czech, sorry."

Well, of course. No Czech. What was I thinking? And I really needed to find out how to flush that darn toilet. I did not realize how international not only Prague but this monastery had become.

On the street, a few men and women hurried with the purposefulness of working people. I wondered if there were any native Czechs among them.

The six-story glass building with oversized red letters "MY" was the grocery store Brother Antonín had told me about. Without his help, I wouldn't have been able to tell what was inside that building. What does MY stand for and how is it pronounced? After the Velvet Revolution, foreign companies had made a mad dash into newly opened Czech territory, grabbing business opportunities — sort of like the Oklahoma Land Rush. The British-based grocery chain MY was one of the high-noon front liners, succeeding in securing this prime location. The store was still closed, but a few people were already gathered at the entrance. "*Dobré ráno,*" I said to a young mom with an infant strapped to her chest. "Good morning," she answered in English.

"Oh, I thought you were Czech. Where are you from?" I asked.

"We are from Australia. This is our third trip here."

Who wants to travel with an infant? The young woman read the question on my face.

"My husband and I keep coming to Prague every year; we love it here."

"And what do you do here?"

"This time it depends on how it will go with her," she pointed to her chubby bundle.

I liked that woman. From all the days granted to us, why not dedicate a few to live in our favorite place?

At seven o'clock, a stocky man in a black suit and short-cropped haircut — the bouncer type — unlocked the door and the first shoppers descended the escalator. I followed my nose to the bakery section. There, in a daze, my vision wavered among the wicker baskets filled with freshly baked twisted cheese rolls, poppy-seed rolls, flat rolls, long, round, plain, twisted, braided, multigrain, salty, sweet, fluffy, dense and of course, the traditional *rohlíky* shaped like uncircumcised penises. I was in heaven. Few pleasures in life can compete with fresh-baked bread. In that moment, nothing stood between me and those godly creations; no saran-wrap, glass counters, or sneeze guards. It was wonderful. And if not for the bouncer man, I would have been tempted to nibble on every one of those divine creations. How to choose? It was overwhelming — bliss or the beginning of a mild nervous breakdown? I took my time, carefully mixing and matching six warm rolls and then moving on to the yogurt section. Such a variety! Pear, gooseberry, sour cherries... Aha! There was the winner, the vanilla and chocolate *Pribináček,* the creamy pleasure of my childhood. *"We've been making them since 1950"* advertised the red letters on the waxy paper cup.

This grocery store was a museum stuffed with my childhood memories. I fingered the *Tatranky,* everyone's favorite chocolate wafers named after Slovak's highest mountains, the Tatra. I was almost in tears when I spotted *Hašlerky,* the hard herbal candies in blue wrappers my grandma used to carry in her purse. Their unique anise and lemon taste always conjured up memories of her. Hašlerky were named after Karel Hašler, the most prolific Czech song-writer. A countless number of his instant hits still remain a huge part of the Czech identity. Hašler died in Mauthausen concentration camp after Nazi soldiers forced him to take a shower and then stand outside naked all night. It was January.

I was moved when I walked by the rows of Swiss chocolates. During Communism we only saw them in the advertisements of smuggled Western magazines. Now, if I wanted to, I could fill up my basket. It was as if I was walking through my childhood drawings where fancy dishes, bowls of strawberries, platters of chocolates and cakes were stacked on overflowing banquet tables. I could have stayed in that grocery store for days.

Larry woke up just as I was placing the ripped deli paper on a tablecloth, setting out an assortment of cold cuts, rolls, chocolate and vanilla Pribináčeks, a bag of Hašlerky, Milka hazelnut chocolate, Carlsbad wafers, and a small paper box with linden tea bags, the dried flowers from the Czech national tree. Out of the blue and yellow box, I pulled a sweet hazelnut wafer the size of a plate, fanning it in front of Larry's face, "You know, these babies are the real thing. The European Union, after six years in the courts with Germans and Austrians, awarded Czechs the sole right to manufacture them. This Czech specialty has more than 150 years of tradition. Mozart, Goethe, Emperor Ferdinand, The Russian Czar Peter the Great — to mention just a few — all loved them. And now, Larry the Greatest is about to fall in love with them too."

"Very exotic," Larry said as he broke off a piece, chewed, then nodded. With a full mouth he said, "They look like family-size communion wafers. Do we have ice cream to go with?"

"Much better, we have Pribináček," I said and realized we didn't have spoons, an item that we would miss throughout our trip.

"It seems strange to go to a museum," Larry said on the way towards Wenceslas Square, "we are in the museum already. Every cobblestone street, every ornate house, all those great old wooden-frame windows, the trademarks above the doors telling of their past, all those churches and towers, statues everywhere; why are we going to the museum on this perfect sunny day?"

Just browsing the streets and the grocery stores would also satisfy me, but instead, I said, "Because I have always wondered what was in that imposing building at the top of Wenceslas Square. This isn't just any museum; it is the National Museum."

Soon the narrow streets widened into modern boulevards; we entered New Town (Nové Město), the section of Prague which King Charles IV began to build in 1348. On

Wenceslas Square — more of a broad boulevard than a square — a young tour guide with bouncy blond curls was lecturing a group of tourists in perfect English:

"On this plaza, many significant events took place. In 1918, Alojs Jirásek, the Czech writer, read the declaration of independence from the Austro-Hungarian Empire. In 1945, the Czechs cheered the end of WWII. The life-loving student of philosophy, Jan Palach, protested the 1968 invasion of Russian tanks by setting himself on fire on the steps of the National Museum. On November 1989, over 300,000 Czechoslovaks filled all corners of this square and rallied for the Communist regime to resign. Under the leadership of playwright Václav Havel, the future Czech president, then a freshly released prisoner, people jingled their keys and chanted to send the message to their government, 'It's time to go.' That was the beginning of the peaceful, Velvet Revolution, as Havel named it."

All those events directly affected the lives of every Czech, including my grandparents, my parents, myself and even my American children. I strained my ears, but the beeping of the truck backing up made it impossible to catch all that the guide was saying.

Shoppers on the square went in and out of stores. A woman, squatting next to a tree, held her little girl between her thighs in the same fashion all Czech girls were held by their mothers while urinating in the open. No one paid attention to them; no one was outraged. People with fixed expressions and unrevealed agendas kept walking by.

8. National Museum

Two icons, the National Museum and the massive statue of St. Wenceslas on horseback, dominate Wenceslas Square. Larry and I sat on the high stairs surrounding the statue, a popular meeting place for Praguers. So many years had gone by, enough for me to establish roots on another continent. Like the Monarch butterfly is programmed to follow his migration pattern, I too followed an invisible string back to my people. Now I found myself at the heart of my country, the St. Wenceslas Monument. A lump blocked my throat and tightness squeezed my chest, but I couldn't stay melancholy for long. Larry began tapping his foot:

Good King Wenceslas looked out
On the Feast of Steven
When the snow lay round about
Deep and crisp and even.

I was doomed, stuck with that Christmas carol for the rest of the day.

Wenceslas, the 10th century Christian Duke of Bohemia, now the symbol of Czech unity, was canonized after his brother murdered him and took over the throne.

In times of remembrance, Czechs lay flowers at Saint Wenceslas' statue. In bad times and in times of hope, they surround the statue with candles. The Communist government wanted Czechs to forget the religious and mythical Wenceslas, but people never stopped coming to their patron at the top of Prague's main square. Václav Havel, before becoming president, got sentenced to nine months in prison for organizing a gathering at this very place to honor the anniversary of Jan Palach's self-immolation.

According to legend, Saint Wenceslas and his army of knights will come back to life, emerging from the nearby Mt. Blaník to rescue the country in the nation's darkest times. Is the worst still to come? Czechs have asked this question during many cruel episodes of their history.

Nazi occupiers exploited Wenceslas' patriotic ideology by rewarding collaborators with the Order of the Saint Wenceslas Eagle, a desperate and despicable act.

Larry and I crossed the street towards the National Museum. What's inside the ornate palace of my culturally rich nation? I harbored high expectations. The countdown banner above the front entrance announced 67 days until the museum would close for renovation. I hoped the bullet holes fired by Russian tanks at the museum's front wall would still be visible. When the Communist government sent workers to patch up the holes, a shameful reminder of the occupiers' aggression, the construction crew purposely used lighter colored stucco to remind people of the 1968 invasion. At least that was the honorable explanation. I suspect there wasn't the right color concrete to be found in the lean Communist paint shed.

From the grand museum entrance hall, my eyes followed the red carpet up the majestic stairs to an ornate glass ceiling, marble and gold all around. A funky long-bearded mannequin dressed in moccasins and a white robe seemed terribly out of place in the fancy museum lobby. He represented Grandfather Czech, a man who led his people from northeast of the Tatra Mountains to Mt. Říp. From the mountaintop, more of a bowler-hat shaped hill than a real mountain, Grandfather Czech declared the surrounding valley the new home for his group of Slavs. A sign placed next to funky Grandfather Czech announced the Old Czech Fables exhibition on the first floor.

I asked the man at the ticket booth how long the museum visit takes.

"Some are done in half an hour," he said in Slovak.

Only philistines would rush hundreds of years of history, I thought and purchased two tickets, one full-priced and one retiree half-priced, feeling a bit of an imposter. The discount probably wasn't meant for those who receive their pensions in dollars. I thanked him, and Larry and I walked up the wide stairway.

The first gallery, like an overstocked warehouse, was packed with stone busts of the emotionless faces of famous Czechs. I thought of my grandmother's poster-size wedding photograph tucked in back of my sister's closet. Not that we didn't love our grandma, but it's that huge picture no one wanted to nail on their wall. The uninspired display of the statues made me wonder if the new generation of Czechs shares my sister's and my predicament. (I must remember not to enlarge too many of Larry's and my photos, or we too would one day cause guilt for our children from the back of their closets.)

In the botanical section of the museum, the stuffed animals in glass cabinets looked as if they had suffered severe cases of ringworms. Still, I was amazed to see all those deer, otters, foxes, badgers, marmots, weasels, bears, wolves, and colorful, exotic-looking birds that have either lived or migrated through Czech land. A group of first-graders pointed and shouted the animals' names as if calling out to old friends. I don't recall American children naming native animals or plants with such ease. When these freckly buggers imitated the geese calls with great agility, I caught myself scheming various methods to silence them.

We escaped into a quiet room where a single animal occupied the entire space. The stuffed mammoth took our breath away the first minute, and bored us at the next, much as did the whole museum. "Big, hmm?" Larry said. "Yep," I replied. Perhaps the mammoth would hold our attention for a minute or so longer if we could at least pull on his fur; many obviously had, but an attendant with beady little eyes followed closely by.

Larry began to yawn. With sad puppy eyes and a faint voice he sang the final verse of the carol:

It fails my heart
I not know how
I can go no longer.

Then he found a cushiony chair in a quiet corner of the hallway. I wanted to join him but feared he wouldn't stop humming that song. I decided to peek into the Grandfather

Czech exposition so we wouldn't give the man at the ticket booth the opportunity to say, "Some only take 30 minutes, but one American couple made it in 17."

Alone, I entered the exhibition. The attendant encouraged me to take four steps to the top of the fake Mt. Říp, where around the year 800 Grandfather Czech declared these famous words:

> *"This is the place I promised to you, the virgin land filled with game, honey, and milk, with the climate favorable and with the abundance of fish. Here you will not suffer shortages, and no one will do you harm."*

If his followers could peek into the future, surely they would protest in one fervent voice, "Keep going, don't stop. Go further south! A tiny state sandwiched between two superpowers, Germany and Russia, can't be good. Run! Plus it's sunnier down there." Instead, those first Czechs rejoiced, sacrificed some weary lambs and drank honey beer in amounts that couldn't have been good for them.

That was the romantic version recorded by the historian Cosma 600 years after Grandfather Czech's supposed declaration. Had he heard the legend from respected elders who had in turn heard it from their grandfathers? Or did he make the story up to silence German voices declaring Czech land as a part of their territory? Centuries later, the writer Alois Jirásek, a patriot like Cosma, rewrote the Old Czech Legends, implying their historical soundness, taking the liberty to fill in the historical gaps. Artists, including Josef Myslbek, the creator of the Saint Wenceslas statue, Alfons Mucha, the famous Czech painter, Bedřich Smetana, the beloved composer and many other nationalists based their life's work on glorifying the idealized Czech origin story. When the nation finally realized that the legends, filled with wholesome people in flowing white robes, were most likely a product of Jirásek's fantasy, Myslbek suffered serious depression, and Mucha's seven-by-seven-meter paintings, on which he spent 16 years of his life, were rolled up and stored away.

Archeological findings had provided evidence for the harsh reality — far from Grandfather Czech's fanciful prophecies of a land rich with milk and honey. Bones and shattered ceramics discovered in ancient burial sites revealed little about mythical groups of Slavic wanderers. Poverty-stricken, hard-working, deeply religious families lived an isolated existence in a jungle of thick woods. Wolves were constant threats to wild honey-hunters and miners who searched for ironstone.

Every nation needs their heroes, and so modern Czechs continue to read stories about Grandfather Czech's son Krok and his three daughters, Kazi, Teta, and the youngest, Libuše, the smart and just woman with a knack for fortune telling. The legend tells us that she became the leader of the Czech people and the founder of Prague.

Once, two rivals came to Libuše to seek justice. One of the men wasn't happy with her verdict and blurted out, *"Shame on men led by a woman, for women have long hair, but a short brain."* Unruffled, Libuše stood up, pointed her powerful Slavic arm and forecasted in a thundering voice, "Saddle my horse! He'll take you to my future husband and your King." The horse led the delegation over the hills and valleys, stopping in front of a man named Thoughtful Ploughman (Přemysl Oráč), a strong and capable farmer who said something like this, "Hey y'all! Watch this!" Then, he stuck his club into the ground. The dry stick immediately burst forth with new buds. "This is the dude for the job! He ought to marry Libuše and become our king," the men insisted. Thus, at the beginning of the 9th century, Czechs found their first king, who began the four-century long Přemyslid Dynasty.

I turned into an anti-fableist when comrade Kratochvílová, my third-grade teacher, covered my desk with specks of her saliva whenever she recounted the Old Czech stories. Comrade Kratochvílová especially loved the fable about the man named Bivoj who wrestled a wild boar with his bare hands, hoisted the struggling animal on his back and carried it to Kazi, Libuše's older sister. There, at Kazi's feet, Bivoj speared the boar and Kazi fell in love with Bivoj. Saliva shot in all directions from my teacher's lips as she reenacted the scene, walking between the rows of ducking third graders. I sensed that Comrade Kratochvílová, the wife of a pale scientist, was in a strange way attracted to the muscular hero. I, on the other hand, knew even then that I preferred the type who was handy with crayons. With that recollection in mind, I exited the exhibition.

Larry and I decided that before leaving the museum, we should take advantage of the free lavatory, an indulgence not readily available throughout the Czech Republic. Upon entering the restroom, with the first pungent whiff, nostalgia overcame me. I haven't smelled an identical reek since elementary school. I took a few careful inhales and said my final good-bye to the National Museum. Thank goodness, after renovation, it will never be the same.

9. Czech Beer Houses: *Hospodas*

"A hot day, a great one for a beer," Josef grinned, extending his arm for a handshake. We met our Czech friend who promised a better exchange rate for our dollars in his bank. Even though we arrived ten minutes early, he was already pacing the Old Town Square. "Let's get this bank business over with and move on to more cultural stuff."

That was a welcome proposal from a native Praguer. I needed help locating landmarks like the Rudolfinum — Prague's largest art gallery — or the Bethlehem Chapel where Jan Hus preached.

Exiting the bank, Josef murmured, "The rate was better yesterday; the dollar is going down fast." And as if the two topics were connected, he pointed to the *hospoda* across the street. A hospoda is a well-lit place where men spend hours visiting and drinking beer.

"I highly recommend this one, good beer there." A few blocks further, Josef pointed again and said with emphasis, "Gold Tiger hospoda (U Zlatého Tygra), a great non-pasteurized beer." The famous hospoda was right across from our monastery. How did we not see it before? Overlooking things among so many monuments was easy.

"Bohumil Hrabal got his inspiration for his novels there, eavesdropping on locals," Josef went on. "It's really something, you know. In school, he got F's in the Czech language. Flunked a grade more than once. They have his report cards on display in the town square where he grew up. But eventually, the beer sprouted the genius in him, creating a literary star." Josef chuckled. "During Clinton's visit in the early 90s our new president Havel treated Clinton to a beer there. Just like that, they sat and drank among the common Joes. Their bodyguards were none too happy." Judging by Josef's rasping belly laugh, he was proud of Havel's hospitality. We poked our heads inside the Gold Tiger hospoda. The place was crowded and noisy.

"Hrabal must have had much better hearing than me," I shouted.

"What?!" Larry cupped his hand to his ear.

I pointed toward the exit.

Outside we tried to keep up with Josef's long steps, straining to hear his lecture about the Czech national pastime.

"Czechs consume over 160 liters of beer per person per year, twice as much as Americans, more than Germans, even beating the Irish." Josef stopped in his tracks, lowered his voice almost to a whisper, his calloused finger erect. "This, my friends, is the world's beer-drinking capital. Imagine 320 jugs a year emptied down our thirsty Czech gullets. Almost a beer a day by all citizens, including every toddler and grandmother."

"Impressive," Larry nodded knowingly.

Not too far from the Golden Tiger, Josef pointed to a renovated two-story yellow building with the date 1466 painted above the tavern's entrance and the sign U Medvídků (The Bear House).

"Their specialty is a dark beer with 12 per cent alcohol — the strongest beer in the world. Regular beers have only four per cent. You should try it." Joseph stopped and let his sentence linger.

I looked at the two expectant faces, then my watch. "Come on you guys; it's not even noon yet."

On our cultural excursion, Josef passed, without comment, the Baroque Saint Nicholas Church where Mozart played the organ. Nor did he point out the Municipal House whose exterior was decorated in Art Nouveau style by three of the most celebrated Czech artists: Alphonse Mucha, Max Švabinský, and Josef Myslbek. Trotting behind, I called out, "Inside is the concert hall where the Prague Spring Festival takes place. Isn't it kind of a musical phenomenon? The International classical music celebrations were thriving during Communism and are still — "

"In the Splotchy Beer House (U Fleků), you can get a shot of *Becherovka* in your beer." Josef didn't let my inquiry distract him. "In Prague's oldest and most famous hospoda the locals have drunk nonstop for over 500 years.

"A half millennium, now there is a phenomenon!" Larry puffed the air out of his cheeks.

The flavor of the celebrated Czech liquor, Becherovka, which contains a blend of two dozen herbs and spices, combined with beer was as attractive to me as the garlic-flavored ice cream I once tasted then declined at California's Gilroy Garlic Festival.

Then there was the Deer House (U Jelínků). "The best beer in Prague," Josef said and wiped his lips with the palm of his hand, "but no place to sit," he added. "You have to drink standing up. Only old-timers earn their chairs."

As we walked by Clementinum, I jumped at the opportunity, "Let's cut through, I haven't been here yet."

Josef wasn't enthusiastic about exploring the formal Jesuit College. To him, the expansive building, among the largest complexes of Europe, was just a detour in the chain of taverns. But my steps were already echoing through one of the empty, spacious courtyards. The College is now home of the National Library, and provides a quiet escape from the crowds and pubs. Behind me lagged one long-faced Czech and his commiserating American buddy.

After the Hussites lost their struggle for religious freedom, the Habsburgs — the most influential royal family of Europe who ruled over the Czech land from 1526–1918 — reestablished Catholicism, and forbade all other religions. *Cuius regio, eius religio:* the religion of the ruler must be the religion of the ruled. After Protestants lost the White Mountain battle in 1620, the Habsburgs invited Jesuit priests to Clementinum to establish a Catholic educational center, offsetting the mostly Protestant Charles University. In these courtyards, 30,000 books became fuel for cultural bonfires set by Antonín Koniáš, the over-zealous Jesuit monk who was outraged by the heretical content of these volumes — probably a sentence here and there rubbed him the wrong way. The nationalistic writer, Alois Jirásek, known to exaggerate and alter things a bit, estimated the large number of burned tomes. It may have been just 30 books. Who can say?

On walks around Prague, I had frequently paused to look up, and often saw wonderful hidden treasures. At Clementinum, on the top of a tall wall, I spotted a modern life-sized statue of a girl sitting with a book in her lap. Her ponytail, tank top, short skirt, and legs dangling, reminded me of my daughter Linda as a little girl. Josef sighed when I took out my camera.

Next, I walked toward the library's gallery and peeked through the glass door. Not even Josef's irritation diminished my excitement, "Oh my gosh, I recognize that vaulted ceiling!" I cried. "It was in a brochure, and there it is. I have to go see it!"

"I'll wait here." Josef offered dryly. Larry gave me his 'sorry babe, can't be rude' look and dug in his heels next to Josef's.

"I promise I'll be quick."

"Take your time!" Josef shouted behind me.

The painted ceiling with fleshy figures partly covered in pastel-colored drapery took my breath away. The medieval scene reminded me of the love-and-harmony atmosphere shared by hippies at Woodstock.

The lady behind the desk zapped me with a laser-beam glare.

"Pardon me, is there any special exposition going on?" I asked, sounding like a fearful schoolgirl.

She searched my face, "You have to ask? Wasn't the sign above the entrance big enough for you?"

Her incivility startled me only for a second. At once, it encapsulated experiences of my youth. That impatient superior rudeness among strangers was a trademark of the Communist era. Much obliged for freshening up my memories, comrade, I wanted to salute to her.

Begrudgingly, the woman murmured. "The work of Czech writers. A celebration of the Czech culture."

I couldn't let those guys wait that long. I took a few moments to study the painted ceiling, feeling the woman's stare on my neck. I'd better go. Barely out the door, I heard Mrs. Politburo yell after me, "Didn't you notice that the door was closed? Shut the door behind you!"

I did notice, but I just kept walking.

Larry and Josef were nowhere in sight. I considered going back to the gallery, but the truth was, I was scared, so I waited on the street.

A mother and her daughter, about age ten, sat on a park bench. The girl rested her feet at the edge of the bench. An elderly man sat down next to them and turned toward the girl.

In Czech, he asked: "Where did you see people putting their feet on a bench? Others also have to sit here." The girl gave him a blank stare. The man went on: "Is it right that people will dirty their pants because of you?" Without moving her feet, the girl continued to gape at him. The man looked at her mother. The woman smiled broadly and said in an American accent, "No Czech, sorry."

The old man was another character of my youth, minding everyone's business by correcting and scolding. Was he the hero Hillary Clinton longed for in her book *It Takes a Village?* Outnumbered, I thought the volunteer educators were gone by now, barricaded against the uncaring world. The old man's approach to violators of decorum and the evil librarian's harassment brought back a latent anxiety. Bugs share the same feeling when the descending shadow of a shoe draws near. I wondered if those "authorities" have something to do with the high beer consumption in this country.

Several minutes later Larry and Josef, both rosy-cheeked and grinning, rushed toward me. Larry shrugged his shoulders and lifted up his arms, a gesture asking, "What is one to do with a thirsty Czech?"

"Beer is proof that God loves us," Josef slurred, "and that he wants us to be happy."

"So let's get another one!" I yelled and ran toward the guys. "I need it."

10. *Prague* Ham Vendor

Larry and I found ourselves wandering past several food vendor booths back on the bustling Old Town Square.

"Don't you feel guilty leaving him there?" I asked Larry.

"You kidding? There isn't any other place he'd rather be. No one will get Josef out of that pub before closing time."

The wonderful smell of roasting pork chased away my concerns. A vendor tended the rotisserie with plump bronze-colored ham. "Let's eat here!" I cried. Larry's eyes were on a man balancing sausage on a paper plate. Like a bloodhound on a mission, Larry followed his nose to the sausage booth while I approached the ham merchant. "One slice, please. I'll take it with rye bread and a small bowl of *haluŝky*." Haluŝky is a Slovak specialty, sort of a gnocchi — a potato dumpling — drowned in sheep cheese.

"How long have you lived out of the country?"

The vendor's question caught me by surprise.

"You speak Czech very well." A sure indication that I no longer speak Czech very well. No one compliments natives. No one tells Larry he speaks English very well.

"America?" asked the vendor while cutting the ham, juice dripping over the wooden board.

I nodded.

"California?" he guessed again, and I scanned his booth for a crystal ball. "How long have you lived there?"

"Over 30 years." No sense keeping information from this wisenheimer.

As he handed me the paper platter with my goodies, his assistant announced, "Two hundred forty korunas."

Steep, I thought. Not accustomed to the pricing, I handed over the bills without question.

Larry came back holding a fine-looking sausage smeared with mustard, secured in a huge roll. I followed him to a bench.

"How much did you pay?" he asked.

"How much did you pay?" I said defensively.

"Seventy korunas."

At once I understood what was behind the ham vendor's interrogation. The bastard was testing me. "I got screwed. I should've known better. I gave him perhaps four times the money it was worth."

"Sweetie, getting screwed is an essential component of the travel experience," Larry offered and took a huge bite of his sausage while I continued my pity party, barely nibbling on my ham.

"I'm Czech for God's sake! I am sick of people on both continents complimenting me how well I speak their language. Just before our trip, a teenager in Burger King asked where I was from. Then she squeaked, "'Neat! Welcome to America!'"

Carefully measuring each bite, Larry was too preoccupied with his sausage to commiserate.

I continued to brood in silence. Then I spotted the white crosses embedded in the pavement.

"I guess there are worse things than being cheated by a vendor. Each of those 27 crosses represents a Protestant who was executed in 1621 at this very spot. The rector of Charles University was nailed by his tongue to the gallows. He had a prime view of his buddies' beheadings."

"Appetizing. Can I hear the rest when I'm done with my sausage?"

After the final lick of greasy fingers and the last bite of halušky we got up and strolled idly through Old Prague, allowing the magical web of the Dark Age to guide our steps.

"Just a few people got away with only flogging. Bodies were quartered, and the pieces were hung all over these streets. Some heads were impaled on metal rods, and for almost ten years remained on display outside the Town Hall, reminding Czechs what happens when you mess with the Habsburgs."

"Did it work?" Larry asked.

"Habsburgs stayed in power for the next 400 years."

"And how did they end up on the Czech throne in the first place?"

"The Jagellons and Habsburgs signed a contract. If one dynasty ended up without an heir, the other would take over the kingdom. The Jagellons lost their last male in the swamps, fighting the Turkish Sultan Suleiman's army early in the 16th century. So in 1526, the Habsburgs married Cesar's grandson Ferdinand to Anna Jagellon, the last Jagellon offspring. Their wedding was the beginning of the Germanizing of the Czech people. Before that, the Czechs had enjoyed uncommon religious liberty compared to their European neighbors."

Getting tired, we spent a good part of the afternoon attempting to find our monastery, but the medieval labyrinth of Prague would not reveal the right path. My toes throbbed. We walked into a nearly vacant church where we collapsed onto a carved wooden pew, appreciating the muted lights and cool air.

"This is incredible," Larry said in a low voice. "Every square inch is gold, marble, and carvings. The ceiling must be what? A hundred-feet high? It's easy to understand the leading role of the Catholic Church in the past centuries. Heck, I'm ready to convert myself."

"That's what the Catholic Habsburgs were after, making a proper believer out of each soul. They put their bureaucrats in government and began closing non-Catholic churches. Of course, the Czechs protested. At the peak of their rage, the Protestants threw three ass-kissing Habsburg officials from Prague Castle's window. And here's the kicker — the bureaucrats didn't even get hurt!"

"And so we have Prague's Defenestration number two," Larry said.

"The uprising triggered a battle between the Czech Protestants and the ruling Habsburgs, a key event in my country's history. It's called the White Mountain Battle (Bitva na Bílé Hoře). The Protestants got creamed, and their 27 leaders were executed near that cheating ham-vendor's spot. Yet, the Habsburgs weren't satisfied. They exiled all non-Catholic priests and forced people to accept a new reality: attending non-Catholic services, baptisms, and funerals became punishable by a sentence of six months in jail. Working or visiting a pub on Sunday could also land someone in jail. And here is my favorite — talking crap about God, Virgin Mary, or a member of the Habsburg family — all members of the same fraternity — meant loss of property and beheading."

"Do you know how to drown a Habsburg?" Larry interrupted me, savoring my confusion like an inquisitor. "Put a mirror at the bottom of the pool."

"A lot of misery would have been spared if someone had thought of that," I said. "Czech intellectuals and spiritual leaders wouldn't have had to move to neighboring countries. I wonder if the nation's IQ would be higher today if all those thinkers would have stayed. Czechs lost one-fourth of their population. For example in Kutá Hora, out of about 600 houses, over 200 were abandoned and fell into the possession of the Habsburg's Catholic supporters. The independent Czech state became a poor province of the Austrian monarchy, and hypocrisy became the tool of survival. In subsequent years, the religious clash spread across Europe, escalating into a grisly conflict with a horrible name, The Thirty Years War."

"All that for tossing three guys out of the window," Larry said as more tourists entered the church. I took pleasure watching their amazed expressions. Cameras flashed, greedily snatching images for those at home.

"It's a House of God!" The angry sacristan's voice interrupted the hushed murmurs. "No photographs allowed! Everyone out!" With arms spread he shooed people out the door, offenders or not. Back among the crowds on the street, Larry said in disbelief, "We were just thrown out of the church! Just like those booted Protestants."

"I know that. What I don't know is which way is our monastery." I looked up and down the street.

"Okay, let's get our bearings," Larry said decisively, taking the lead. "There is the museum, so to the northwest must be Orloj. I think I remember now. Let's head this way."

A parked caterpillar-green vehicle sparked Larry's interest. "It's like a toy," he said and stepped closer for inspection.

"A Trabant!" I said. "My family used to have one just like that, the good-luck color. For 15 years our loyal Trabant was the butt of friends' jokes."

Manufactured in the former East Germany, these two-stroke-engine vehicles looked more like smiling M&Ms than real cars. Larry took a photo and, as we continued the search for the monastery, I told him our family's Trabant story.

"In 1959, my parents paid the deposit and put their name on the long Trabant waiting list. Nothing came easy in Communism, but Mom and Dad had big plans; the new Trabant would take our family on a dream vacation to Bulgaria's sandy shores of the Black Sea. Before that, Mom would faithfully check the blackboard in the window display on the main plaza in Brno, where our order for a new car was waitlisted. Nearly a decade later, their number appeared written in white chalk, and my mom knew that within a year they would own a car, becoming something of an upper middle-class family."

"The upper middle class? Wasn't everyone equal in Communism?" Larry asked as I followed him around another uncertain turn.

"In the apartment building where I grew up, musicians, doctors, hairdressers and factory workers lived side-by-side. Seemingly, we were all the same. But there *were* differences. Though today they appear minuscule, I felt them. For example, our friends Jana and Eva, the Sedlák family, who lived on the fourth floor, owned a Škoda, a car superior to a Trabant. They had been on vacations to Bulgaria twice during the decade when my mom kept checking the board for our number to show. Their Christmas tree was a long-needled pine that didn't shed while ours was a cheap spruce that lost its needles the minute someone sneezed next to it. The Sedláks owned a nice vacation house in the country, and although our vacation house was not far from theirs, it was just a small one-room cottage. Mr. Sedlák was a member of the Communist Party, so they were better off than most."

A strikingly tall, red-haired beauty walking ahead of us stopped my chatter. Larry and I stared as she searched for balance and firm footing, teetering on her Jimmy Choo four-inch stilettos, struggling to take a stride longer than eight inches.

"Hiking boots would have been a better choice," I whispered.

To shift our attention away from our own aching feet, while still hopelessly tangled inside the labyrinth of medieval cobblestone streets, I cheered Larry with a Trabant joke:

The Saudi Arabian Sultan decides to buy the best car there is. Leafing through the delivery schedules, he reads, Lincoln — six days, Rolls Royce — six months, Trabant — six years.

The Trabant must be something special, the Sultan thinks and decides to order one. The East Germans were honored and sent one right away.

The Trabant arrives, and the ministers run to tell the good news.

"It must be a superb company; they delivered a functional cardboard model!"

"Were Trabants really made of paper?" Larry laughed.

"Duroplast, a resin strengthened by used cotton and paper. The Trabant was probably the first recycled vehicle. On the other hand, this cute, friendly car produced five times the amount of carbon monoxide compared to other European cars. Whenever Dad needed to fill the gas tank, he would lift the hood and insert a dipstick into the six-gallon tank to see how much fuel it had. He carried spark plugs, a replacement belt, and some basic tools, always ready for repairs. Still, he said his Trabi was a reliable vehicle."

Larry stopped and frowned. "Wait. What's that? Is that...? Yep, it's the green Trabant. We've been here before; I have photographic evidence." Larry sighed and added, "This is absurd. We made a full circle."

"What's absurd," I said, "is that a used Trabant sold for more than the new one, just because it was available right away."

We trudged and retraced our steps, taking more wrong turns, but eventually, just like that, our monastery door appeared in front of us. In our room, when I took off my shoes, I discovered a good-sized blister on my toe. I hated to imagine what Ms. Jimmy Choo's feet looked like.

11. Insulting Interlopers

For the first week in Prague, I kept waking up just before 5 a.m., struggling to adjust to the nine-hour time change. If I had to get up, I might as well take advantage of that thin sliver of time when the vacant streets offered pure magic. Taking care not to wake Larry, I crept out of the room, tiptoeing through the hallways out into sleepy Prague. The creak of the front door spooked a flock of pigeons. Their wings flapped in panic as they fled the cobblestones.

Excited, as if entering a time machine, I was about to travel back eight, nine-hundred, a thousand years. I stepped into the narrow street lined with adjoining three-story buildings. The sumptuous decoration around the windows resembled whipped cream curlicues from a skilled chef's pastry bag, offsetting the apricot, lemon or blueberry colored icing, just like a three-tiered wedding cake. Everywhere I looked, I saw antique details: curved iron handles, large keyholes for great heavy keys, cast iron streetlights, arches, stone thresholds worn thin in the center by the steps of generations of Praguers.

With no destination in mind, I let my feet carry me toward the heart of this mystical city.

A shop window displayed three open books of poetry. Just three books, nothing else. In this prime commercial tourist district with expensive restaurants and overpriced hotels, where everyone was trying to make a buck, someone attempted to slow down this fast pulsing city with poems from Shakespeare, Frost and Whitman, gems worth pausing for.

On a whim, I turned a corner. The wrong corner. I was almost in the middle of the street when a group of young Germans were exiting a nightclub, robbing the morning of its innocence. Their obscene gestures and sounds gushed in my direction like raw sewage. They were too drunk to care that I was obviously more of a mother type than a hooker. I turned back, but within a few steps, an even larger party of arrogant Brits insulted sleepy Prague. Their shouts were getting closer. I felt my heart's panicky beat. I was still close to my monastery, but could I reach it in time or would I be sandwiched between those vulgars?

I used to have a recurring nightmare of being chased. While trying to outrun my pursuer, I would search for my house key. Now I was living it. Just a few more steps. I squeezed my magnetic chip in my pocket — the key to the monastery. I stretched my arm to match the door magnet. In my peripheral vision, I saw the two brazen groups meet.

How could these foreigners torment and disrespect Prague in such way? How dare they? Something erupted in me, and I turned, stepping out of my sanctuary. I positioned myself in the midst of those drunks. With my index finger over my lips, I just stood there.

They walked by me roaring and howling. They had to continue with their belligerent and rude noise if they didn't want to lose face in front of their buddies. I locked eyes with one of them and noticed his discomfort, perhaps even a sense of shame. Being bad in front of one's mother is never fun. Within seconds they staggered past me, and the neighboring streets swallowed their shouts. Did I behave like one of those scolding Czech moralists? I didn't care.

I climbed the stairs of the monastery, my knees trembling. Larry was still asleep. I slipped under the cover and pulled the blanket over my head.

A few minutes later Larry stirred. "Good morning, sweetie. Are you awake?" he asked softly.

12. *Prague's* National Theater

The National Theater, or simply The National, as locals call it, was one place I didn't want to miss. As the author Petr Hora said, there may not be another building in the world in which its nation invested such passion, anger, hope, and self-sacrifice. With my persistent, "Our tour starts at nine. Come on. Let's hustle," Larry and I pressed toward the National. I wanted to be the first in line.

We expected to meet our guide in front of a modern building that resembled a giant ice cube located behind the National; instead, we found only an empty plaza. Inside the ice cube the receptionist said with that sleepy, didn't give a rat's-ass way, "There may be a tour today, but I think they meet at the door on the left."

It was five minutes till nine. We rushed across the plaza, under the overpass, and along the National where I reached for the doorknob of what we decided must be the door on the left. It was locked.

"She must have meant the other left. Come on." My knight-in-shining-armor grabbed my hand and pulled me along the side of the building. Soon scaffolding blocked our way. I checked my watch as we jogged back in the direction we came from, searching for a door, any door.

I knew the National's story from my school days, but I didn't know anyone who had seen a performance there. Not only were tickets too expensive for most families, including my own, they were usually divided up between Communist party members. As my mom would say, "we have nothing to wear anyway." For me, the National was just a chapter in my history book.

We scuttled around the theater that stood as colossal as the Czechs' 400 years of resentment toward the Austro-Hungarian Empire under those powerful Habsburg rulers.

In the 19th century when the theater was built, the official language used in schools and offices was German. The Czech language and Czech folklore were kept alive by the lower classes and villagers. Thankfully, a group of nationalistically minded poets, writers, and artists, sons of ordinary dressmakers and shoemakers, realized that Czechs needed their own theater where they could learn the heroic stories of their ancestors. People's pride in their heritage could reverse the culturally downward-spinning spiral, thought these intellectuals. Since the Habsburg's Emperor Franz Josef wouldn't build a theater for them, the Czechs decided to build one for themselves, as glamorous as the theaters in Vienna or Paris, a world-class symbol of national identity to reflect the Czech people's desire to be viewed as a separate nation with its own language.

We trotted back and forth along the side. The theater looked bigger with every wheezing breath. At last, when we turned the corner, there it was, an entryway as stately as I remembered from my school book. It takes an extraordinary bozo not to find an entrance this grandiose. Hot and sweaty, we stood in the lobby, the gateway to my cultural heritage. We purchased two tickets and joined a group where a lady with a short girlish hairdo and a ringing voice introduced herself as our guide. I never imagined a green knit dress could look this good on anyone. I was enthralled by her fluent moves. Was she an actress? Whoever she was, she was able to convince her appreciative eight-person audience of her performing talent. For the next two hours, we barely took our eyes off her.

"Dances, trips, lotteries and auctions were organized throughout Bohemia, Moravia, and Silesia to collect money to build our National Theater," she said excitedly as if sharing the news for the very first time.

"The theater would never have been built without the contributions of ordinary people. Meticulous records were kept, and the lists of donors were endless. A street accordion player sent one full week's earnings. Mr. Adam contributed monthly with money he saved on cigars. Gamblers' jackpots arrived from all over the country, billiard players' windfalls followed. A one-legged beggar brought his blind friend, and together they dropped their coins into the nation's piggy bank. A little girl sent her contribution from the sale of her crochet lace. A grandmother brought an extra coin she saved on groceries. The money came from Czech patriots living in America, Asia, and even Africa. Someone from California sent a gold nugget. A hat maker supplied the theater's dressing room with six hats; a shoemaker gave 48 pairs of shoes. Mr. Karásek lent his carriage for two weeks. Building our theater unified the nation. Czechs wanted to prove that their cultural and artistic spirit was equal to any nation." Our guide's voice quivered, and I envisioned colorful butterfly wings aiming for soaring heights. The toe of her silver slipper pointed, her arms moved through the air with the grace of a dancer. Mesmerized, we followed our ballerina's one-woman show to a basement where she halted before a display of large square boulders, each engraved with a name of a different Czech town.

"As word spread, stone blocks began arriving from all over the country. Every region wanted a piece of their backyard to be the base on which their National theater would stand. Each boulder was pulled by six white horses, their collars decorated with ribbons and flowers. Music and dancing accompanied them as they entered Prague." Here our dancer rose to her tiptoes.

"On groundbreaking day the owners of taverns and coffeehouses opened their doors to lodge the multitudes who came to Prague to participate in the largest 19th century

Czech festivity. The army handed out blankets and straw beds. Do you know what a straw bed is?" our performer asked a teenage girl, the youngest in our group. The girl shook her head.

"It's a mattress stuffed with hay or horsehair."

"Eew!" the girl smirked.

I remembered lying in my grandma's bed, my fingers looking for the little nubs, pulling long horse's hair through the coarse white sheet. I have never thought of grandma's bed as being gross, just comforting. Pulling horse hair through the sheet was something one does in grandma's bed.

"No one was sleeping that night," our ballerina continued. "People everywhere swung their bright paper lanterns. Fireworks shone multi-colored lights on two-tailed lions, Czech icons displayed on all public buildings. The Vltava River reflected the glimmering symbols of Czech, Moravia, and Silesia. Sounds of music carried from the boats." Our ballerina paused, smiling broadly, her happy eyes locking with ours. We smiled back, even Larry, despite the fact that he didn't understand a word she said.

"The next morning villagers dressed in traditionally embroidered dresses launched the parade. The young men of the athletic association named Falcons (Sokol), followed, all two thousand of them. Behind the sea of red, white, and blue flags marched butchers, coopers, bakers, millers, and goldsmiths, then faculty members, university professors, and students. Merchants, bricklayers, masons and carpenters went next. The band introduced the miners who comprised a 3,000 man procession of laborers." Lowering her voice and ever so slightly drooping her shoulders, she added, "Still, it took 37 years before the doors of the Czech National Theater finally opened in 1881."

We moved on to the upstairs lobby. Every ornate piece of furniture and gold-framed painting was accompanied by our ballerina's animated explanation. She spoke much faster than I could translate for Larry, so he kept to himself at the outskirts of our little group. At one point he came closer, leaned toward me and whispered, "This is going to cost you a beer." Then he stepped back and resumed his guard posture with his hands folded in front of him.

We all were impressed with the upper lobby that looked like a fancy art gallery, the royal blue ceiling full of golden stars above statues and oil paintings.

"Attending the theater was an all-day affair and during the long intermissions, people socialized."

I studied the oversized paintings and the statues crafted by Czech artists, at the time when they were still boys in their early twenties, art academy classmates. Almost without an exception, they came from low-income families. Today, Julius Mařák, Mikoláš Aleš, František Ženíšek and Josef Václav Myslbek are household names in the Czech Republic and beyond in the world's art centers.

I loved the stories told by their paintings. One of my favorites showed a father and mother with their two kids, at first glance a portrait of an idyllic family. The children were observing their parents at work, learning their customs. But unnoticed, lurking beyond the outside window, watched creepy old Morana, the symbol of death, holding scissors in her crooked bony hand. She was preparing to cut off the string of life, to remind us to treasure the time we have together, for we don't know when she will bring it to an end.

My group had already moved on, but I kept standing in front of another painting where young lovers, sitting in the grass, appeared mesmerized as they listened to the wanderer's song about ancient times. I wondered if my children would pause and listen to my ancient song.

Entering from the highest balcony, we finally got to see what we had all waited for, the opulent interior of the National. Gold frescos complemented the 1,000 red-velvet seats. The ceiling was decorated with eight scantily dressed women representing the muses of architecture, sculpture, dance, pantomime, epic, lyric, music, and painting. "Now that's art," Larry the connoisseur, whispered.

Our eyes rested on the stage curtain, the largest painting in the country. There was the old grandma donating her coin, there were the poor with their contributions, carpenters, poets and a sculptor, actresses like fairies in flowing robes, waiting for their golden chapel to be finished. The grandiose emotional scene was a lively play in itself.

I imagined the curtain lifting and the tones of Bedřich Smetana's Libuše, the opera celebrating Grandfather Czech's youngest daughter, the founder of Prague, filling the space. It looked like our ballerina was also imagining, perhaps every velvet seat occupied and every eye focused on her. She gazed off into the distance, ready for her final act.

"The Czech nationalists took the Old Czech fables as their historically accurate Bible celebrating their courageous and wise ancestors. The mythical stories awakened pride in the Czech underdogs. However, good intentions, led by passion at the beginning, matured into hatred toward their German neighbors. Fights between Czech and German students occurred daily. During the summer of 1881 when the National Theater finally opened, someone broke windows in the nearby German theater. Soon after, tragedy struck. A fire of suspicious origin destroyed the interior of the newly opened National Theater. Within a few hours, only the outside walls were left standing. The fire was still burning, and the weeping nation spontaneously started collecting money for repairs. In six weeks, there was enough to rebuild and not long after, the National reopened with Bedřich Smetana's Libuše performed once again."

"That was another sad story." I said to Larry, "Smetana, the aging Czech composer, wasn't even invited to the grand opening. He had lost his hearing and became something of an embarrassment. Also, Josef Zítek, the main architect, never again stepped in the theater after it was rebuilt. The newspapers ripped him apart, blaming him for not designing a more fire-resistant structure. Much bitterness is buried in all this splendor."

When our group returned to the lobby on the first floor, the panicky ticket lady rushed toward our guide. "Quick, another group has been waiting for over an hour already! Eva didn't show up."

Our star bowed for us and, not waiting for applause, rushed toward her new audience. We heard her calling out, "Dances, trips, lotteries, auctions were organized throughout Bohemia, Moravia, and Silesia to collect the money to build the National Theater — "

From the sidewalk outside, we looked back at the National's icons, the statues of triumphant horses frozen in flight beneath the rounded copper roof. God Dio's eight daughters, the Muses of art, held their instruments, all glorious even underneath decades of layered soot.

At the intersection we waited for the green light. A woman leafed through her guidebook, matching the picture with the National. "I think this is their National Theater," she told her husband in English, but his attention was on his ice cream cone. The light changed, and she closed the guidebook. Together they walked on by.

13. David Černý's Black Babies

From our view at the National Theater, the medieval Charles Bridge looked crammed, reminding me of a photo of the Golden Gate Bridge on its 50th anniversary, when thousands of San Franciscans crossed it on foot. Not a fiber in my body wanted to mingle with the multitude of slow-moving colorful dots. Even though the historical Charles Bridge is a must-see for Prague visitors, Larry and I decided to cross the mighty Vltava river to Lesser Town (Malá Strana) by one bridge over, the Legion Bridge, which we shared with only a handful of pedestrians. "Prague off the main drag," Larry sang happily. "That's the way to go." Without the horde of strangers competing for the view, we took postcard-perfect photos of expansive Prague Castle (Hradčany) in the distance and the stunning Charles Bridge lined with Baroque statues of religious figures in the foreground.

The Legion Bridge stretches over long, narrow Shooter's Island (Střelecký Ostrov), named after the bowmen who have perfected their skills here for the past 700 years. Green branches of grand old trees caressed the sides of the bridge from below, hiding the tranquil oasis including a very fancy restaurant with very bad reviews. Later, back in California, we asked each other, "Why didn't we check the island out?" We just looked at each other and shrugged our shoulders.

On the other side of Legion Bridge, we turned towards Kampa, Prague's romantic river district. At once I recognized what I was looking for. I had first seen this river path decades ago on a postcard a friend had sent me. It inspired two of my paintings. I labored in my home studio to bring alive the giant buckeye trees and the curving stone wall, trying to capture the idyllic atmosphere on canvas, wondering if I would ever experience it beyond its postcard size. "Do you suppose we'll ever see the end of Communism?" I asked my Czech friend, a fellow emigrant. He was stunned by that concept. "You are a dreamer, Lenka," he said then.

Now, I was here. All was as lovely as on that old postcard, despite the graffiti that covered the wall. In a few places, peeling stucco exposed the bricks. It was as if the wall was trying to rid itself of the blue and black spray paint.

I wrapped my arms around Larry's waist. A light breeze brought the sweet fragrance of lilac. I closed my eyes. The hum in the chestnut trees accompanied by the Vltava's splashes created a concert performed by the timeless duo. "This is a dream," I said as we continued to stand there, savoring the perfect moment. For so many years I could only imagine being here. All I had to do now was to open my eyes.

A life-size statue of Sri Chimnoy, the Indian spiritual master stood by. His meditating image went viral in the wet summer of 2002 when the Vltava rose over its banks, flooding Prague's streets. Only the guru's bald head and his hands raised in prayer showed above the water.

I imagined painting the holy man, squeezing a blob of alizarin crimson hue, a dash of sap green, and some titanium white on my pallet. For the lilac bushes exploding with violet blossoms and the sensual statue of a young girl holding a bunch of plump grapes at her breasts, I would tap the canvas in Monet's impressionistic style. For the chestnut trees whose blossoms framed Old Town across the river, I would use a huge canvas and my finest brushes.

Larry and I sat on one of the wooden benches facing the river, a perfect place to read a poem by Jaroslav Seifert, my favorite modern Czech poet, but having Larry next to me, spreading soft cheese with a plastic fork on crunchy rolls wasn't bad either. Larry must have sensed some poetic vibes. With his full mouth, he began, "There was a young girl from Nantucket..." I shoved another chunk of roll in his mouth.

After we had snacked, we walked toward the courtyard of a renovated three-story building, a former mill. The motto on its snow-white wall read:

If the culture lasts, the nation will survive.

Forty years of Communism had left the old mill in a dreadful state of neglect, but after the revolution, it was saved from crumbling away by the wealthy art collector Meda Mládková, a Czech-born emigrant, who is now spending her golden years in Washington, DC. Mládková turned the old structure into a modern art gallery.

"During the Communist era, Mládková supported the underground artists, representing them in the West, saving them from the isolation of those God-forsaken times," I said.

"How did she enter a country that was wrapped in barbed wire?" Larry asked.

"The Communists were hungry for foreign currency and were happy to make an exception to their own rules. Eventually, Mládková's public comments about the oppressed Czechoslovakian artists cost her the privilege. After the revolution, she donated her art collection back to the Czech people. 'Fulfilling my moral obligation,' she said in a TV interview."

We looked over the courtyard where some contemporary art pieces were displayed.

"What is this?" Larry pointed to three stone elephant-size infants crawling on the lawn.

"The babies!" I yelled. "David Černý's famous black babies. I was hoping to see them." I love how his outrageous art yanks people out of their daydreams.

"Remember the statue of a man hanging from the roof by one hand? That's also Černý's creation."

The realistic statue shocked Larry and me when we were browsing through the Old Town. For a moment we thought it was a live man ready to commit suicide.

"The very first thing Černý shocked the nation with was his 'Pink Tank'," I said. "In 1990 he painted an entire Russian WWII tank, a monument honoring the liberation of Czechoslovakia by the Soviet army, in flamingo pink. The Soviet Foreign Ministry screamed to prosecute Černý. Apologies were given, and the tank was repainted its original olive green. But just a month later, the tank was pink again. This time it was done by members of the Parliament who were immune to prosecution. The nation was fed up with Soviet dominance over the past 40 years and people stood behind the prank. Key chains, T-shirts, and postcards with the pink tank were sold on Charles Bridge, raising money to pay Černý's fines. Mládková organized the sales."

"Cool," Larry grinned and rested his foot on something that could have been either scrap metal or a priceless piece of art.

"Černý's 2009 art piece, 'Entropa' displayed at the European Council building in Brussels, again scandalized the world. Major newspapers all over the globe commented on his controversial work. I heard on the BBC how mercilessly Černý pushed the limits, poking fun and stereotyping the European countries. He presented Romania as Dracula's theme park and France as a country on strike. Bulgaria got it the worst and demanded an official apology and removal of the Turkish toilets representing their nation."

"That reminds me — " said Larry and I knew what he was going to say: "That photograph on Linda and Ben's refrigerator! Ben's back is to the camera and he is grinning over his shoulder, mimicking two statues of men peeing in the water fountain shaped as the Czech Republic."

"Speaking of which, I could use that water fountain right now," said Larry and looked around rather urgently.

It took us a little while to find a sign announcing:

Public restrooms
Open 9:00–18:00
10,KC or 0,50E

Larry rushed in. Two seconds later he was back out.

"I need some change. Mrs. Pee-pee-ová didn't let me in."

I pressed a coin into his hand. Larry returned momentarily. "I didn't need it after all. Men only pay for number two. Number one is free," he informed me with a grin and I couldn't help but wonder how that conversation had gone.

We struggled up the hill toward Prague Castle, the home of Czech kings and now the President. A huge crowd filled Castle Square, anticipating the changing-of-the-guard ceremony.

"Christ, are they giving out the president's bobble heads?" Larry cried. "We would have to climb a street pole to see something."

"Let's go to Petřín Gardens instead. It's not far," I offered.

Following the sidewalk, we dragged ourselves further up the hill. At Petřín, by sheer luck, we got the last shady bench with a view of the city, our wide-angle matinee. The cherry trees had transformed their blooms into small green fruit. Dandelions thrust their happy faces from the grass. Couples sunned on the grassy slope using their sweaters for blankets. Larry pointed out Saint Vitus Cathedral, the Charles Bridge, the two-towered Týn Church, the green roof of the Saint Nicholas Church, Powder Tower and the National Theater.

"Look at all those towers," he marveled. "There is so much more we haven't seen."

On the horizon, Prague's controversial TV tower poked through the haze like a launching spaceship. Černý's babies were crawling toward the top. Once drivers pulled over, wondering if the city was being invaded by giant black infants.

The afternoon heat set in. Larry and I strolled the park, occasionally pausing, taking refuge in the shade of the huge chestnut trees.

Back at the monastery, the cold walls provided immediate relief from the unseasonably muggy, hot spring. The building was deserted. Where was everybody? And who was everybody anyway? Beside Brother Antonín, we had only seen a couple of other people. One was an older unshaven monk whose white habit looked like an ill-fitting woman's dress. He was startled each time we ran into him.

"How did you get here? Who let you in?" he demanded as if he'd just caught trespassers. Unsatisfied with our explanation, he would murmur something under his breath and totter on.

Once, I attempted to engage him in a conversation, hoping to find out something about his life. "How did you survive Communism?"

"Construction," he mumbled, looking away. "And 40 months of a labor camp."

I wanted to know more, but he was not interested in my questions, and, as if I was no longer there, he said to himself, "Where did I put it? It was someplace here." Hastily, he disappeared down the corridor.

We took a shower and sank in between the white covers.

It was dark when we woke up three hours later. Reaching for a laptop, we began to research the train schedules. The next day we planned to relocate to Čáslav, a small town about an hour east of Prague.

Date out of admissible range. We were unable to come up with any timetables. Every date we picked was out of that freaking "admissible range." All of a sudden, the light went on in one of my mind's dusty file cabinets. In Czech, we write the day first, then the month! So five-twelve would be the fifth of December, not the American May 12th. Once we got that squared away, I clicked on the seventh day, the Sunday.

"That's Saturday," Larry corrected me.

"No, my little love bug, the Czech week starts on Monday, so the seventh day on the calendar is Sunday."

Larry shook his head. "Do you even count starting with one?"

"Depends what you're counting. Did I tell you the story of Linda and Ben trying to rent an apartment on their first visit here?

"At the rental agency, an employee handed them a key, wrote down the address and told them their apartment was on the first floor. Linda and Ben arrived by taxi at the charming old four-story building. They stared at the sidewalk-level door, a slab of scratched metal. The key didn't fit. They peeked through the crack below the door and saw a broom and a bucket in the middle of the cement floor."

"They got scammed," blurted out Larry.

"That's what they thought, so they fetched a taxi back to the agency where Ben slammed the key on the counter and demanded their money back.

"The manager listened to their troubles and at once solved the problem. Czech floor counting (like many other European countries) omits the bottom level. Back at the apartment building, Linda and Ben climbed the stairs to the second floor, which was really the first floor, and their key unlocked a lovely sunny apartment someplace in this neighborhood."

"At least they didn't wander into an elevator shaft," Larry added thoughtfully.

"And then, there is the thumb," I said. Number one isn't the index finger, it's a thumb up, like when hitchhiking."

"And how does one hitchhike then?" Larry said exasperated. "You mean to tell me I won't even be able to communicate with my hands?"

"You guessed it, and that's why you need to be especially sweet to me. You could start by providing me with a nice orga... Wait, hold on." I wiggled myself from his embrace. "At this moment I desire a nice organic cup of tea, please."

14. Train to *Čáslav*

We pulled our rattling suitcases through the sleepy streets of Old Prague at 6:30 in the morning. Bars were closed, and the German and British partyers were back in their hotel rooms, suffering excruciating hangovers, as I liked to imagine. A light drizzle glazed each cobblestone and the laundered air intensified the loveliness of the deserted streets. At last, we had Prague to ourselves. But our minds weren't focused on her treasures; we were in a hurry to catch the train. Larry took the lead, clutching the street map, referring to it at each corner. We passed the Museum of Alphonse Mucha, perhaps the most recognizable Czech painter, the leading European Art Nouveau artist. Mucha's posters featuring Sarah Bernhard, the French actress, adorned the living room walls of my Czech friends. I regretted not having visited the museum. Through a side street, I caught a glimpse of the statue of St. Wenceslas on his horse.

I thought of little Honzík, a character from a story my first-grade teacher read in class. The boy was on the way to visit his grandparents in the country. From an open train window, Honzík waved to his mother standing on the platform. The six-year-old traveled alone. Did I really live in times where parents sent their kids into the world alone and no one found it the least bit worrisome? Little Honzík sure didn't appear as nervous as Larry and I were now.

The Political Prisoners' Street we walked on was to commemorate the victims who had been tortured at the Gestapo headquarters once located here. The horror of those words was jarring. In the historically accurate movie "Anthropoid," German secret police smashed a school-age violinist's fingers to make him reveal the hiding place of men in the resistance movement that his family harbored. And that was just the beginning. Eventually the interrogators placed a bucket holding his mother's head in front of him.

Behind which windows were the innocent folks humiliated and tortured? How long did it take for the people living on this street to utter those words — political prisoners — without thinking about their meaning?

At the top of the street, we turned toward Prague's Central Station. As anxious travelers do, we arrived over an hour before our train's departure. The station was modern and sleek, not at all like the train stations from my youth. Then, swarms of weary travelers crowded the waiting area, some slept on long heavy-duty wooden benches, others slumped on their roped luggage. The stench of urine crept out from the door marked "WC," which my dad told me stood for "water closet." Throughout my childhood, Mom warned me against using public restrooms; if my sister or I had to go, Mom instructed us to squat behind a bush. On weekends, groups of tramps filled the stations: Carrying rucksacks with dangling canteens, wearing faded khakis, guitars slung over their shoulders, they awaited trains to take them into open country. Those free spirits appealed to me, and I fantasized about joining their ranks when I grew up.

Travelers looked stylish and rested now, some pulling wheeled luggage, an indulgence known to modern man for a surprisingly short time. Others were consumed by their phones. I imagined the odorless restrooms equipped with hand-driers and automatic flushing toilets. What happened to those sturdy wooden benches, now replaced by modern pedestal seats?

We purchased two tickets to Čáslav. The electronic timetable informed us of our terminal number. Easy enough, just like locating a gate at the airport. We climbed the stairs and entered the domed platform area.

"Straight out of the 1940s movies," praised Larry.

"The ceiling must be 100 meters high, don't you think?" I asked.

"I'll say it's about 57 liters." Larry reminded me that he doesn't do European measurements. I never understood what was so hard about decimal-based measures.

The electric-powered trains hissed, arriving and departing on other tracks. The PA announcements both in English and Czech echoed into incomprehensible gibberish.

I confirmed with a woman who was boarding what I thought to be our train. We settled into a vacant boxy compartment, hoping that other travelers would join us. I could hear my mom's warning, "Don't touch anything." With a handkerchief she would fan the black soot off my sleeves, scolding, "Look at you, we haven't even left, and you're like a pig already." Trains fueled by coal are history, and soot from smoking locomotives no longer covers everything along the tracks, including the train compartments. Our area was clean and cozy.

We felt a tug and the train set in motion, taking us through Prague's suburbs into the country.

At the edge of the woods, a motionless herd of deer enveloped by soft fog watched as our train went by. Further along, two colorful pheasants cautiously crossed the pasture. Here and there, long-eared rabbits hopped across the field, disappearing in tall grass. The green fields alternated with huge yellow carpets of rapeseed flowers. It looked like the farmers were growing sunshine. When the sky was gray like today, the golden acres made the world bright and joyful again.

At the next stop, a nice family entered our compartment.

"Dobrý den. Are those seats available?" the father asked in perfect Czech.

I happily gestured for them to come in, thinking, are you kidding? Those seats are customized to your fit, my beautiful countrymen. Boy, am I itching to eavesdrop on your conversation.

The nice family thanked us, hung up their jackets, lifted their luggage onto a rack above the seat and then engaged in conversation among themselves. In Russian! I tried to restrain myself from bombing them with hard looks of displeasure.

I stared out the window, wondering what Čáslav was going to be like. With our reserved *pension* conveniently located across from the train station and trains arriving every hour or so, it seemed a perfect choice for our base camp. We wanted to visit nearby Kutná Hora and two or three neighboring towns. A few centuries back, Kutná Hora had competed with Prague for the title of the Bohemian capital. I wanted to see Saint Barbara's Cathedral which took 500 years to complete and looked so impressive in the brochure.

Before the next stop, the Russian family gathered their belongings, repeatedly apologizing whenever their coats ever so slightly brushed over our knees.

"Naschledanou," they said in turns, nodding their heads and with timid smiles they backtracked toward the door, making me regret the evil thoughts I had harbored toward them.

A man with long gray hair and body odor entered our compartment next.

"Dobrý den," he said, and Larry gave me a look which I read as — here you have it — your conversation companion delivered.

After exchanging a few pleasantries, I asked about Kolín, the city we had just passed.

"Kolín is very nice. Especially the square around St. Bartholomew Church. I used to play guitar with my buddies there, earning money for tramping," he said with a shy smile.

Would I be like him had I had become a tramp? The perfectly pointless wondering about what would have become of me, had I stayed in my country surfaced in my mind. To ground myself, I asked, "How much is an acceptable price for a beer to a Czech person?"

"About 30 korunas. Czechs wouldn't pay those Prague prices. Not even well-off Czechs." His claim followed complaints about the inflated rates in the capital. But what bothered him, even more, was the early closing time of public restrooms.

"Six p.m! What is one supposed to do after that?"

I gave it some consideration but restrained myself from giving any tips.

We spent the next few minutes watching the passing greenery brightened by the rain.

"You can walk around Kutná Hora in one day," the man disturbed the silence, "I am sure there are over 100 restaurants there. During summer, something is always going on, concerts, festivals, music competitions, wine tasting, you name it. I never miss the Renaissance fair. It goes on into the night, celebrating King Wenceslas II who promoted Kutná Hora to the second most important city after Prague. In 1300, the city boomed, thanks to its silver mines. Torches, fireworks, the fair is something to see. You should come back in the summer. My sister works there. I could get you in for free."

And, as if wanting to cheer us up for missing the big events, he added, "But a lot is happening all over this region even now. And a lot to see. Are you going to Čáslav?"

I nodded. "To Pension Česká Koruna."

"Good choice, they are famous for their cooking. Legendary."

He ignited my interest, but as the train came to a halt, the man said, "This is where you get off."

In a hurry, Larry and I gathered our jackets and suitcases and stepped into the murky morning just as the conductor in a maroon hat blew her whistle. I turned and waved to our traveling buddy. His arm was already stretched out the window. He smiled broadly as the train took him away.

Our waving arms conveyed the unspoken: "Goodbye stranger, I am glad chance brought us together. Safe travels!"

15. Pension in *Čáslav*

At Čáslav's small train station, untouched by modern times, a handful of travelers sought refuge from the chill by burrowing deeper into their coats. The dullness of a rainy Sunday sat heavily on the small town; no one in the streets, shops closed. As a teenager, I often wondered where everyone was on days like this. The same old Communist propaganda on both TV channels, no good book to read, the phone remained silent. The weight of those murky days brought unbearable loneliness as if all my friends were having fun in someone's house whose parents were not home and I wasn't invited. Now, the steel gray skies draping over deserted streets brought back the essence of those boring Sundays. I reached out for Larry's warm hand and squeezed it tight.

Across the street, the Pension Česká Koruna, a mixture of a hotel, guesthouse, and inn, was where we had booked the next few nights. It looked as it had in the 1870s when Mr. Tichý opened the door to his first customers. Seven windows faced the train station and two rows, 15 windows each, faced the side street. There was one exception. The picture on my computer screen showed people in front of the building. This place looked dead, and indeed, the *Closed* sign in the window confirmed that it was.

A jolt of panic shot through my stomach. From my mobile (as Czechs call their cell phones), I dialed the phone number on the window sign.

"You are here already?" The man's voice barked, quickly adding in a more pleasant tone, "I'll be right there."

I looked forward to meeting Mr. Tichý, the great-grandson of the original owner. I looked forward to sitting in his restaurant, learning about the turbulent years of their family business. Mr. Tichý would be delighted by my interest and would declare: "You are my guests. The drinks are on the house!"

Minutes later, a harried middle-aged man with a worried face popped up from behind the building. Rummaging through his pockets, checking for the right keys, he introduced himself as Mr. Tichý's brother-in-law.

The man unlocked the restaurant and the trapped smell of cigarettes and spoiled food hit us like an escaped beast. We followed him through the dim dining area, out the back door to a hallway and up the stairs, all divided by locked doors. The man handed us the keys as we went, four so far. Streams of sweat ran down his sideburns. From his office on the second floor, he handed us some papers to sign, checked our passports, and gave us the fifth and final key. Then he left, locking the door behind him. We stood in a foyer in complete silence. I looked at Larry with big eyes and whispered, "We are completely alone in this whole building."

Our room was surprisingly bright. The salmon-colored walls complemented yellow and orange bed covers. It all looked immaculate and strangely familiar.

"Ikea!" Larry exclaimed as if running into a long lost friend. "All this stuff is from Ikea. Look, those are our lamps."

"And those bed covers..." I said, recalling the guest bedroom in Linda and Ben's San Diego home. I hoped to discover old familiar things on this trip, but this wasn't what I meant.

From our window, we saw a corner bakery shop, a *Closed* sign on its door. My stomach growled.

"If we want to eat today, we had better take a train to Kutná Hora and hope that one of those hundreds of restaurants will be open," I said.

From the heated compartment of our train, we watched the countryside through the sliding raindrops. I dreaded the thought of exchanging our cozy sanctuary for the dampness outside.

"The good thing is, we'll get to test our brand new rain gear," said Larry, ever upbeat.

We got off the train and the moment it was out of sight, we realized, judging by the surrounding jungle of greenery, we had gotten off one stop too early. There was nothing else to do but to throw on our ponchos and start the 40 minute march along the fields toward Kutná Hora.

Accidentally, Larry forced his poncho over his head backwards. The hood wrapped his face, outlining his nose and lips. He looked as if he had zip-locked his head in a green vacuum freezer bag. His mouth, like a pump, quickly sucked all the air out. I found it hilarious. But then it dawned on me that a plastic bag tightly wrapped around a person's head could not be good. I reached to free the hood from his face, but the plastic wouldn't budge. In a sudden panic, I ripped a hole through it. Larry, a bit disoriented, took a few deep breaths, and as if he hadn't just suffocated, headed in the direction of

Kutná Hora. I followed on a narrow pathway next to the puddle-filled, two-lane road.

The rain got heavier. Larry's ripped hood flapped in the wind, rainwater dripping down his face and behind his collar. Avoiding the geysers from the wheels of passing trucks that threatened to drench us, we kept our eyes on the vehicles, jumping out of the way. When we were passing one of the lagoons in the road, an eighteen-wheeler fast approached. "Oh no!" I yelled, and both of us raced ahead. We looked back just as the truck, without slowing down, barreled through the water, generating an enormous wave where Larry and I had stood seconds earlier.

"That one could have thrown both of us over the fence," Larry nodded.

We, the unwilling participants of the "outrun the passing cars game," raced toward the city center. The brown tourist sign ahead pointed toward Kostnice, one of the major attractions. Since we were just steps away, we decided to go for it even though we would have preferred a sign pointing to a pizza parlor. The line of tourists waiting to purchase tickets was moving quickly. Soon, Larry and I stood in the middle of an ossuary, a kind of a church whose interior was decorated entirely with human bones. Chandelier, altar, candleholders, coat-of-arms — all were made with bones. Scallops made out of skulls and thighbones draped from the ceiling. Skull- thighbone, skull-thighbone. Wars and the black plague had provided plenty of building material. Some pamphlets stated 30,000 people were buried here, others threw in an extra 10,000. The place was dim, dusty and weathered. Even though the ossuary was packed with tourists taking pictures, it was strangely quiet. Some fractured skulls had earned honorable display on narrow vertical shelves. Larry and I stared at the heads with holes big enough for a good-size stone to fit through. Others had small round holes from bullets, yet other ruptures had resulted from metal bars, or so we guessed. Some skulls had long cracks.

"Let's get out of here," I whispered. Larry agreed. Outside, the persisting drizzle glazed the red roofs, cobblestone sidewalks, and everything in between.

In preparation for this trip, I had amused myself by studying Kutná Hora on the map, dreaming and planning. Now, we were here. Wet, cold and starving.

We entered the first restaurant. Despite the steep beer prices, sure sign of a tourist trap, we gladly took a table by the window overlooking the city. With *svíčková* (the traditional creamy gravy) and five dumplings steaming on the plate in front of me, the world became an agreeable place once again. Larry ordered *guláš* (paprika beef stew) with golden crisp *bramboráček* (fried potato pancakes). Only after we licked our plates clean did we marvel at the view of the St. Barbara Cathedral towers in the distance.

The rain stopped, and the timid sun began to peek from behind the clouds.

Back on the street, Larry said, "This place is amazing, and as breathtaking as Prague, minus the crowds."

In front of one of many historical buildings, we discovered a statue of the first Czechoslovakian president, Tomáš Garrigue Masaryk. I had never seen his full-size statue before. In his three piece suit he looked elegant, tall and handsome. The Communist regime didn't teach us about our first president in school. Nor, did they teach us about our second and third presidents. Our education began with the fourth president who had been, of course, the first member of the Communist party, the square-faced Klement Gottwald.

Dad kept Masaryk's photograph on his dresser and told my sister and me, in a hushed voice, that Masaryk was the founding father of Czechoslovakia. Masaryk's son, a member of the Czechoslovakian government, refused to resign when the Communists came to power. He ended up being thrown out of a window, Prague's Defenestration number three. I only learned of his mysterious death, and of his father's life, through rumors. No wonder Czech history had never made sense to me.

Raindrops like stars shone on the black marble statue of Tomáš Garrigue Masaryk, the Father of our nation. The adamant antagonist of the Communist regime stood in full poise and grandeur at last.

The first Masaryk bust I ever saw was in the rose garden in San Francisco's Golden Gate Park. It was donated by Czechoslovakian emigrants. It brought tears to Dad's eyes as well as to my own when in silent reverie we stood in front of it in 1990, one year after the Velvet Revolution, when Dad was first able to visit us in California.

16. Silver Mine in *Kutná Hora*

We gathered with a few other visitors in the small courtyard of a medieval house that had been converted into a museum. Presented with two choices — touring the mint or visiting the silver mine — Larry and I said simultaneously, "The silver mine." Our guide, a girl of perhaps 16 years, led our group to a huge wooden gazebo where we put on miner's hooded coats.

"They will protect your clothing. Wearing a white coat underground may seem impractical, but in the 14th century, when this mine was most active, plain cotton cost substantially less than dyed," she said in Czech, then repeated her explanation in English.

Larry, the dress-up enthusiast, was checking for a coat his size.

"They are all damp!" A French lady complained, looking at her husband as if it was his fault.

Reluctantly, I took a damp cotton coat off the hanger. I had barely recovered from the earlier rain and was still chilly. Larry, on the other hand, was decked out in full gear: his wet coat reaching to his knees, a hard hat strapped under his chin, a lunchpail-sized hydrogen lantern in his hand. On his face was the grin of a five-year-old before his first train ride. Glued to our guide, Larry hung on her every word.

"A handful of 11th century miners who lived in this area were unaware that their tiny mining settlement was sitting on silver deposits. Around 1290, Kutná Hora's thick deposits of silver ore started producing wealth beyond anyone's wildest imagination and the last Czech kings of the 420-year Přemyslid Dynasty — the only Czech Dynasty — became one of the richest and most influential European...hmm..." Our guide looked over the semicircle of the shivering pseudo-miners, searching for the right English word.

"European leaders?" I offered.

"Yes, that," she smiled, relieved.

In single file, like Snow White's dwarfs, we walked through Kutná Hora's streets to the nearby mine entrance. Giggling passersby stopped and pointed. Larry hummed, "Hi-ho, hi-ho, it's off to work we go."

The stairs of a well-lit shaft took us 500 meters beneath the street. At the bottom, the shaft narrowed and darkened. In the spots where we had to squeeze through the tunnels sideways, the dull thumps of the hard hats hit the uneven, dripping ceiling. Our guide asked us to turn off the lanterns. We found ourselves in darkness thick enough to drive a person crazy. A splash disrupted the stillness. The French woman yelled, "You dropped my thousand-dollar Nikon in a puddle, you dumb shit." I don't speak French, but I was pretty sure that was what she said.

We turned the lights back on, and our guide pointed to the displays along the wider sections of the tunnel. "Here are some examples of miner's tools, the ...the... how do you say?"

"The chisels, stakes, hammers?" I filled in.

In short side tunnels, mannequins in hooded white cotton coats identical to ours were frozen in motion. I was pleased to learn that in centuries prior to any worker protection acts,

King Wenceslas II granted miners a six-hour workday in recognition of their hard physical labor.

Further along, around more tight twists and turns, our guide asked us again to switch off our lanterns. We were instantly consumed by a thick blackness which offset the violent gurgling of a powerful river in the earth's belly, not so far beneath our feet. Larry and I lingered behind our group, savoring the mixture of excitement spiced with apprehension. How useless our hard hats would be should the river decide to claim a new corridor now.

Outside, at the end of a quiet street, we caught up with our group on a flat grassy knoll. The sun finally came out to warm our shoulders.

Someone asked if King Wenceslas II was a good king.

"Wenceslas II was the wealthiest of the Czech kings, due to the Kutná Hora silver mines," the girl said. "To understand Wenceslas, one needs to know about his ambitious father King Ottokar II who doubled the size of the Czech kingdom.

"Ottokar's great success generated even greater problems. Others, especially the Habsburgs and Hungarians, along with the papacy in Rome, became increasingly nervous over the Czech king's — " Her eyes met mine, and I mouthed the word "expansion."

"Ottokar gained some territory by force, some through his two marriages," she continued. "He was 19 when he married his first wealthy wife. She was 50. Ottokar had his eyes on the crown of the Roman Emperor. He calculated that in the next election the nobility would cast their votes in his favor. But the nobles didn't wish for a strong, capable ruler. Instead, they picked the unknown Count Rudolph Habsburg, whom they hoped to manipulate. Ottokar stood up to Rudolph Habsburg in battle, but the great Czech King was defeated and died in 1278. His son, seven-year-old Wenceslas II, the successor to the Czech throne, fell into the claws of his wicked and abusive guardian Marquees Branibor, who took the future king out of the country. With Branibor in the lead, other vultures joined in plundering and looting the king-less Kingdom."

The Branibors! I finally understood why Mom called me Branibor when I ripped my doll's head off. "You behave like Branibor's army in the Czech land!" Czechs would scold 700 years after the gory chapter in their history ended.

"An unprecedented famine settled in Bohemia," the girl went on. "Rich became poor and poor became beggars. Processions of peasants staggered toward cities hoping to preserve their lives. With no clothes to protect them in the winter, at night some crawled into piles of horse manure seeking warmth. Others stole hanged bodies from the gallows and, like ravens, consumed their flesh.

"When the nation cried out for Branibor to return the King to his people, greedy Branibor demanded an outrageous amount of silver in exchange. Eventually, with great pomp, the 12-year-old Wenceslas was brought back to Prague. His advisors, of course, had to make decisions for him at the beginning. Still, with age and experience, he proved to be a capable king. Between Kutná Hora's silver and the marriage to his second wife, the 12-year-old Polish princess Eliška, Wenceslas expanded the Czech Kingdom from the Danube River to the borders of Greece and Russia."

That was half of Europe! I realized now how ambitious my earlier plan was, to travel the area once dominated by Czech kings. Its original core, today's Bohemia and Moravia, was proving more than sufficient for our seven-weeks travel.

"The foreign kings lusted over Czech treasure," our guide continued. "Some manipulated political spheres, others mobilized their armies, ready to take Kutná Hora by force. In 1304, the Habsburg military surrounded the city, planning to starve its residents. Instead their soldiers, camping in the muddy autumn fields, became infected with disease and began to die. From the disastrous Habsburg siege, 30,000 hired men never returned to their families."

I leaned closer to Larry and whispered, "Imagine the mess. Scattered corpses as far as the eye could see."

"You'd tell a joke, and no one would laugh," said Larry.

"Even though King Wenceslas II had defended the city, the cost of constantly building armaments eventually exhausted his treasury. When Wenceslas suddenly died of tuberculosis, his treasury was depleted. Fourteen months later, the murder of his 16 year-old son, King Wenceslas III, brought the mighty Přemyslid dynasty to its end."

Slowly, our group walked toward the miner's village where we moved between mannequins engaged in various stages of coin-making. Some melted ore, separating minerals from silver; others scaled out the silver sticks or sculpted the coins, one at the time. It was as if we were touring a functional silver coin manufacturer.

"The King Wenceslas II mint coined the Prague groschen, the well respected hard currency which lasted 344 years," the guide said.

That's a long time in comparison to now. In modern times, Czech currency has gone through four major reforms. In 1918, the new Czechoslovakian government issued its first money for the new nation, freshly separated from the Austro-Hungarian Empire. Until then, Czechs used money from the countries geographically closest to them.

In 1939, Hitler invaded Czechoslovakia and took over the Czech banks to help finance his war. The war money, one German mark to ten Czech korunas, sucked the Czech economy dry.

Then, there was the turbulent summer of 1953. Later that day, over the phone, my dad recalled:

"Thirty-six hours before the financial reforms took place, Communist president Antonín Zápotocký told people not to panic. He assured them that there wasn't going to be any reform. At that time I was in my mandatory two-year military service. I heard the bastard's speech from the post office radio where I was assigned to guard bags of the new money.

With an empty rifle they made me hold, I was protecting the worthless money that would build an illusory world."

Mom, at the time a student living in a dormitory, described her experience:

"At 3 a.m. they woke us up and divided us into groups of ten, sending us to factories. The Communists used students to spread their lies about the stable Czech economy, hoping to prevent panic. The next day people woke up in poverty. We could exchange 300 korunas at the rate of 5:1. If anyone had more money, the rate became 50:1. Once I got my savings converted into new money, I had barely enough for my bus fare. The working class who, after WWII, voted in the Communist system, got screwed. And finally woke up. Angry people went to the streets, protesting. But it was too late. The government quickly crushed the uprisings. The Czechoslovakian korunas became worthless, and our nation became further isolated from the rest of the world."

As Czech people do in hopeless situations, my parents laughed telling their stories. It was a bitter laugh.

The last money reform was in 1992 when Czechs and Slovaks separated after the peaceful 1989 revolution. The Czechs issued gorgeous bank notes adorned by Alphonse Mucha's paintings while Slovaks converted to euros.

On a display, I studied the thick and wonderfully uneven handmade groschen. On one side it read, "Wenceslas II, by God's grace"; the opposite side showed the two-tailed lion, the symbol of Bohemia.

"Money, the devil's tool," I said studying the coin, "whoever holds it, holds the power."

"Actually, I don't like money either, but it does calm me down when I have it," said Larry.

We walked toward the exit gate where we parted from our sweet guide.

"Your English is very good," she said. "How did you learn all those words?"

"Oh, just speaking it every day over the past three decades," I laughed. "I live in California."

"Really?" the girl's eyes widened, "and you came all the way here?"

In Prague, no one is astonished over meeting someone from California or Timbuktu. In Kutá Hora, it was different. I was touched and flattered. Some things money just can't buy.

17. The Vietnamese Girl

We hustled down the hill beside pretty pastel colored houses to catch the train back to Čáslav. A young English-speaking Vietnamese woman approached us on the long cement platform between the tracks. She asked when and where the train to Prague would arrive. The girl looked at me innocently, expecting me to read the information on the timetable. I am Czech after all, no? But her request took me by surprise. Being a visitor here myself, I was the one asking those questions. I had no idea what the numbers and the abbreviations squeezed in rows on the timetables represented.

The girl didn't speak Czech, but that didn't stop her from taking a day trip to Kutná Hora, which she liked very much, as she kept repeating in broken English. The girl had recently left Vietnam and joined her family who owned a small restaurant in Prague. I was fond of her right away, and wanted to help. I walked with her toward the train timetables where I stared at the yellowish paper, not having a clue how to crack the hodgepodge of tiny symbols. What the hell do the crossed hammers stand for? And a cross? Could it be a symbol for Sunday? I followed the line with my index finger and read in a small voice, "Eighteen thirty-four?"

"Thank you, very much," said the girl, "and from where?"

A crowd of people gathered on the track opposite from where the three of us stood. So many people, they must be going to the capital. I wasn't sure, but I pointed anyway, "Over there." The Vietnamese girl was so thankful; she took out her camera and asked Larry if he would take a picture of us. Then she rushed toward the underground passage to join the people on the platform across the way from us. A train came exactly at 6:34 p.m.

The girl turned and waved to us.

"What have I done?" I mumbled as the train left, hoping I'd put her on the right train. Otherwise my photograph may be attached to a refrigerator door somewhere in a Vietnamese restaurant in Prague, with a note underneath — No service! Ever! The second part underlined in red.

18. The Policemen in *Čáslav*

In Čáslav, before returning to our Pension Česká Koruna, we decided to examine the church whose tower could be seen from the train station. As we strolled up the deserted street, I noticed two police officers walking down towards us. With their black uniforms, baseball caps, laced boots, guns in shiny holsters, nightsticks and tasers, they looked like a special unit ready for serious action.

In Communist Czechoslovakia, I usually crossed to the opposite side of the street to avoid confrontation because the police took pleasure in exercising their authority. They would stop people randomly to leaf through their 31-page citizen books, smirking over the personal information, while the poor citizen shook in his boots. Official stamps from current and previous employers stimulated an array of questions: when, where, how long, why? Current address, former address, temporary address — more questions. Parents' names, mother's maiden name, children's names, single, married, divorced (how many times), criminal record, immunization record, library record. (I made the last one up.) Seriously, anything could trigger suspicion, especially the absence of the current employer stamp. Unemployment was a crime punishable by a jail sentence. I didn't make that one up.

The police officers were a couple of steps away from us now. They may be the only people we'll meet in this town, I thought, and, with the sweetest smile I could summon, I said, "How is it going, officers? Nice evening we have." Those few words opened up the floodgates of response. Unable to control the flow, Larry and I swam in a reservoir of their enthusiasm. "No crime this year yet. Just petty theft. Not a single car stolen." The older one shook his head in a way a fisherman might complain, "Too quiet, not a single bite."

Learning that we were new in town, they moved on to a new subject.

"These houses here," the older officer swung his arm and paused, building up momentum, "have underground tunnels leading all the way to the central plaza. And that tower there," he pointed toward our destination, "is the Peter and Paul's church, from the 13th century."

"It may be 12th," said the younger policeman.

"Whatever, nothing changes the fact that Jan Žižka of Trocnov was buried there."

Then the senior officer pointed to Larry, "Has the American gentleman heard of Miloš Forman, the Oscar-winning filmmaker?"

Larry leaped at the opportunity to get involved in the conversation in which he finally understood a few words, "One Flew Over the Cuckoo's Nest," he said with his bright smile.

"*Ano, ano!*" The officers cheered, proud of their famous Čáslavian.

"What a shame that you don't stay longer. Our Iron Mountains are so beautiful. It's too bad to miss the Lovětín Canyon."

"And Hedvica's Meadows. All protected reservations."

"Tomorrow we'll go see the ruins of castle Lichnice," I said, hoping to cheer them up.

"You don't even have to pay the entrance fee," the older one said. "Just go around the backside, you'll be able to get in."

What? Did a man of the law just tip us on how to commit a crime? Or is it a trap? Are they going to wait for us behind a bush, to jump on the chance to use their tasers?

Both officers continued talking over each other, filling us in on wonders we could not squeeze into our schedule. We learned about lookout towers, churches, synagogues, castles, the region's first stone theater, the list went on until Larry discreetly pulled on his earlobe, our secret signal, a plea to move on.

"Don't forget the church by the lake, the best view of the city. With the original city wall, built by King Ottokar II," they yelled after us.

In a few minutes, we were in awe over the enormous stone church, a massive giant disproportional to the entire town. I reached for the front door but jerked back when a face appeared in the opening within the door. The woman's few remaining teeth matched the brown colors of the stonewalls.

"Service is over," she said in a tone that one uses to chase away stray dogs.

"She may be the reason for the policemen's tasers," Larry said as we descended back toward our pension through the abandoned darkening streets.

19. The Oak Tree in *Podhrádí*

"Dobrý den," the next morning Larry tried to repeat the Czech greeting after me.

"Let me hear those r's rolling. Then we'll practice on *prosím* — please, and *děkuji* — thank you."

Equipped with four pleasantries, Larry agreed to venture across the street to the bakery and get us breakfast. "I'll go as long as you promise not to complain, and eat whatever I bring."

The door clicked after him, and I was alone.

I checked on the damp socks and underwear that I had hand-washed in the sink and now hung around the room. I was anxious. Today we were going to visit my dear friend's family house. She once told me that it is next to an 800 year old oak tree, a protected monument. We will also visit her resting place. For too many years I had wanted to do that. How is it going to be standing in front of her grave? Would it finally chase away my longing for all that might have been? I inhaled deeply and looked out the window. People in the sunny street below were going about their business. No more ghost town. The city was revived. Larry was crossing the street back toward the pension, victoriously holding a brown paper bag above his head for me to see. A few bakery customers formed a line in front of the counter. Our two police officers sat at a small table, donuts, and coffee in front of them. Some things are the same wherever you go.

The smell of fresh pastries filled our room.

"Five? You brought us five poppy seed rolls?"

"That's the lowest number I can pronounce. I only wanted four, though."

I couldn't blame him. The Czech word for four — *čtyři* — is impossible to pronounce for a foreigner.

Larry and I boarded a single shuttle train, a toy-like blue and white electric car that looked as if a little boy neglected to put it away in a toy box. We were off to the small town of Třemošnice. The lone passenger, an older gentleman, looked up from a window table covered by his neatly pressed handkerchief. He was slicing a poppy seed *koláče* into bite-sized pieces. "Dobrý den." We greeted each other. Larry got comfortable on the other side of the car in a sun-warmed seat while I struck up a conversation.

"Are the ruins of the Lichnice Castle walking distance from Třemošnice?" I pointed to our map. Without even a glance at it, the man answered, "Ano, but a bus from Třemošnice leaves six minutes after this train arrives."

Larry would prefer the bus, I thought. I let the soft-spoken man return to eating his breakfast and moved to be closer to Larry.

"Ahoj Jano!" the man greeted. He rose to help an elderly lady, perhaps a childhood friend, lift her shopping bags up the metal stairs. The train and its four passengers lurched forward. I eavesdropped as the woman described in great detail all her smart purchases. She was particularly pleased with her quality metal cheese grater. The magazine clippings and discounts she had earned in various marketing promotions reduced her total expense. Remembering that their generation had been used to uniform, government-regulated prices, I silently congratulated her on her smart buys. Thriftiness and resourcefulness are ingrained in the Czechs. I imagined my mom and dad at their kitchen table, cutting and organizing their discount coupons.

The train slowly rolled through green and yellow fields. Here and there, pink blossoms of plum trees were like fluffy bouquets on a checkered tablecloth. The bright landscape reflected in Larry's sunglasses.

"Those screaming colors make me wish for a pair of earplugs," said Larry without looking away from the window, his face serene, smiling just a bit.

At frequent stops, one or two passengers embarked or disembarked from the train. A conductor dressed like an airline pilot in his pressed dark blue uniform and crisp white shirt checked tickets. All seemed orderly and neat.

A peculiar sight caught my eye: four short chimneys from a small white factory nested in the middle of the fields.

"Excuse me," the elderly gentleman appeared from behind. "Those chimneys back there belong to an old lime-powder factory. You could tour it for about 10 korunas (50 cents). It would be a nice stop for you, I think."

A lime-powder factory? A baggy of lime-powder as a souvenir? I just couldn't summon excitement towards the idea. Later that day, I found a flyer promoting the site — visitors even get to look up the chimneys!

"We'll get off at the next stop, the end of the line," the gentleman called out to us.

Larry and I could barely keep up with him. All the while, he explained how to get to the castle ruins. We parted at the bus station. A few steps along his way he turned and said, "May our land warm your hearts."

The bus strained on a curving road up the hill toward the woods. We were instructed to get off at the first stop, a crossroads in the middle of nowhere. The gentleman on the train said the ruins were walking distance from the train station, but our drive had lasted a while already. I made a mental note — don't ask Czechs if something is walking distance. They always say, "ano, ano, of course." We labored up hill toward Podhrádí, a tiny village whose name means "beneath the castle." We passed the first house, a woodcarver's showroom. The garden was filled with statues of kings, princesses, dragons, trolls and other mythical figures. "I wonder where that old oak tree is," I mumbled, out of breath.

"Over there." Larry pointed to the pile of logs in the woodcarver's garden.

"Funny," I said and continued up the hill. I needed to find that tree.

The left side of the road opened to a view of lush countryside, its right flank hemmed in by immaculate houses, manicured gardens and mowed lawns. It was too perfect. Where were the chickens, the smell of manure, the tractors and the old farm machinery? Why did I feel discontent in this pretty place? Then it dawned on me. People didn't live here; the village houses had all been converted into vacation cottages. I imagined the wooden troll jeering after me, "Life marched on while you were gone, my dear. Why should we live in dung just to please a stranger from California?" Things changed, got better, people would say. But still, this wasn't how a Czech village is supposed to feel, it wasn't how I remembered. "Yeah, yeah, yeah," the troll taunted.

A few steps more and we stumbled upon the old oak tree with its hollow trunk, and arthritic branches full of yellowish green sprouts. A small sign was nailed to its trunk:

I saw the castle Lichnice being built, and I saw the castle being destroyed.

I shifted my attention to the window of the vacant gray house caressed by the oak branches. I imagined two small faces looking out, watching tourists who came to admire their oak tree. Little Lucinka and little Marky, whose mother, my best friend, had grown up in that house. I met Lenka in Trai-skirchen, a refugee camp in Austria. We had liked each other instantly, not only because we were both Lenkas with blond hair and blue eyes, both pregnant with our first daughters. We bonded through our laughter and tears. So infectious was Lenka's laughter that often mere eye contact triggered a new attack of the giggles, leaving us wheezing and struggling for breath. Our girls were both born in August 1979. Later, we both had sons. And then Lenka died. That was the year I reevaluated my belief in God. After the funeral, little Lucin-ka's and Marky's father moved the small family and I never saw them again. Twenty-five years later I found them on Face-book. Lucy wrote about the oak tree next to their grandma's house, where their stepmother had sent them each summer. "The only good thing about her."

No wonder my friend Lenka remained nostalgic for this fairytale land: a house at the edge of the woods, in the shadow of the castle ruins — her playground. The old oak's fingers tapping on her window and the wildflowers scattered around her childhood home reminded her where she belonged. No wonder she got homesick in America. In those Communist years, she couldn't go home, not even to visit. The borders opened less then two years after she died. Too late for my dear friend.

Larry and I scrambled up the steep hill on all fours. Every so often something crunched under foot. Finally, the remnants of the stone walls of the once mighty castle rose in front of us. We could almost make out the window arches, moats, and falling bridge. Yellow dandelions, like forgotten coins, were scattered all over the green football-sized field. We had it all to ourselves. How fantastic it was to walk through imaginary rooms where important decisions had once been made. Larry found a perfect stone to sit on and took out the poppy seed rolls for our picnic. Accompanied by chirping birds, we looked far into the country, a perpetual quilt of dark and light greens and bright yellows. Here and there a nest of red roofs squeezed in a tight bunch. Blossoming cherry trees that reached to the skies outside the castle ruins teased with their sweet fragrance.

In 1250, when a close friend of King Wenceslas I built this castle, Mongolian armies stormed like starved grasshoppers through the Czech land. They killed, stole and destroyed. Their trophies were the heads of fallen Dukes. Since then, ownership of Lichnice Castle passed through many royal hands; the good and bad took turns. Elaborate receptions greeted visiting dignitaries and kings. Blood was spilled during the time of the Hussite wars. In the end, fire swallowed it all, damaging the castle beyond repair. The ruins were left at the mercy of locals who used its stones as building material for their own houses.

I told Larry the legend of a local Duchess who was unable to give her husband a son. As punishment, he imposed a slow death on her when he built a windowless and doorless room and forced her into it. Her friends helped her escape, and when — years later — she unexpectedly walked across the Duke's path, he died of a heart attack.

On the way back down the hill, I picked white, red, blue and yellow wildflowers, arranging them into a bouquet.

Crunch!

"What was that? Something keeps crunching under my feet."

"Look," Larry bent down and pointed in the grass at a large streaked snail. "Holy Mother, look at that sucker!" I shook, "let's walk on the road."

"I have never seen such hefty guys!" Larry said enthusiastically.

Down at the edge of the woods there was a rusty sign with an announcement. Larry read aloud the English text at the bottom:

"In this area subsists a rare species of snail Bithynella Austriaca, the glacial relic."

"Sweetie, you just killed — like five of those glacial relics," Larry said, suppressing a chuckle. We continued walking along the road, my eyes scrutinizing the path, trying to avoid further butchery.

On the outskirts of Třemošnice, we entered a small cemetery that resembled an immaculate flower garden shaded by tall poplars. When I found my friend's name engraved on a tombstone, a jolt of painful disbelief shot through me, just as when I first learned of her death.

"Now we have her back home with us, in the meadows below our beautiful Iron Mountains." I had read in a letter from Lenka's mother years ago. I laid a bouquet of wildflowers on the cold stone. Perhaps it was those cracking snails, those glacial relics that triggered my giggle. Soon I imagined Lenka was laughing with me. We laughed till tears rolled down my face. We laughed till my jaws locked, and the drool dripped. It was Larry's concerned look that made us laugh even harder. Till it hurt. Till it really, really hurt.

Larry and I had an hour or so before the train would take us back to Čáslav. In a pastry shop above the plaza, we took seats on the spacious terrace among mothers and toddlers. While the moms sipped coffee with whipped cream and nibbled on fancy cakes from pretty porcelain plates, their children played with colorful plastic toys in the sandbox. In this maternity haven, Larry rejoiced when I sat a tall frosty mug of Czech draft beer in front of him, the thick white foam slowly running down the glass. From underneath the garden umbrellas, we looked at the unhurried life on the modern plaza below: benches, water fountains, a boutique shop. An idyllic town in an idyllic setting. Only a few *paneláks*, the unimaginative four-story apartment buildings that looked like concrete boxes, spoiled the scenery. They symbolized an era when the individuals' longing to separate from the masses was a crime punishable by death, jail, or permanent segregation. Because Lenka left the country without Communist approval, she wasn't allowed to go back home.

20. The Train Conductor in *Žleby*

We pulled ourselves up the two metal steps of a single train car. The engineer, sitting by the door, greeted us in Czech: "You seem tired, where have you come from, Lichnice Castle?" I nodded, and he fired up the next question. "And did you see the Girl's Rock?"

"The Girl's what?"

"And how about the reservoir Seč? You didn't miss that, did you? You could have seen two more castle ruins, all in a day's walk." It was evident he would have liked to continue, but he glanced at his watch and jumped to his feet. "Time to roll," he said and disappeared in the engineer's cabin. With a gentle tug, the train began to move. To my dismay, the engineer reappeared, walked up to us, motioning to the empty seat. "Do you mind?" he asked and, not waiting for approval, he sat next to me.

"Who is driving the train?" I squeaked.

"I'm training a young lad." With a satisfied grin he added, "after 30 years on this route, I am going to retire."

"Things must have changed from the early days," I said.

"Since the Velvet Revolution, there hasn't been any maintenance done on the track. You can hear the dumpting. The train isn't going smooth. Dumpt – dumpt – dumpt, you hear that?"

I didn't, but nodded anyway.

"In winter, it's all white, and when the sun goes down, it's like hot lava spilling over the snow," the engineer said looking out the window. Then, as if yanked out of a pleasant dream, he added, "But now the government talks about shutting down the small trains."

I acknowledged the unfairness of it with a solemn nod, and then asked, "I hear a Slovak accent. Are you Slovak?" (Before the 1993 split, Czechoslovakia had three main ethnic groups: Czech — also called Bohemians — Moravians, and Slovaks.)

"Living here 36 years, I am Czech now, I think." He leaned closer to me and lowered his voice, "Moravians are much better people, though."

He must have recognized my Moravian dialect. Otherwise, he wouldn't make such a statement.

"When I take a bus with the Moravian tourist club, we sing all the way. The Czechs sleep all the way."

In the middle of laughter, the engineer frowned, concentrating on the cadence of rolling wheels. He jumped to his feet and sprinted to the cabin. "What's going on?" Larry stood up, nervously looking around. "Are we gonna derail?"

In a couple of minutes the engineer returned, took his seat and said, as if nothing had happened, "You should have gone on the trail from Třemošnice to Ronov. One of my favorite hikes." And he pointed out the window toward the steep forested hills. In Ronov's distillery, they give samples of *slivovitz*," he said waggling his eyebrows.

Knowing that Czechs are avid walkers, I wasn't surprised that this beer-bellied almost-retiree was suggesting his favorite hike that any tour book would classify as difficult. But sampling the hundred-proof plum brandy on top of it? And then what, roll down the hill to the train station?

"The next stop is the Žleby Castle, a definite must," the operator said.

"Can we get off and then catch the next train?" I asked.

"If you get off midway, you can't get back on. You'll have to buy new tickets," he said.

I must have looked surprised, for the engineer said, "I know, it's a stupid rule, but only destinations longer than 200 kilometers can be interrupted. If the conductor is *vůl* (a beloved Czech word for an idiot, ass or a fool), he'll make you buy new tickets. If he is a decent person, he won't."

We got off at Žleby. The engineer shouted after us, "The castle is beautiful but make sure you see the park. They have white deer there. Straight across the bridge, then turn left. Two hundred meters along the river and you are there."

"Naschledanou!" Larry and I yelled back, waving.

Approaching Žleby Castle, we passed a parking lot, surely jam-packed during summer, but empty now, in early spring. The castle's elegant white towers were adorned with gold lightning rods; they soared above enormous cypress, cedar and chestnut trees. We entered the garden, hoping to spot the white deer, but soon gave up our search. We opened our blanket in a meadow next to the river with the pretty name Doubravka. Larry laid down, propped his head with the backpack and closed his eyes. Within seconds his breath became shallow and even. I laid next to him and interlaced my fingers under my head. The romantic sugar-cube towers looked even taller now. Ivy climbed crenelated walls, and I imagined cupids firing their arrows, peeking through the gaps of the wall's even teeth. With rhododendrons bursting with white flowers in the foreground, only the white deer were missing from my postcard view accompanied by buzzing insects, chirping birds, and the River Doubravka bubbling over the shallow dam.

Someplace along this river, my brave high school teacher had taken 30 hormonal teenagers on a field trip. Trying to hide from her watchful eye, we smoked cigarettes in an effort to look like adults. We must have succeeded in driving her wild because back in the classroom, she assigned us an essay entitled "What was the River Doubravka Whispering?" After chewing the end of my pen and staring at the ceiling for a long time, I wrote about Doubravka foretelling my future, promising a happy life with Prince Charming.

A golden green beetle circled the edge of Larry's sleeve. I was certain if a fish jumped out of the river, it too would be golden. If that magical creature would offer to fulfill my dearest wish, I would say, "But you already did."

Back on the train, with slight trepidation, we handed our desecrated tickets to the young conductor. The words of our engineer echoed in my head; if the conductor is vůl, he'll make you buy a new ticket. The conductor glanced at our ticket, waved his hand and moved on. He must be a decent person, I thought. I love how Czechs choose to ignore the rules when they disagree; even officials who are paid to enforce them.

21. Dinner in Pension *Česká Koruna*

Earlier this morning, when we walked through the crowded dining room of our pension, the workmen were already drinking beer and wiping the red paprika gravy off their plates with dumplings. They looked content. Now, having returned from our day trip famished, Larry and I couldn't wait to dine in the hotel restaurant. I was already choosing my meal from among the many dishes listed on the laminated menu. But we were out of luck. From the outside, we could see chairs turned upside-down on the tables and the beautiful, though solemn Mrs. Tichý was mopping the floor.

"Come, come, we'll still have something left to eat." She waved us in and lowered two chairs onto the wet floor.

"A couple of people on the train told us how much they like your cooking," I said cheerfully, trying to bring a smile to her sad eyes. Without revealing the slightest surprise or joy she just muttered, "That makes me happy," and disappeared behind the swinging door. She came out holding the menu that Larry and I, before our trip, printed from the website and studied with great interest. In no time, Larry navigated among 37 traditional Czech dishes listed: roasts, ribs, goulash, poultry in creamy gravy, deep fried cheese and deep fried mushrooms, dill, horseradish and paprika sauces with fluffy dumplings. Tripe, sauerkraut, lentil and cream-of-pea soup, all the hearty meals of my childhood. They had potatoes prepared in seven different ways.

My mouth watered as I rubbed my hands in anticipation, "I was dreaming of this moment," I said as Mrs. Tichý placed the menu on our table.

"That's what's left," she said and with a red pen circled meatloaf with svíčková, beef chuck with svíčková, and something named after the city Čáslav. I suspected it had svíčková in it too.

"Oh," I said, picturing the cook tilting the almost empty pot and scraping its crusty walls.

"I've never eaten in a restaurant with all the chairs stacked around me," said Larry when Mrs. Tichý placed two tall glasses of beer and two plates of svíčková in front of us.

We ate while studying the yellowish-brown photograph of the inn that hung on the wall. The story of Tichý's family restaurant represented the fate of countless Czech businesses. I was hoping to hear the details from Mr. Tichý, but instead, he handed me a memory stick and said, "It's my son's school project. You can download it to your computer."

So I learned about their ambitious great-grandfather Alfonse Tichý who, in 1870, borrowed money from Count Karel of Auersperg, the owner of the romantic white castle Žleby, to build this hotel and restaurant. His establishment prospered until shortly after WWII. In 1948, the newly adopted Communist ideology stripped the rights of citizens to own a business. Small and large businesses were confiscated and declared state property. The Royal Auerspergs fled from their white castle to Austria while the Tichý family was forced to hand their restaurant and hotel keys over to the Communist thugs, mostly young brainwashed enforcers. The widowed Mrs. Tichý was allowed to end her days in one of the rooms of her ancestor's decaying dream. For over 40 years after her death, the building — like a giant ghost — stood empty. Windows cracked, the roof collapsed, mold infested the walls, and fractured pipes flooded the floor. In the 1991 restitution, after the Velvet Revolution, the dilapidated structure was returned to the family. By then, the Tichý's fourth generation was in the computer business and no one had any restaurant experience.

"What do you think Linda and Peter would do if they'd get their great-grandparents' confiscated farmland?" I asked Larry. "How would my city kids care for horses and cows?"

"Don't sell them short. We know they can grow an herb garden and they had a turtle and a dog. So the basics are covered. They would just have to get used to wearing overalls."

Mrs. Tichý replaced Larry's empty stein with a full one and returned to her mopping.

"My dad told me about the day in 1948 when the Communists marched into his village," I said. "My grandpa had refused to hand over his animals to a cooperative farm, so they came in person to take his workhorses and milk-cows. The Communists informed my grandparents that along with their farm animals, their farmland now belonged to the state, allowing them to keep only one pig, some chickens, and a few rabbits.

Grandpa, like his father and grandfather, loved to dig in the soil and treated his animals well. On Christmas Eve, he would take some of the best foods into the stables to share with his livestock. Only then did the family sit at their dinner table. It was his gratitude ritual. The day their cows and horses were stolen, grandma symbolically broke a loaf of bread to pass to their beloved helpers one last time. But the government men pushed her away, accusing her of wanting to poison the animals."

I smeared the cold gravy on my plate with my fork. "My grandparents refused to work in the cooperative farm. As a punishment, their citizen books were stamped with the word *kulak*, the black mark of nonconformists. With that, no one was allowed to hire them. My dad's brother was at that time in the mandatory military service. As a son of kulaks, he wasn't trusted with a weapon and was assigned to hard labor in the coal mine. Black epaulets on his uniform set him apart from regular soldiers. Czechs nicknamed those military outcasts, with some degree of veneration, the Black Barons. My dad's brother, on a rare home visit, used some kind of chemical to erase the word kulak from my grandparents' citizen books. Eventually, both of them found employment in Brno, an inconveniently distant city: grandpa as a laborer in Mosilana, the textile factory, and grandma as a cleaning lady in the public restroom at the central bus station."

Mrs. Tichý collected our dishes and switched off the lights over the front counter. Walking up the stairs to our room, I wondered what would have happened if that chemical had burned a hole in my grandparents' citizen books. I reached out and squeezed Larry's hand.

22. Social Realism in *Kolín*

"Nine-o-four, right on the money," Larry checked his watch as our train took off from Čáslav.

We settled into an empty compartment and began to study our tourist road atlas where Kolín was not only highlighted in yellow — the sign of a tourist destination — but also was framed in red, the sign of a national cultural monument. The names on the page burst with highlighted yellow towns like Čáslav or Třemošnice. Fewer places, like Prague, Kutná Hora or Kolín, were also framed in red. We were eager to explore.

In front of Kolín's train station, we hopped on a crowded city bus heading toward the historical center. We held on tight to the metal overhead railings as the bus came to frequent jerking stops. The passengers stared numbly at the fogged-up windows. In contrast to their stylish spring coats, Larry and I looked like hunchbacks with backpacks underneath our raincoats, but our eyes sparkled. Seven minutes later, just as our plastic-wrapped bodies began to sweat, we got off the bus a block from the old town.

The imposing St. Bartholomew Church, the reason for Kolín making it to the national monuments list, was closed: *"under construction for two more years,"* said the sign taped to the church door. The lookout tower was still open but only on Sundays. "What's plan B?" Larry asked.

"Wandering around. Inhaling this wonderfully laundered air," I said perfectly content. A few steps up the narrow street we chanced upon a regional museum located in an old stone building. I rang the doorbell.

"Why would anyone leave their house in this weather?" We heard a woman mumbling before she had came into full view. She sold us two tickets and then followed our every step. As we leaned over displays with broken pieces of pottery, her body language screamed — "Hurry up!" And so we did. Not because she wanted us to, but because these archeological treasures — the broken ceramic pieces that the Celts in this area spun on pottery wheels 2,400 years ago — had become just what they were: a collection of unexciting blackened ceramic chips.

A few doors down from the Celtic museum, in a row of residential homes with well preserved old-world charm, we discovered a house that had been converted into a museum representing a wealthy townsman's residence. It had everything the Celtic museum lacked, including a cheerful guide — a plump lady in a red sweater. From the basement to the maid's room, kitchen, and the living room, it felt like we were visiting someone's home while the owner had toddled off to a fish market. The guide commented in Czech on every single article, all the pieces of the Victorian walnut furniture, the vases and dozens of porcelain knick-knacks. Larry took a special interest in a toilet bowl painted inside and out with bird heads, and the 18th century women's bloomers which weren't sewn in the crotch. All of it was interesting, but things slowed down considerably as the house tour concluded with a walk through an adjacent art gallery. The long wall was adorned with paintings of Kolín. The red sweater lady stopped in front of each one, pointing out where the city differed today. It was like viewing someone's never-ending collection of vacation snapshots. Larry started sending the 'I'm bored' signal, pulling on both of his earlobes simultaneously. Then the telephone rang down the hall. The woman excused herself and rushed off. Larry and I jumped on the opportunity and hurriedly by-passed the long exhibition, aiming toward the exit sign. We froze when we heard her footsteps and pretended to study one of the paintings. Our dedicated guide stopped where she left off and said, "But have you seen the mill on this painting?" Caught, Larry and I obediently backtracked.

At last, we made it to the exit door. But our guide didn't stop there. Ignoring the rain, she followed us outside. In the middle of the street, she pointed in the direction of the synagogue and the Jewish cemetery. "Also you can't miss the museum in the city hall — the knight-and-sword show."

We promised we wouldn't and, out of sight, aimed straight toward one of Kolín's many fine bakeries.

I eyeballed the rustic loaves of bread displayed in wicker baskets, perhaps five or six pounders that sold for less than two dollars. In California, we pay over six bucks for artisan bread one-fifth that size.

"Sales personnel aren't used to browsers," I remembered my dad's words before he nudged me out of a small store once, "don't drop by if you don't buy." Ignoring the etiquette, Larry and I continued dripping rainwater from our raincoats on the bakery tiles, indulging in the aroma of freshly baked bread.

The pastries looked exactly the same as they did in the Communist period when pastry chefs had to follow identical recipe books regulated by the state. I had ingrained in my brain the flavors of every tartlet on display: the creamy eggnog inside the chocolate Indians, the pleasant tartness of raspberry jam in Linzer tortes, the crunch of hazelnut meringue. I could almost feel the pleasant tickle in my throat as if I were inhaling the cocoa powder that the marzipan potatoes had been rolled in. My eyes rested on the chocolate-covered vanilla cake rolls neatly stacked on a narrow silver tray. When Mom, on her way from work, sometimes brought a couple home for my sister and me, we gladly interrupted our street play, rushing to greet her, happily skipping by her side. The pastry package she carried generated such an excitement one would think she had brought us a live kitten. "No, you can't have it now," Mom would say, "All your friends will want to have a bite, and we don't have enough to go around." No matter how hard Czechs had to work to scrape up a penny, they always managed to indulge in pastries. I wondered if it was a government tactic to keep the masses happy.

I considered buying one of each of the little cakes; luckily Larry helped me narrow my choice. I handed 40 korunas to a salesperson behind the counter, less than three dollars for a box of sweet memories.

Kolín's main square opened up in front of us, and we gasped. The magnificent 13th century city hall was the most attractive building on the plaza. A statue of a knight looked down from the roof's pedestal, no doubt in memory of the town's founder, King Ottokar II, nicknamed King Iron and Gold, for his great army of knights. Even with the rain and overcast sky, the place looked amazing. We circled the plaza, nibbling on our pastries from the white paper box.

The shops along the square advertised in bold letters just like during Communism: MEAT, FOOD, TOYS, CLOTHING STORE. I almost expected the stiff mannequins to be holding signs with political slogans: "With the Soviet Union for Eternity!" Or, "Communism Forever!"

We began to get chilly, so we decided to investigate the restaurant that faced the plaza, hoping to sit by the window to watch life in Kolín roll by. Judging by the white leather armchairs and original oil paintings in opulent gold frames, I wondered if this place was too fancy. A couple of elegant ladies sat behind large exotic plants, sipping coffee from porcelain cups. I glanced at the menu by the door. "It's a pizza place for God's sake!" The waiter led us to a table by the window. He put two mugs of beer and two sets of silverware on a white tablecloth before us. Just as we leaned back and I was about to comment on our great observation post, a blue delivery van parked directly in front of our window.

"We're about to eat pizza with silverware," Larry feigned excitement. After taking a sip of his beer, he wiped his mustache with the back of his hand, just like a Czech guy would. "My Little League team would have loved this. Pizza Hut has much to learn."

"Eating pizza in an 800-year-old building is weird," I said and dove into the culinary work of art adorned with a sunny-side-up egg.

At the train station, with few minutes to spare, Larry and I studied three oversized murals dating from the 1950s, painted along the station's walls. They were emblematic of my parents' era, done in a style known as Social Realism. After surviving the terror of Nazi invasion and fascism during

WWII, many Czechs were vulnerable to the emerging Soviet-styled leftist doctrine. Murals like these promoted the new ideology: a strong-armed woman in overalls holding a shovel, a robust man's arms filled with an abundance of golden wheat, children in white shirts and red neckerchiefs harvesting apples, young factory workers. They all looked content in a dopey sort of way as if working for the state was all they ever wanted from life. The vision of normalcy and abundance, of strong and resilient people was what this doctrine projected, and it is easy to see — after the deprivations and violence of war — how such images could entice the population.

In those days my parents awoke to the marching tunes of labor songs like this jewel:

Happily Happily,
To the factory goes the worker.
Happily, happily
To the factory he goes.

Happily he sings
When his lathe rings.
Tell me, tell me, my lovely mommy
What're the machines in factories
Humming.

They sing, they sing
Just like the stork
That people are happy
And treasure their work.

During this period my mom entered a contest with one of her still-life paintings. The rejection letter read: *"Comrade, your painting doesn't inspire socialism and the working class."* She never again attempted to show her artwork. Instead she bartered her paintings for whatever friends and relatives offered. Four kilos of plums or a mug of lard, she remembered with laughter.

My parents spent their best years in a tightly controlled world. My mom, the artist, labored in the textile factory. While some read novels before going to bed, my mom fell asleep holding the world atlas, imagining. I once attempted to capture my memory of her in a poem.

Tired perm,
Worn out coat,
Hands buried deep, deep in pockets
So desperately, so tight
Holding on to her paint brushes
And a poem written on the back of a train ticket,
Dreaming of the world
Far from the beat of marching drums.

On the train back to our pension, a lady asked me about our visit to Kolín, then she lamented, "Too bad you couldn't stay till the evening to see St. Bartholomew's church lit. It's so dramatic, so beautiful. And you didn't even go inside the city hall? Oh, that's really too bad, the twisted stairs, the painted ceilings, gorgeous, just gorgeous! What a shame that you missed it."

I wanted to push her off the train.

23. The Museum in *Čáslav*

Larry reassured me that he wouldn't mind if I went to Čáslav's plaza without him.

"In the meantime, I'll have a beer with the locals," he announced and bravely stepped towards the crowded bar at our pension Česká Koruna while I aimed toward the city center. I wanted to say good-bye to the one-eyed warrior Jan Žižka of Trocnov. His statue was standing at the corner of the plaza across from the city hall where his warrior skull was displayed in a glass box. In the center of the square named after the famous fighter, I passed a Baroque statue of Virgin Mary. From a high column, she looked down at four saints guarding her, one at each corner of the obelisk. Old men in sun-bleached fedoras sat around the fountain, their folded hands resting on their walking sticks. A mom pushed a stroller, school children skipped and chirped like happy kids everywhere. In front of a shop, a woman swept the sidewalk with a diligence only private ownership stimulates. Čáslav's plaza wasn't as fancy as the one in Kolín, but the vast, lovely square was a harmonious composition with each person adding a vital note. Where did I fit? Suddenly I was enveloped in melancholy, and I wished to have someone besides a statue to which to say good-bye.

Before I could fully immerse in self-pity, my nagging bladder shifted my attention. I had neglected the number one travel rule — use the restroom wherever you see one. I looked around in panic, searching for the WC sign. Forget the one-eyed warrior, forget the harmonious plaza, forget the sweet little children. A single goal in mind, cold sweat popping at my temples, I rushed back toward the pension, not sure I would make it. Halfway there, I ducked into a large museum in the desperate hope of being able to use its restroom. Only after I took care of my business did I notice the sumptuous decoration adorning the arched ceilings. I was delighted to come across a display of sandstone tiles salvaged from the ruins of the Castle Lichnice. I rejoiced like I had found my favorite long-lost earring.

What a serendipitous discovery this 1884 museum turned out to be. The glass cabinets made of ornate mahogany frames had craftsmanship worthy of admiration. A cherry pit-sized hummingbird egg next to the giant egg of an extinct Madagascar ostrich — *Alpyornis Maximus* — was among my favorites along with the colorful glass collection from 200 years ago. I examined the antique vases and goblets, looking forward to the day when I would say to a fellow traveler, "What? You went to the Czech Republic, and you skipped the museum in Čáslav? But that is really too bad, my friend, such amazing collections. What a pity you missed it."

The attendant standing next to an antique iron velocipede with a tall front wheel said, "It's impossible to ride that thing. I tried in the hallway, but couldn't balance myself."

Attempting to ride the hundred-plus-year-old velocipede in a museum hallway filled with antique statues... hmmm... how about drinking coffee from that two-hundred-year-old glassware? I nodded as if testing a museum showpiece on a whim was the most ordinary thing.

Back in the pension, I heard Larry's laughter from behind the door of our room. I stepped in and was immediately captivated by Homer Simpson speaking in Czech. I stood in the middle of the room, enthralled. Soon, though, I begged Larry to switch the channel. What is it with guys? They just won't let go of the remote control. Occasionally, Larry grants my wish and changes the channel, but he wouldn't release his magic wand. Larry flipped through the channels and paused on a show where rival towns competed to see who had the smarter residents. On the street, the TV interviewer shoved a microphone in people's faces with questions like "Against whom did Don Quixote fight a war?" I found it superbly entertaining when one man answered — WWII. Another said, "Thirty Years War." Some gave the I don't-know-shrug. It was hilarious, but Larry, unable to understand, gave me that "I want my Bart Simpson" growl.

"Why are you not drinking beer with your Czech buddies, anyway?"

"I chickened out," he admitted flatly.

"I didn't get to say good-bye to Žižka either."

We snuggled in bed, and watched as Bart yelled in Czech at his sister Lisa, "Don't have a cow, dude!"

24. World War II Celebrations in *Plzeň*

Larry and I got comfy in our cozy train compartment on the soft seats covered in cheerful red, yellow and blue fabric. The sun warmed the cubical just right, creating an inviting reading nook, despite the three strangers with whom we had to share it.

A girl, whose black hair looked like she had used shoe-polish to spike it, leafed through the Czech equivalent of the *National Enquirer*. A pimply student frowned over a pile of papers on his lap. A matronly woman pulled a culinary magazine out of her bag and adjusted her glasses to the tip of her nose, carefully inspecting each recipe. Larry burrowed into Tim Cahill's *Road Fever*. I looked out the window, letting my thoughts wander to our new destination: Plzeň.

In 1990, the year after the Velvet Revolution, I drove through Plzeň with my teenage children, Linda and Peter. We traveled 12 brutal hours from France in a rented Ford. At 3 a.m. we found ourselves tangled in the streets of Plzeň, Czech's third-largest city. "Linda, wake up," hissed Peter, elbowing his sister in her ribs, "this is better than Disneyland."

I still remember their big eyes asking, is this for real? A few street lamps cast a faint yellow light on rows of what used to be magnificent 19th century residential buildings. They were blackened by centuries of burning coal, with stucco peeling in huge chunks, exposing the crumbling bricks underneath. "Like leprosy," muttered Peter. Our car was the single moving object in that ghost town. The two lone shops we passed carried survival gear; one sold hunting goods and the other, guns, as if civilization had reached an apocalypse and each man had to fend for himself.

I was curious to see the Plzeň of today, more than 25 years later.

Our train was leaving the fertile lowlands surrounding the River Labe where expansive yellow rapeseed fields alternated with plush vegetation. Here and there, small lakes glistened through the green fields and shrubbery. The electric train hummed a midday lullaby and, one by one, the members of the reading club rested their hands, freeing their books and magazines in their laps, surrendering to a collective nap. Left alone, I explored my memories.

I was well into my teens when my sister told me, with the smug satisfaction reserved for juicy gossip, that she knew for a fact that U.S. soldiers had freed southern Bohemia. Her best friend's grandmother, an eyewitness, reported the far-fetched news.

Born 14 years after WWII, I had grown up on the heroic stories of the Russian mighty Red Army. Honoring anything American, especially the U.S. Army, was unimaginable, but so was hiding the truth. No wonder Czech history didn't make sense to me. So many pieces were twisted or erased altogether.

Czechoslovakian children may not have known about the U.S. liberation, but Plzeň's residents never forgot. How could they? The locals built a statue to remember the U.S soldiers. Soon thereafter, the Communist government removed it, leaving only a bare cement stand. In subsequent years, during the first week in May, a few brave souls lay flowers at the vacant base to commemorate the liberation. Now, on my way to Plzeň, the thought of openly celebrating this history seemed surreal. Once again, Larry was my emotional anchor, and I was thankful that he was with me.

From the train window, more and more houses popped out between the large chestnut trees. We were approaching the suburbs of Prague, aiming toward the central station. The sound of squealing brakes made children on the platform hop and giggle, pushing their hands to their ears. We had exactly eleven minutes to switch trains. First, we had to race to the lobby to check the digital timetable that announced which platform was assigned for the train to Plzeň.

"Let's hustle!" Larry yelled, slaloming between travelers. I could barely keep up with him when I saw a blind man, groping with his white stick, trying to find his way among all those bodies and heading the wrong way toward the loaded escalator. "No, not that way!" I stretched my arm toward him, but a faster hand had already grabbed his elbow. Czechs are quick to help. Sometimes we take our goodwill too far. Once a man cursed me as I shoved his scruffy dog into my car, sure that the dog was lost.

Larry was already running back towards me, shouting, "It's platform four!" pointing to the stairs. We sprinted through the underpass, our suitcases rattling as we dragged them behind.

Inside our next train compartment, an elderly lady greeted us, "Dobrý den." On the seat next to her, locked in a plastic animal carrier, stared a Garfield look-a-like. The conductor, in his neatly pressed uniform, waist-long dreadlocks and a tire-like earring that stretched his earlobe enough for a good size carrot to fit through, checked our tickets. Soon the train rolled beside the River Doubravka, through green hills sprinkled with attractive villas.

"As soon as the weather gets warmer we are out of Prague," the lady next to us said. "Who could stand being cooped up in a panelák?" She peeked lovingly into the animal carrier. "We are on the way to our summer cottage, right Mourek?"

Czech cities empty out in the summer months. After the long winter, the city folks are hungry for sunshine. They relocate to their country cottages and remodeled village houses. Even simple wooden shacks will do, as long as the lake and the woods are nearby.

I told Mourek's owner that we were going to Plzeň's WWII celebration and was surprised when she said, "I was there that spring. The camouflaged jeeps and soldiers in olive green uniforms turned Plzeň into a giant street party. It was the first time I ever saw a black man — an American soldier with very white teeth. They gave us kids chewing gum, another first."

"I guess liberating a city known for the best beer in the world was a bonus, no? But why did the Americans stop in Plzeň? Why didn't General Patton's Army go on to Prague?"

"It was ordered by Moscow," the lady said. "Stalin knew that Czechoslovakia would be easy to swallow if the Russians, not the Americans, liberated Prague. He was already licking his chops, dividing postwar Europe."

"But Prague needed help," I said as if I could change the outcome of history. "The fighting was still going on, and the Americans were right there."

"Yes. Hitler was dead, and the Third Reich had collapsed, but those Nazi bastards wouldn't quit." The lady paused and shook her head, then chuckled as Czechs do when remembering desperate times. "Our people took over the Prague radio station, sending out pleas for help. But General Patton's hands were tied. He received orders not to pursue north of Plzeň. And he was only an hour away from Prague! The Russians didn't get there 'till days later. One-thousand-seven-hundred-dred Praguers were killed in the meantime." Her light blue eyes bored into me as she said, "And I blame Stalin for that." I began to wonder if I should change the topic, but it was too late. "Once people found out that the Russians, not the Americans, would liberate us, they were horrified. Even the German prisoners would rather have been captured by Americans. The Russian soldiers were nothing but teenage peasants in scruffy uniforms. They raped women and stole anything not tied down. Some carried half-a-dozen stolen watches on each arm," the lady said with a snicker.

Before the woman and her cat got off the train, she told us about The Convoy of Liberty: "It's something to see. The salvaged and restored American jeeps lead the parade. Many are the originals that Patton's Army left behind. After the war, people hid them in barns and caves, or buried them in hand-dug underground bunkers."

Plzeň's worn-out train station still held its 19th century charm, but just barely. Shortly after Larry and I visited, the spacious lobby was restored under the watchful eye of historians. Handmade floor tiles (predicted to last another 120 years), revitalized frescos, and a massive dome, brought the building back to being one of the most beautiful historical train stations of Europe — adding another gem to the jewelry box of Czech's cultural heritage. I'd seen pictures of the renovated station from magazine clippings Dad had sent me, but right now, Plzeň's train station held one sole concern for me: the door marked "WC." The restroom keeper swapped my eight korunas for three pitiful squares of toilet paper, the waxy kind, like the pan liners for baking.

An underground passage spat us out at street level by the cable car stop. We needed to go to Plzeň's suburbs where my friend Pepa had reserved a room in a military dormitory.

We stared dumbly at the automat selling the tickets, a metal box with too many buttons, the instructions printed in a minuscule font.

Some people actually follow the directions, and some shove their wrinkled bills up any opening of the adversarial box, push all the buttons, including the bolts, while clutching their fists, spitting, kicking, blaming their spouses and providing far more compelling entertainment for bystanders. I am a senior member of the latter group. To Larry's unhelpful "What does it say?" I snapped, "Bloody Communists!" Our tram had arrived, and we still didn't have the tickets.

"Buy them inside," a man advised.

We climbed into the cable car. "Two tickets to Slovany station please."

Before the driver could hand them out, a lady got up from her seat and rushed toward us. "It'll cost you too much if you buy them here," she said, as she fished in her bag for her wallet, looking for her spare tickets. My puzzled expression motivated another woman to explain the public transportation system, which confused me further. The first lady handed me the tickets, but I didn't have exact change. Then a third woman with the right change and a strong voice got up, and while digging around in her purse, she offered tips on how to get around Plzeň. They jabbered over each other, like a trio of opera singers performing a humoresque. Larry later told me that standing there and not understanding what was going on made him feel as if he was my slow-witted cousin. Wondering if we were in trouble, he was ready to duck for cover.

In the suburbs, at the terminal loop, Larry and I got off and walked toward an appealing modern building. A passerby assured us that it wasn't the military dormitory and pointed to the rundown panelák across the street. Well, of course, what was I thinking? I recalled Pepa's enthusiasm, "You can't find a cheaper place in the whole of Plzeň."

We rang the bell and were buzzed in. Words like lobby, front desk and receptionist were too fancy for that panelák converted into a dormitory. Through a coaster-sized opening in a glass door, an unsmiling lady asked for our identification. We handed over our passports, which she studied with unmasked confusion. She returned them with a key and a handwritten receipt. Larry examined the piece of paper as we walked toward the elevator. "Mr. Ohio? That's my birthplace!" Baffled, he concluded, "For $20 a night one can't be too picky, I reckon. She could have chosen to call me Expired, I guess." With cement floors and whitewashed panel walls, the place resembled a giant bunker. Without carpets, pictures, plants, or anything else suggesting creativity and coziness, the bare hallways echoed from the vibrating elevator and lonesomeness. On the third floor at the end of the hall, we unlocked door number 24 and stepped into bleach-scented darkness. I groped for a light switch. The fluorescent tube blinked before spilling a blueish glow into a square hallway converted into a kitchen.

"Oh, crap," I blurted. In a chipped brown pot on the stove, a spoon was stuck in some leftovers. "I didn't realize we'd have a roommate," I murmured, avoiding Larry's eyes. In a daze, he slowly moved around, then pulled open a vinyl cabinet, and like in a bad comedy the handle came off in his hand.

There were four doors off the kitchen, two solid with black plastic handles, and two with frosted-glass panels, also with black plastic handles. One of the solid doors opened to a tiny room with a shallow foot basin with a hand shower, a stained shower curtain and a sink. I turned on the faucets and steaming hot water burst out as if from a mad espresso machine. No cold water, not even lukewarm.

"Maybe that's why commie plumbers didn't install bidets," Larry said. "It would scald off hemorrhoids."

I grew up in a panelák and knew that there was always something that didn't work, usually the plumbing. In our 1990 visit, when the rented Ford finally got my children and me to my parents' panelák, Linda, the true American teenager, headed straight for the shower.

"But we don't have hot water," Mom had lamented.

"At least my mirror won't fog up," Linda hollered over the sound of running water.

The other plastic door from the kitchen led to an even smaller cubicle where the flushing toilet was adjustable to high or low water flow. Considering the totalitarian regime, a person was probably beside himself with the sudden freedom of choice. Judging by the worn out red-handled toilet brush standing at attention in a pickle jar by the toilet, the water control switch to high flow didn't work that well.

I tried the key to one of the frosted glass doors. It was locked.

"Aha, that's where the serial killer is hiding. We have the other room," I said.

Our room was light and fairly large. It had a table, two nightstands, two simple armoires, a couple of chairs, and in opposite corners, two narrow beds.

"Why do we have place mats on our beds?" Larry asked and held up a cloth with two blue stripes for me to see.

"That's a towel!"

"A towel?" Larry studied the stiff cloth. "Why is it so small and hard?"

"I don't know. We never asked. We just accepted it."

I was strangely pleased to see the bedding boxes adjacent to our beds. It was like running into an almost forgotten friend. During the day, tenants converted their bedrooms into an office or living room by storing the linen in the bedding boxes, then converted the beds into seats.

The room that would be our home for the next few nights was run down but clean, unadorned but almost functional. Its best feature was the window with a glass door leading to a balcony which stretched the entire length of our room. We rejoiced just like inmates would if they'd discovered that their cell had a balcony.

Larry locked our bags into the armoires. With care, he also locked the frosted glass door to our room and then the apartment door. On the way out we handed our apartment key to the matron who hung it on a hook with our room number.

From the tram windows heading toward the central plaza, the Náměstí Republiky, I didn't see the crumbling buildings I remembered from my previous trip. Although lacking the snug charm of smaller towns, the city was pulsing with life. There were signs that shops and restaurants were prospering; people drove nice cars and wore stylish clothes. We had seen only well-maintained structures, and I realized that the panelák we were staying in was among the last Communist relics. Its barely functional, mass-produced shoddiness captured the spirit of its era. I made a mental note to pack in a souvenir, one of the blue-striped towels.

"Honey, staying in our panelák is educational," I declared. "Instead of just reading about Communism, you get to experience it."

"A walk-through would do just fine," Larry said. "I don't have to spend a night to feel how it dispirits a person."

Other paneláks we had seen from the cable car glowed with new pastel colors and slick, efficient canopies. Attractive lofts had been built onto flat roofs. Resourceful Czechs had transformed housing for the masses into pleasant contemporary homes. I saw a documentary of a famous Czech actress who, like many other celebrities, lived in a panelák among ordinary people. At the end of the show, she looked out from her balcony where begonias cascaded over the railing. "It's like being on a cruise ship," she said with fondness as the sunset spilled the red glow over her mini-garden on the tenth floor.

Our cable car was taking us through General Pika's Plaza. Helisdor Pika was yet another icon once swept under the massive Communist carpet. He was a General of the Czechoslovakian army during WWII. Before the end of the war, he sent a warning from Russia, where he was stationed, to President Beneš: "Stalin isn't interested in a free Czechoslovakia; he is interested in installing his Bolshevik ideology in Czechoslovakia." After the war, when the first Communist President Gottwald took office, Pika was accused of treason and was dragged through a kangaroo court. He was executed by hanging in 1949. Pika's 26-year-old son was imprisoned in the same jail for fighting Hitler in the RAF. Hours before his father's execution, they were allowed to spend the last night together.

"Even though it was the longest and most brutal night, I gained strength from his words. His wish became my mission: "'Don't harbor anger and bitterness. When the time comes, clear my name. And take care of Mom." The execution of General Pika was the first in a long chain of political trials that took place during the 1950s. After the Velvet Revolution in 1989 the truth came out, and Pika was posthumously awarded the highest military honors.

We got off the cable car a block before Náměstí Republiky. Larry and I waited at the intersection for the light to change; a convoy of U.S. Army WWII vehicles with shiny brown jeeps and trucks rumbled by. An American girl next to us panicked, "What's going on? It's freaking me out!" I briefly explained about the celebrations. As the light turned green and we stepped into the intersection, she said, "I should probably take a picture," and she pulled out her cell phone.

St. Bartholomew's Gothic Cathedral dominated the plaza. Its slender tower, the tallest in the country, soars 103 meters into the sky. The square was packed with spectators. Red, white and blue American and Czech flags fluttered in the breeze. A Czech jazz group on stage played Duke Ellington. I couldn't stop moving to the beat, aware that those around us observed motionlessly. Out of respect or lack of spontaneity? I couldn't tell. The next singer, a thin, pale Czech, sang "Hello Dolly" in a great, raspy Louie Armstrong voice.

"After such an excellent English rendition, it's strange to hear the Czech děkuji (thank you) at the end," Larry said.

We walked by stalls selling sausages, fried potato pancakes, fried sugar almonds, fried curly potato chips, and other artery-clogging delights. A little girl with a boy's haircut sat on her dad's shoulders, wiping her cotton candy fingers in his hair. A group of rowdy Germans parked on the church stairs, drinking beer from flimsy plastic cups, and then tossing them around. A garbage can was no more than ten meters away.

You sauerbraten brains, pick up your trash! I wanted to shout. By now I was tired of German and British groups of young men acting like American college kids on spring break in Cancun. I wondered if the German kids even understood that all these people were celebrating their grandfathers' greatest defeat.

The band stopped playing, and the speaker on the podium introduced a small group of American heroes, the WWII veterans who in 1945, as young soldiers, liberated this city. Two of them were unable to climb the stairs on their own and were lifted onto the stage. Larry teared up.

"That could have been my dad," he said. "He enlisted, then married my mom, and ten days later, his unit deployed to Belgium. All my mom remembers now, is how fast she ran to the train that finally brought him back home two-and-a-half years later."

I pulled Larry closer to me, then turned toward the church stairs where empty plastic cups rolled back and forth in the breeze.

🍺🍺🍺

25. Pilsner Urquel

Late in the evening we returned to our panelák. The giggling receptionist was flirting with a guy who leaned over the counter. I don't know what threw me off more: the fact that he was almost naked — wearing only a red Speedo, the mullet on an otherwise bald head, or his striking resemblance to Good Soldier Švejk, a short and chubby character in a classic Czech novel by the same name. Apparently, we were disturbing their midnight rendezvous.

"Key number 24 please," I said.

"Twenty-four? That's my room," Švejk said as if it was a real good thing. I stared at him until Larry's gentle nudge prompted me to close my mouth. On the way to the elevator, I hissed, "That's our roommate. The red underwear guy — "

"Shh, he can hear you," Larry said.

"You don't understand; the naked guy is sharing the apartment with us."

Later, lying in my bed by the thin wall, I realized that my head was less than a foot from the toilet bowl the Švejk guy would use sooner or later.

"Honey," I moaned, "do you want to switch beds?"

"I'm already comfortable," Larry sighed. Wrapped tight like a mummy, bare feet sticking out of the thin sheet, he looked anything but comfortable.

I shut my eyes, willing myself to sleep before Švejk would come upstairs.

The bright morning sun squeezed between the window blinds. I heard the squealing water pipes, slamming doors, and muffled coughs of the panelák's invisible co-habitants. Behind the frosted glass door moved two blurry figures. At once I recognized the receptionist's giggle. Oh, my gosh, Švejk scored last night! I pulled the cover over my head, trying to ignore my bladder. What would I say to two lovers on my way to the restroom? Soon the click of the front door announced their departure, and Larry and I sprang to our feet. We had a full day ahead: first a brewery tour and then a concert.

Larry came out of the shower steamy pink, holding a towel to his mouth, "Dammed hot water! I burned my tongue brushing my teeth."

"So, no beer tasting for my poor baby?"

"Shut up your face," he lisped.

The prospect of touring the famous Czech brewery Pilsner Urquell was as exciting for me as visiting Yankee Stadium would be for Larry.

When I was a kid, not yet knowing my times tables, I already knew that Pilsner was the beer capital and the home of Pilsner Urquell. Urquell in German, Prazdroj in Czech, means the ancient source.

The story of Pilsner's beer began in 1295 when King Wenceslas II, the same guy we already met in Kutá Hora's silver mines, gave 260 noblemen the hereditary right to brew and sell beer in their houses, a popular and lucrative business. But during The Thirty Years War and its aftermath, Czechs lost much of their population to the Black Plague and mass emigration. Czech culture spiraled downward. Not even the brewing business was spared. Without proper training, inexperienced beer makers began producing nothing more than murky sludge. Locals, calling for a quality beer, once dumped 36 casks of so-called beer in front of Pilsner's city hall. City councilors decided to invest in a new, large brewery and invited a Bavarian beer master with an excellent reputation to teach Pilsner's how to make good beer. When the first batch of clear, delicious golden nectar with thick white foam poured out of the wooden barrel in 1848, it outdid everyone's expectations, especially the Bavarian beer master's. Some credited Pilsner's soft water and the high quality of hops for the unprecedented clarity and the delicious taste, concluding that the secret that gave the local brew its character could not be duplicated.

In the city center, as we walked beneath the Arc De Triumph-like gateway to the attractive grounds of the beer metropolis, I asked Larry the question that had been rolling around in my head: "How many beer songs do you know?"

"Hmm..., Ninety-nine bottles of beer on the wall... That's it."

"I know about six. All in Czech," I said. Later I would discover a book where someone with a lot of time on his hands had published the lyrics of 700 folk songs celebrating Czech beer, the life blood of its nation.

The Czechs' pride in beer tradition was evident everywhere. The original malt storage barn was reconstructed into a slick visitor center — stone, brass, glass, and bizarre, beer-related contemporary art. My favorite was the motorcycle made of beer caps.

In a few moments, our English speaking group met the guide, a preppy, plump woman, the kindergarten teacher type. As the brewery bus passed beautifully restored buildings where the fermenting took place, she began our beer education. "Pilsner Urquell is the world's first-ever brewed pale beer. Its fame quickly spread into the world, and our brewery became the official beer supplier for the Austro-Hungarian Emperor Franz Joseph. From 1900, the refrigerated beer train left daily for the seaport, shipping Pilsner's beer to America. Fortunately, glass manufacturing took off around the same time, and the general public enjoyed the golden color of the world's first crystal clear pale lager for the first time through glass steins instead of ceramic chalices. Pilsner beer became a model for nine out of ten beers produced in the world today."

The bus stopped, and our wide-eyed group followed the guide to the biggest elevator in the Czech Republic, which led into the revolving cinema and to the sci-fi heart of the brewery where the copper kettles were reflected in white marble walls. The futuristic plant has the capacity to fill 120,000 bottles an hour. I was hypnotized by the sea of green bottles funneling single file, disappearing into the tunnel like Metro travelers in an underground escalator at rush hour. Larry and I felt like Charlie visiting the Chocolate Factory.

"Today we make over 132 million gallons of beer a year, that's about twenty Olympic-size pools," the guide said.

"That's nice, but I haven't had a single beer yet," Larry murmured. As if our guide heard him, she invited us to the historical underground cellars to taste unfiltered and unpasteurized beer right from the oak barrel. We all lined up for a cold glass mug filled with Czech's golden pride.

"To the beer of unsurpassed quality!" Our guide lifted the tall glass above her head.

"To the Czech people!" shouted an American man.

"To my chic Czech chick," Larry whispered in my ear.

Our preppy guide tilted the mug to her lips. A flap in her throat opened up, and she hammered it down.

"She sure takes her job seriously," Larry said, wiping the foam off his lips.

In my beer-loving country no one used to question drinking on the job, especially not beer. Without a proper beer supply, construction workers wouldn't lift a finger. Not offering a beer to a hired plumber or electrician was just rude. Still, today, certain hot professions, like glass blowers, can legally drink beer on the job.

From his first sip, Larry was hooked. He hasn't stopped searching for that unfiltered and unpasteurized brand of Pilsner Urquell ever since.

In a delicatessen we stopped to get two open-face sandwiches, found a grassy spot by the river and, underneath a shady chestnut tree, opened up our blanket. Balancing our sandwiches on a paper plate, we tried not to lose the arrangement of sliced ham, hard-boiled egg, crisp pickle, a pinch of curly parsley and a snippet of red pepper from a slice of French bread spread with finely chopped potato salad.

Larry leafed through a colorful 16 page brochure that he had picked up at the information center. The thick, shiny paper and the beautiful color photographs were of high quality. The text was translated into multiple languages. Larry began to read the English version:

> *The town of Pilsen became a natural center of West Bohemia since the time of its foundation in 1295. It is due not only to the goodwill of the Czech rulers for its dominant position but also to its advantageous location on the intersections of land roads. We can observe the testimony of the material wealth as well as that of the cultural wealth also while taking a walk through the municipal monument reservation...*

"Was it the beer or did I just read an English 101 student project?" he asked.

I remembered it wasn't long ago when English began to be taught in Czech colleges by teachers who had never met an English-speaking person. Their students mostly just memorized the vocabulary. I remembered well my own struggles learning English.

In California, on my first job in a bakery, a customer asked me to write "Happy Birthday" on a cake. "No problem," I said, and in red icing inscribed: *Hepi Brsdej.* The customer kept staring at my creation without a word. Then he asked for the manager.

Another time, writing a check at a grocery store I discreetly asked my ten-year-old son, "Peter, how do you spell 19?"

"N-I-N-E-T-E-E-N. I told you three times already," he yelled for all in line to hear.

I thought that the computer spell check would be my savior. Once I emailed Linda that we had just rescued a dog of unidentified breed from the local shelter: "We got a mud from the pond."

And there was my accent. A salesperson recently handed me chopsticks, after I had asked for Chap Stick for my lips.

Larry closed the brochure and I checked my watch. I didn't want us to be late for the concert. I was curious what kind of pop-music Czechs listen to now. The 70s hits were my final singalong before the Iron Curtain slammed shut behind me, the last songs I learned in my mother tongue. More than a decade later, on my first visit back home, my sister pointed out that the songs I hummed weren't even among the golden oldies. They were just out.

My first years in America I would come to the bakery where I worked all excited, "Guys, I just heard this awesome song:

"...there goes my baby
with someone new,
she sure looks happy
I sure am blue..."

"Everly Brothers. 1956." The counter girl would roll her eyes.

I was so out of it. On both continents. My Czech language was already getting rusty, while my English was far from being polished. My Czech music repertoire stagnated in the 70s, while the old American classics were my new hits. I become one of many in-limbo immigrants, wondering where I fit in.

I tucked my hair behind my ears in a feeble attempt to look presentable. The concert hall was every bit as ornate and glamorous as the outside of the building: marble, gold,

chandeliers, draping velvety red curtains. The frill and painting on the ceiling made me think of the Sistine Chapel.
Radůza came out dressed in black, wearing army boots. She
has been compared to Suzanne Vega, although I think of her
as a modern Edith Piaf. Originally a street singer, she has a
strong, raspy voice. Between songs about cold feet, lonely
Sundays, hangovers and sharing the last cigarette, Radůza
gulped from her water bottle with gusto, then wiped her lips
with her forearm like a lumberjack. She was fabulous, switch-
ing between six instruments: guitar, flute, piano, harmonica,
accordion and, when the audience at the end of the show kept
calling her back with rapturous applause, she reappeared from
behind the curtain dragging bagpipes. "This will teach you!"
she announced.

On the way to our panelák, sitting in the cable car, I leafed
through the tourist brochure again. So many great places we
wouldn't have time to visit, such as the second biggest European synagogue with its red onion towers, more museums, art
galleries, castles, and chateaus... My eyes stopped on a picture
of a simple garden. The description below read, *"The Memorial
to the Victims of Evil, a life work of political prisoner L. Hruška."*

Back in our room, Larry switched off the light by his
bed and turned away from the glow of my laptop screen. I
propped a pillow behind my back and wrapped my legs in
the starchy white sheet. Then I inserted the earphones and
scrolled through websites dedicated to a former political
prisoner, Luboš Hruška, admiring the serene corners of his
meditation garden, sometimes called "The Garden of Forgiveness," officially known as "The Memorial of the Victims
of Evil."

I imagined taking a shady path among ferns and conifers, inhaling the aroma of the pine needles. I pictured sitting down on a wooden bench among pink rhododendrons,
Mr. Hruška next to me, telling his story, teaching me how to

accept the past, how to be at peace with suffering. How to be happy.

In 1946 when Hruška was 22, the border patrol caught him crossing the woods into Austria. He became prisoner number 590, sentenced to 18 years. He was sent to Leopoldov prison, the most dreaded among all Czechoslovakian correctional facilities, where inmates died from hunger, tuberculosis, and suicide, and many lost their minds. Some swallowed metal spoons in the false hope of being taken to the clinic. It was there, with 80 prisoners in one cell sharing one waste bucket, every evening one man shared something he knew. "Those were among the most wondrous moments in my life," Hruška said.

> "In contrast to the inhuman conditions of the Leopoldov prison, some noble men performed selfless deeds for others, like sharing the little food they had. Their inner peace amazed me, their lack of hate. They didn't crave revenge. It was as if only their bodies were in prison; their souls were free. Among them was the highest representative of the Jesuit order, František Šilhan. I was curious where his serenity came from. We discussed issues of faith for hours. It dawned on me that all people suffer in some way. It's part of life. We all carry our cross... That's when I got the idea of building a garden that would contribute to acceptance of our cross, a place for people to sit and think."

After ten and half years Hruška was unexpectedly released. During that time, he had inherited a fruit orchard from his father and began realizing his dream.

> "I learned patience, not to force solutions. If I couldn't solve a problem, I waited a month, a year, or two. Often the problems solved themselves. Sometimes fate brought just the right people in my life. The men from the nearby alcohol rehab center came to help. The garden became a part of their recovery.

"Roman Podrazský, an academic sculptor who endured hardships from Communists because he was religious, created 12 sandstone statues for different corners of the garden. He began with the statue of Jesus being whipped. Two distorted faces behind him weren't just portraying the Roman soldiers: they represented the Nazis and the Bolsheviks, all servants of cruelty and hatred. They were the prison guards.

"In the garden, thinking, praying, conversing with God, but also listening, I came to many new conclusions. I learned about forgiveness, fear, and joy. Hatred deforms a person. Still, it took me ten years to shed my hatred. And when that happened, I felt an enormous liberation of my soul. My mind cleared. Evil no longer had its power over me and would no longer block my spiritual growth. It happened because I wanted it to happen. The first step is always willingness to change.

"In the garden, I learned about the incapacitating results of fear. The more afraid we are, the more helpless and vulnerable we become, depriving ourselves of joy. Closeness to God taught me to leave worries that I can't solve to Him. By doing so, I create room for happiness."

In closing, Mr. Hruška made this incredible statement, *"Today I don't think that I got shortchanged by life. Being in jail was my destiny, which I don't regret."*

I stared at the blurry rectangle of light on the wall. Mr. Hruška's success in extracting beauty from suffering was empowering, his noble spirit inspiring. While most Czechs focused on sheer survival, he labored on "The Monument of the Victims of Evil." A few noble souls acted boldly in those years. Most people learned to live like nails, avoiding being hammered by not sticking out.

Before I realized it, I, too, had become a nail. When I was 18, a year before I left the country, I was hospitalized and shared a room with five older women. One day, two strange men entered our hospital room. The first one handed each of us a slip of paper with a single name written on it. Then the other man shoved a paper bag in our faces. One by one, we all dropped the slip with the name in the bag. The men checked our names off their clipboard and left.

"What was that?" I asked my roommates.

"Elections," someone answered. Later, I heard on the radio about the unanimous vote for the Communist candidate.

Now, I lay motionless, overwhelmed with a mixture of sorrow and joy. Sharing this earth with an individual capable of such nobility gives us all hope. Mr. Hruška followed his conscience, refusing to live a lie, choosing to live in truth instead. That was what Václav Havel, another angel of our times, wrote in his essay "Power of the Powerless."

I wished to see Mr. Hruška's garden, but my cousin Veronica was expecting us. Rushing the spiritual walk would defeat the purpose for which it was built.

Before I turned off my laptop, I filed Mr. Hruška's story in a folder marked my favorites; then I took a deep breath, pulled the scratchy sheet closer to my chin and gave silent thanks for making the acquaintance of this inspiring man.

26. Baroness in *Blatná*

Our next destination was the Southern Bohemian mountain range called Šumava, where my cousin Veronica's family lives. Since neither Larry nor I had seen the area between Plzeň and Šumava, we chose to exchange the comfort of a train for the independence of a car so we could zigzag through a countryside rich with history.

"It's here!" From Larry's lookout post on the balcony, he announced the arrival of our rental car. I peered over his shoulder. Parked in front of the panelák was the little red Škoda Fábia.

A young man from Kazakhstan arrived with our car and patiently answered our questions. A professional and efficient rental agent, unlike the slick-talking cheater my dad warned would squeeze us for every koruna. Dad's suspicious attitude came from a lifetime in a regime corroded with lies. The butcher slipped some green pieces of pork in your order, the mechanic wouldn't move a finger without a bribe, a doctor would prescribe medicine only after you supplied him with a plumber. Or electrician. Or whatever the hell one had access to. No wonder Dad is still paranoid. Could his unfortunate generation ever be healed?

After inspecting the car, Larry signed the contract indicating the missing hubcap and scrapes on the driver's door. Then we swapped three 5,000 koruna bills for a key chain with a dangling pink Converse All Star and two keys. We loaded the car, and within minutes Plzeň was behind us, the little pink shoe happily swaying below the ignition.

"What a waste of worries that was," I told Larry. "The guy was really nice."

"I put him in his place with my don't-mess-with-me cowboy handshake. That's why."

Our red Škoda slid through the Southern Bohemian countryside while the sun smiled in the blue sky. The road ahead danced like a ribbon between undulating green hills and flowering yellow fields, sometimes vanishing in patches of forest, then teasingly reappearing in the distance.

"Oh, this is beautiful," we took turns exclaiming. "Picture perfect!"

"And we have the road to ourselves," Larry clicked his tongue in delight.

"So why would I start getting a migraine now?"

"You need to eat." Larry said. In the next small town, he pulled over to a restaurant that had just opened for lunch. We walked through the empty dining room to the back patio facing a lake below. The proprietor, a short man in a dark blue apron, approached our table shaded by an umbrella advertising Pilsner Urquel. Instead of handing us a menu, he measured us with curious eyes, squinting a bit.

"I could make you a nice piece of butt roast with fries," he said. But he kept appraising us the way an artist would evaluate an unfinished painting, "No, no fries," he said. "I'll make it with sautéed vegetables."

All agreed, he went into the kitchen only to appear a few moments later, announcing, "I better not make you the roast. I'll make grilled chicken breasts." Then, noticing me rubbing my forehead, he added, "I see that you have a headache." His sentence lingered, waiting for my nod. "I'll bring you a fresh green salad instead. More refreshing than sautéed vegetables, much better for you."

He arrived holding two plates. "Bread is better with this than fries," he said and placed in front of us our customized lunches: juicy chicken breasts sitting on thick slices of home-made rye bread, surrounded by crisp butter lettuce, sliced tomatoes, and sweet green peppers. He also prescribed his own carbonated lemonade. "To cure your headache," he said. The simple lunch was a perfect fit. His special lemonade, as promised, chased away my migraine.

Back on the road, we passed brown signs that indicated points of interests. How many since Plzeň? Ten, fifteen? On a whim, we followed one to Blatná's small town square. Larry pointed to an open window where puffy down comforters hung over the windowsills.

"I remember my grandmother airing bedding like that," I said, surprised at that memory. "Although never in the street-facing window."

We parked the car and walked a short distance toward Blatná's historical site.

The 13th century castle Blatná didn't gain its strategic position from the height of a hill, like most castles, but from the isolation of an island encircled by marshes.

The white romantic chateau was reflected in the still water where yellow water lilies adorn its image. The stone bridge — a former drawbridge — led us toward the grand wooden gate and into the courtyard.

"The next tour starts in five minutes," someone announced.

We followed a self-assured woman in her 50s — who vaguely reminded us of someone — to the first chamber called the Ethiopian Room. An Ethiopian? Here, 30 kilometers from Plzeň? On the woven African carpet lay a shield made of hippopotamus skin, a war horn and a drum.

"The articles are souvenirs that the royal Hildprand family brought back from their Ethiopian exile," the guide began. "In 1948, the Communists came to power and confiscated Blatná castle which the Hildprands' had occupied for the previous 150 years. The royal family was ordered to move no closer than eleven kilometers from their former home. Baron Frederic Hildprand got a job in an electric power station, and Baroness Kornelie taught foreign languages.

"In 1959, the Ethiopian emperor, Haile Selassie, a friend of Kornelie's father, pleaded with the Communist President Novotný to allow the family to move to Ethiopia where he would sponsor them. And so Ethiopia became the family's new home for the next three decades. After the 1989 Velvet Revolution, the castle was returned to the Hildprands, and Baroness Kornelie moved back home, although she found living in an elegant estate behind the castle far more comfortable. You may still see the 90 year-old Baroness Kornelie strolling in town or in the English garden. She walks slowly these days. Other than that, she looks no different than any other woman from Blatná."

As I tried to concentrate on the guide's words, my mind kept wondering where I might have seen her before.

Before we entered the next elegant salon, the guide ordered us to put large felt slippers over our shoes to protect the hardwood floors. Our small group shuffled and slid behind, turning our heads as she pointed.

"The furniture on the left is a present from Maria Luisa, Napoleon's second wife, a frequent visitor to Blatná." The guide pointed toward a gold-framed picture by the door. "On this painting is the Hildprandt's family house in Venice, and here," she pointed to another painting, "is Baron and Baroness Hildprandt escorting Maria Luisa on her wedding day." Our eyes followed the outstretched arm and our heads, like puppets joined by an invisible string, kept bobbing in soundless synchrony. In the large 1940s painting at the center of the wall posed Baroness Kornelie. I stepped forward to study the soft features in Kornelie's youthful, pretty face. She had no clue then that the fan resting in her lap and the royal blue dress exposing her shoulders would soon have to be exchanged for the practical clothing of the working class.

"Don't touch!" A man's hand froze over the inlaid coffee table. Sheepishly he looked up and with an apologizing smile stuck his hand into his pocket. With a noisy exhale, like a teacher disappointed in her pupil, the guide ordered, "Follow me."

The next room was a testimony to the previous dwellers' hunting madness — deer antler bed frame, table legs, armchair frames, chandeliers. Animal pelts lined the walls.

"Do.Not.Touch.Anything," the guide articulated.

I don't know how I found the courage to ask about additional points of interest in Blatná. My simple inquiry unleashed a beast. "This isn't good enough?" she said and let out a kind of a gurgle, a forewarning of spitting venom.

"What do you think of us? You think we are just past the Stone Age? You think there is nothing to see in the Czech Republic?"

I stuttered, "No. Not at all. Of course not." Instinctively I took a step toward Larry. Did that woman just cast me among foreign snobs who look down on Czechs through the tinted windows of their BMWs? Me? A girl who grew up in a panelák? For the rest of the tour, I couldn't concentrate on anything she said. I was too busy thinking of things I should have said to her.

There is no need for Czechs to feel second-rate. Didn't they pioneer Cubism, invent soft contact lenses, the propeller and sugar cubes? Don't they have the best beer in the world? Didn't they produce Dvořák, Hrabal, Klíma, Kafka, Kundera, Havel, just to name a few? And why do so many Americans move here? Because big nations have something to learn from us! The importance of family, the economizing that lessens the burden on the environment for example. Sure the West brought the global market, business, and profit, but all Czech women have two years paid maternity leave! Czechs have security, tradition, and culture. They have medical and dental insurance! Czechs learned to live sandwiched between super-powers, adjusting and surviving, coming out the better for it.

But at the end of the tour, I took off the felt slippers, folded them into each other, returned them in the desig-nated slot where the guide's finger pointed, and whispered, "Naschledanou."

Behind the castle, a carpet of greenery opened up as far as the eye could see. A herd of deer lay motionless on the short grass. From a distance, they looked like a large patch of dry shrubbery. The tame animals didn't seem to be disturbed by children whose parents sent them to pose for photographs. My eyes darted between the top of the ostentatious circu-lar stairway of Baroness Kornelie's mansion and the deer. I didn't want to miss the moment when the parents dropped their cameras and rushed to defend their youngsters, should an erratic buck decide to charge, or should Baroness Kornelie appear at the top of her stairs and yell, "You kids, get off my lawn!"

All of a sudden Larry exclaimed, "I know who she reminds us of! Kathy Bates in that James Caan movie. What was that called?"

"Misery," I said, astonished. He nailed it.

27. Marie from *Sedlice*

As a pickup got within an inch of our bumper before shooting ahead, Larry grumbled, "Passing must be the Czech national sport." A few minutes later another truck avoided a head-on collision by cutting us off. Larry, the rookie in the game, wiped the sweat from his forehead.

I wasn't sure how much more he could take. Time to get off the road and look for lodging. In the next town, Sedlice, a pension sign pointed to a neighborhood of well-kept villas, green lawns and colorful flowerbeds. We found the pension, rang the doorbell and waited. No answer. I dialed the phone number displayed on the sign.

"Yes, we have a vacancy," the woman's voice confirmed. "Give me five minutes. I'm on my way.

Larry reclined in his seat and folded his arms behind his head. Brooding, I stared ahead. I wanted to spend the night in a more significant town that had a national monument, or an interesting tourist destination. From what I could decode from the map, this town only had a church built in 1744. Not even a really old one.

A few minutes later, a four-door silver Suzuki pulled in front of the house and a woman in her late 50s wearing a man's flannel checkerboard shirt and faded gray pants, hopped out to greet us. "I am Marie," she said. Her blue eyes were as warm as her handshake.

"I just came from the fields. We have two new lambs," she said jubilantly.

We followed her through a glass veranda into the house. The skylight, slanted ceiling and wood paneling of the upstairs bedroom felt like a romantic cabin. I saw satisfaction in Larry's face. We paid $40 for one night's stay.

"I'll return to my lambs now," Marie said and handed us the key.

"Can I go with you?" I blurted out.

"Of course, just put on old shoes."

She wasn't the least bit thrown by my request. Larry assured me that he'd be fine resting and reading in our sunny nest upstairs.

I climbed into the passenger seat and fastened the seat belt. The car weaved into the neighborhood.

"We love our lambs. They take care of the meadow, keeping the grass low," Marie told me as we turned into the main road. After a mile or so we exited to a dirt path. The four-wheel-drive vehicle began to bounce in and out of deep potholes. "My heart calls me to our meadow every day. It always did, even before we had the lambs."

Soon I saw why. The fresh smell of spring came through the open windows as we drove past lush greenery. Some branches brushed against the car. The dirt path curved, revealing an old rusty gate. Marie stopped the car and jumped out.

"Welcome to my sanctuary," she said, fiddling with the gate.

The late afternoon sun shone through a thicket of young leaves that encircled the green meadow, a small wooden cabin and a pond. A group of sheep welcomed us with anxious bleating. The smallest lamb was black. I wanted to cuddle with her, but she was too skittish. Marie and I strolled toward the cabin. We must have stepped on some wild thyme hidden in the grass. Its tiny leaves released a familiar scent that reminded me of my mom, who always kept dry thyme in her dresser.

Marie pointed to the growth of white birches, "Let's sit in the shade." The simple bench hidden among the trees faced the fishpond.

"It's so beautiful here," I said incredulously.

Marie smiled. "We have people stopping for a night and they end up spending a week. A German couple comes in the fall when we harvest potatoes. They like to see how they come out of the ground. We always give them a bag to take home. An American woman who came here to trace her genealogy had never seen poppy seeds growing. I showed her how I harvest, dry and grind them, and together we baked poppy seed koláče."

My mouth watered in a vision of the sweet dough with its dense black filling.

A fish jumped, creating water rings.

Marie pointed, "There's one, see him? Our Christmas carp. We celebrate Christmas here. The whole family comes. Everything is covered in snow. We build a fire, and then we fish out our carp."

"How romantic," I sighed. "My dad used to buy a live carp two days before Christmas. In our apartment he plunked him in the bathtub and my sister and I watched him swim. The first Christmas in California, I tried to buy a carp in Chinatown. I was lucky to get a frozen one. I breaded and fried him, just like we did at home on Christmas Eve, but it tasted like mud, not the delicious treat I remembered. After that, I started cooking turkey, the tradition my American children now know."

More ripples disturbed the surface of the pond. After a few moments I said, "I came home to remember, so I could tell my children."

Marie looked at me with those sincere blue eyes, put her hand on mine and said, "Take it in. Take it all in until your heart is full."

I felt that familiar tightness in my throat that always paves the way to tears. Somehow, I wasn't even embarrassed.

"How did you end up in the pension business?" I asked, my words muffled through a wrinkled handkerchief Marie handed me.

"My husband got laid off in 1989, right after the revolution. At the same time I got sick. A spider bit me. I was hospitalized in Prague for a whole year. I couldn't walk or move my hands. We needed money."

Being incapacitated for a whole year? No wonder Marie was so content now, so appreciative. Is it through suffering that she found happiness? The verse from Kahlil Gibran came to me:

> *The deeper that sorrow carves into your being,*
> *the more joy you can contain.*

"Our daughters got married and moved out, so my husband converted their bedrooms into guest rooms," Marie continued, "now we have steady clients, the cross-country truck drivers. Some have been coming for ten years. When we are not home, they know where the keys are. They know all about us and we know all about them."

Marie rubbed her arms. "It's getting chilly." We got up. "Let's go see my husband. He is fishing near by."

Marie locked up the sheep, and we hopped in the Suzuki and continued down the winding dirt road. Just as I was about to say that there wasn't a man-made structure in sight, we passed a large neglected building.

"A mill," Marie said. "A couple bought it, and then the man died two years later. Now the woman stays there alone, even in the winter with the roads snowed in. My husband checks on her twice a week. She has two dogs and two goats. What a sight when she takes them for a walk! All jumping and teasing each other."

> *And is not the lute that soothes your spirit,*
> *the very wood that was hollowed with knives?*

To our right, a long and narrow lake mirrored every shade of yellow and green the surrounding landscape offered, creating an elongated work of art that Monet would have envied. I asked Marie to stop the car so I could take a picture.

"That bluish horizon," she pointed ahead, "is the Šumava mountain range. My husband and I also can't pass through here without stopping, soaking in all the beauty. Look, he is waving to us." I could barely make out a tiny figure at the far end of the lake. Marie waved back vigorously, yelling, "Ahoooj!" Then she said, "I need to pee," and without the slightest hesitation, she squatted behind a bush just a few feet from where I stood.

On the way back to the pension, as Marie drove through the town, a homemade sign in a window caught my eye: *Lace classes here.* I asked Marie about it.

"Sedlice is known for bobbin lace work. The tradition goes back centuries."

"I saw it on TV!" I exclaimed, suddenly remembering old ladies braiding and twisting threads on dozens of wooden bobbins. It looked impossibly complicated. From the tangled mess of strings, underneath their nimble fingers, emerged a dainty lace. "In the National Theater, the wall of the Presidential box is decorated with lace made by the women from here," I reported to Marie while she nodded enthusiastically, filling me in on more lace history.

"Rich German ladies used to order fancy hats here, some even with gold-wired threads. Nine women worked on one of them, weaving in wine-colored Czech garnets. In those days, when a local couple got engaged, they didn't exchange rings, but fancy lace handkerchiefs."

"I saw beautiful contemporary bobbin lace made into jewelry in expensive gift stores in Prague," I interrupted.

"They were probably from here," Marie said, pulling into her driveway.

I couldn't wait to tell Larry how the stranger I left with a couple of hours ago had come to feel like a sister. I wished he could have seen her piece of heaven.

Marie and I walked toward her front door, passing neat flowerbeds where small, uniformly spaced plants poked from the soil. "What are these?" I asked.

"Statice. For wreaths. On the Day of the Dead in October, all my neighbors come to buy wreaths from me."

"A tricky business, no?" I commented, "selling to people you know."

"That one," she pointed to the house at the left, "brings me Becherovka. That one," she pointed to the house at the right, "always gives me eggs. And that one," she pointed to the slick plane cruising above, "also gets them from me. That's our neighbor. He has lots of money, so he bought himself an airplane," Marie said with triumph.

In the evening, lying in bed on big fluffy pillows, I told Larry about the famous Sedlice lace, Marie's meadow, the Christmas carp and the adorable little lambs. Then something struck me. I took the pillow, unbuttoned its side and unzipped the next layer. We stared into the pillowcase filled with soft frizzy wool.

"You'll get to hug your sheep after all, Larry said, "and I think I'll count mine." And with a big yawn he wrapped his arms around me.

I snuggled in that soft spot between his neck and his shoulder. I'll miss my new friend, Marie. I wished that today had just begun. Again, Gibran's words rang in my head:

When you are sorrowful look again in your heart,
And you shall see that in truth
you are weeping for that which has been your delight.

28. Helfenburk Ruins

"Look at that idiot behind us!" Larry kept glancing nervously in the rearview mirror at the white Kia glued to the bumper of our Škoda. Finally, the Kia driver took a chance to pass. For a second it looked like three cars would have to cram into space for one. We caught up with the Kia at a crossing where we all waited for a train to past. "How did that work out for you?" Larry mumbled with a dose of satisfaction.

We took a detour from the main highway to have a picnic lunch at the ruins of Helfenburk Castle. Although there were almost no other cars, the slow going on the narrow, curvy road was going to put a serious dent in my overambitious planning, I realized too late.

"It's frustrating to be so close to the birthplace of Mr. Jan Hus and have no time to visit. And no time for the medieval city of Prachatice, either," I lamented.

"Well, honey, you just can't stuff a gallon of fun into a Seven-Up can," Larry said, and I wondered if he just made that up.

"The paneláks have probably ruined the scenery anyway," he tried to comfort me.

We drove through dense woods and green round hills sparsely populated with tiny settlements. Then, a farmhouse just like I remembered from my childhood fairytale book emerged in front of us, and I enthusiastically recalled, "Any minute the devil will shoot out of that chimney and be gone forever. The happy villagers will run to the town square, dance the Beer Barrel Polka and eat poppy-seed koláče. Clever Honza will finally marry Manka, and everyone will live happily ever after."

"Huh?" Larry tossed me the look.

"Until now I had only seen pictures of these Southern Bohemian jewels. They're built in the unique architecture called Rural Baroque," I said and leaned forward, hoping the road would reveal more of these beauties. In pastel blues, yellows and pinks, scattered like rare species of wild flowers, they were all there, waiting for us.

"Those puffed roofs remind me of the 1960's bouffant hairdos with ringlets at the sides, like my high school teacher used to wear," Larry said.

"It would be a good comparison if she'd had a tribal tattoo on her neck, too. The Rural Baroque is a complete mismatch of styles."

The pine forest opened up to a dirt lot with a handful of parked cars. Before locking up our Škoda, I arranged our sweaters over some knick-knacks, hiding them from the thief my dad had warned us about.

"Come on, there's hardly anyone here. It'll be fine," Larry said, impatient to get going.

Dad's burglar stories rang in my ears as we hiked on the forest trail toward the ruins. The vision of our broken car windows and the empty trunk haunted me. I searched for a sign of malice in the faces of a couple returning to the parking lot. "Are they the ones to vandalize our car and steal all our stuff?" I muttered, fingering my money belt. "We have enough to get us to my parents' house. There, we would have to accept handouts," I said. Larry just rolled his eyes.

A pile of waist-high pine needles at the edge of the woods, a sight I hadn't seen for decades, got Larry curious. He stepped toward it to take a better look.

"It's all moving! For god's sake, those are ants!" Larry took a hurried step back, squinting at the large black ants.

As a child, I was fascinated with these ant skyscrapers. With the swish of a stick, I could destroy the hill. I relished that feeling of power. My dad must have read my mind, for he had taken the time to explain about the lives of these enterprising creatures. "The queen lays the eggs, the workers gather food, the builders build, and the soldiers protect the colony with their claws." I could almost hear him. "The wall facing south is always the wider one because it gets the most heat. But when it gets too hot, and the pine needles are too dry, the workers tunnel deeper underground to bring in cooler air. See how hard they work? They take care of the forest by keeping it clean."

I would lower my eyes, convinced he knew my evil thoughts.

We continued the climb toward the ruins, and I told Larry about Ferda the Ant, the Czech kids' beloved cartoon character. "For over 80 years, this dapper black ant with a red polka-dot bow-tie is sort of a Czech Mickey Mouse. I forever pestered my mom to read his adventures. I feared for Ferda when he got lost exploring the world and was relieved when his comrades found him and brought him back to the safety of his colony. I didn't get the subtle message that celebrated the workers, promoted loyalty and the subordination to the colony. I would clap when Ferda was pulling sleepy ants out of bunk beds, yelling, 'get up you lazy ants, we need to complete the Five Year Plan.' You see, Ondřej Sekora, Ferda's creator, was a fired-up Communist."

"What is Ferda up to now?" Larry asked, setting a brisker pace.

"On YouTube, I saw how Ferda watched the soap opera, "Dallas," staying up late and over-sleeping the following morning," I said.

"Next thing, he is going to have *insex* with a lady bug," Larry chuckled.

"The Nazi sent Sekora's Jewish wife to a concentration camp, and banned him from publishing," I said, trying to catch my breath.

"Did she survive?"

"She was lucky. After Hitler lost the war, she was reunited with her husband. That's when he began cheering for the Communists."

Trudging on, I speculated, "What would we do in his shoes? Imagine that against all the odds I would come back from a prison camp and you get the job you loved back, even your fame. Would we kiss our liberator and accept his new ideology without questioning? Would our gratitude choke the reason?"

"Or would the reason choke our gratitude?" Larry said.

"Perhaps Sekora, like many after the war, wanted to repay the Soviets by contributing to their new ideology. When I was about ten, I found in the back of a closet, a shoebox full of my parents' love letters. You can't imagine my shock when in my dad's handwriting I read: 'My Dear, on the International Worker's Day, May first, listen to the radio. In one voice, the Czechoslovakian army is going to cheer to the Soviet Union. My voice is going to be among them.' When I asked my dad about it, he tore up the letter, saying he'd been young and stupid.

"They fooled my dad! My dad who, for as long as I can remember, cursed the Communists every time he turned on the news. That same guy was once cheering in the Communist carnival!"

We stopped to rest, and Larry handed me a water bottle. A massive round stone tower arose between the trees, a short distance ahead. We crossed the wooden bridge toward the ticket booth where a cashier offered us a pamphlet.

"Make sure to sit at the stone table, the only original piece of furniture left. Face the tower, then close your eyes and feel the energy of the Rožumberk brothers, the royal builders of this castle. It's almost tangible at that spot."

I leaned toward her and lowered my voice, "How safe is the parking lot? Are there many burglaries?"

"Here? Of course not!" she exclaimed as if I'd asked if they sold dog meat at the snack bar.

The ruins reached above the tallest pines. The yellow mustard flowers, purple lilac, and golden dandelions — the last devotees — beautified what was left of the once imposing castle. On the other hand, the wild ivy, like a patient traitor, climbed the walls, determined to repossess what once belonged to her.

In one of the ceiling-less chambers, we found the massive slab of the stone table. But previous picnickers' candy wrappers, stained paper plates, and broken plastic forks stole the magic. Larry and I sat, staring at the trash at our feet. Then we closed our eyes. After a few moments, we looked at each other, shrugged our shoulders and got up.

We explored the broad, crumbling walls of meeting rooms and sleeping chambers. The gaps where the windows used to be looked like hollow eye sockets. The five-petal rose, the Rožumberk's family crest, was still visible above the Gothic doorways. From the top of the tower, Larry pointed to a perfect picnic spot below. We descended the uneven steps, and in the grass next to the wall we spread our feast on crumpled deli paper: radishes, rohlíky, and wonderfully aromatic slices of pink smoked ham. A gardener's arrival didn't spoil the idyllic setting. He cut the grass with a charmingly old-fashioned and blessedly silent sickle. He worked his way toward where we sat.

"People have been picnicking here for many years," he said and pointed to crooked numbers scratched in the stone: 1782. "An 18th century tourist left his mark. Even some ancient love messages. You can still find them if you search the walls."

"And I thought that graffiti was a modern-day thing," I said.

"When the castle still stood, it was often deserted and attracted vagrants. Today, people can pitch a tent right here in the courtyard. With a permit, of course."

"Imagine that!" "A night with the Helfenburk's ghosts," I said dreamily.

On the way out, we located more messages carved in the stone. Smoothed by rain, wind, and time, they were no longer legible.

Down at the parking lot, I rushed to the red Škoda. Anxious, I peered in through the window.

"Oh, shit!" I turned to Larry, yelling frantically, "It's all gone! The car is completely empty! They even took my flip-flops!"

"And I bet that even the key wouldn't fit." With a grin Larry dangled the key over his head. Then he unlocked another red Škoda parked two cars down.

🐝🐝🐝

29. Šumava, The Sudetenland

I traced the line on the map leading to Šumava, the southernmost part of Bohemia. "This road will take us all the way to my cousin Veronica's house," I said to Larry, refolding the map and placing it in the glove compartment. I reclined my seat and opened up a bag of salty peanuts, ready to soak up the scenery.

Around the city of Vimperk, the landscape turned mountainous. The historical river town with a castle and timber-framed houses is the gateway to Šumava National Park. With the Bavarian Forest on the German side, it forms the largest forested area in Central Europe, aptly nicknamed the Green Roof of Europe.

I spent many childhood summers with my sister and cousins in Šumava, jumping and splashing in the dark blue waters of Lipno Reservoir, the largest body of water in the country. The reservoir bordered my aunt's backyard. To four freckly kids with sunburned noses and bleached hair, Lipno was an ocean where we became beautiful mermaids and Captain Nemos, certain that summer would last forever.

Years later, when my sister Hana married, she passed her adoration for Šumava on to her husband, and together they put many happy miles on their hiking boots. Occasionally Hana shared her love affair with Šumava in her emails:

Sitting in front of our tent with my first cup of coffee, I see hills like lazy giants poking their backs out of foggy white

139

blankets. The burbling creek stretches all the way to the valley. Daisies are opening their palms, offering the pearls of morning dew. I sip my coffee and wonder. Where did Šumava get its name? Was it from the sound of the wind in the trees or from the morning harmony?

The year my sister found her beloved Šumava devastated by tree-eating parasites, she wrote:

Groups of pine trees are awaiting their fate at the hands of a deadly army of bark beetles. Some thick pines are guarding the scattered pale bones of their predecessors haphazardly resting in the grass. The stumps are lining the distorted curves of sorrowful mountain lips. This is also Šumava. The vulnerable Šumava, the scarred Šumava.

None of the destruction left by the bark beetles was evident from the road. Our Škoda passed isolated settlements surrounded by dense woods. I felt the warmth of Larry's hand on my knee.

It had been more than three decades since I'd visited Šumava, that bittersweet land whose isolation didn't shield its residents from political cataclysms. Quite the contrary.

In 1938, Hitler's followers stirred troubles among Czech and German neighbors in border towns. Nazi agitators manipulated the political climate, preparing for their Fuhrer's proclamation about the suffering of ethnic Germans among the Czechs.

In the infamous Munich Conference, the representatives of the world superpowers nodded as Hitler's jaws parted and his razor sharp canines got ready to rip off the border region, known as Sudetenland, from Czechoslovakia. The English, French and Italian ministers naively hoped that by allowing the beast a bite, it would satisfy its craving and silence the war drums over their own countries.

On October first, 1938, German tanks crossed Czechoslovakian borders. From army generals down to commoners,

Czechs were ready to fight for their country even without western allies. However, the Czech President Beneš refused to lead the masses into a battle he believed would be a one-sided slaughter. Hitler gulped Šumava along with one-fifth of Czechoslovakia, taking over almost 5,000 towns and 4 million people. It left the country economically devastated and strategically weakened.

After Germany lost the war in 1945, my Aunt Mařenka, Dad's younger sister, landed in Šumava from a traditional southern Moravian village named Dambořice where custom dictated when to eat, what to wear, how to sing, or whom to marry. There Mařenka fell in love with handsome and industrious Kuba. But Kuba's people were Protestants. Mařenka's were Catholic. Both families opposed the marriage.

After the war ended, the Czechoslovakian government forcibly expelled three million Germans. Now was the Czechs' turn to punish the Germans. As a result, 70,000 businesses closed their doors, and weeds overgrew 350,000 small farms. The Czechoslovakian government needed to secure the next year's harvest. So with convenient loans they lured newcomers to the vacant border towns. Mařenka and Kuba jumped at their chance and eloped. The couple found themselves in the remote Sudetenland among adventure seekers and opportunists.

My aunt and uncle didn't adapt well to the harsh climate of Šumava, its long dark winters, thick, lingering fog and summer storms with gusting winds that bent mature trees like blades of grass.

My aunt's voice cracked when she talked about "my golden Moravia." Overwhelmed with emotion, she would engulf my little body, squishing me like a comfort pillow. My torso shook with the convulsions of her sobs. Although I loved my aunt's farm, especially swimming in Lipno, I too felt the strange void in Šumava. With the last German old-timer gone, there was an absence of tradition, culture and folk art. What a contrast with Southern Moravia where colorful embroidered skirts spun to the rhythm of fiddles and the claps and whistles of onlookers.

Mařenka and Kuba didn't discover poetry in Šumava the way my sister and her husband did. My Uncle Kuba worked as a lumberjack and my Aunt Mařenka as a milkmaid on a run-down cooperative farm. They became numbers filling in the Communist quotas. Many settlers had difficulty adapting to a lonely place faraway from civilization and their families. With no home to return to, Mařenka and Kuba found themselves stuck.

Even though all was beautiful and calm now, Šumava was once saturated with tears. Trees along the road, the silent witnesses, remembered the hate and the fear, German and Czech alike. First, the Germans chased away the Czechs, then Czechs chased away the Germans. The Germans marked the Czech Jews with the yellow Star of David, later Czechs marked the Germans with the white armbands of subordinates. Germans liquidated Jewish cemeteries, later Czechs liquidated the German graves. During the war, traveling was restricted for Czechs. After the war, traveling wasn't allowed at all for the remaining Germans. After the war, Terezín, the concentration camp near Prague, became the detention camp for Germans.

The shallow western tail of the Lipno Reservoir emerged in front of us. I felt the gentle drumming of Larry's fingers on my knee.

"Almost there," I said.

30. Aunt Mařenka from *Horní Planá*

"So, who's house are we going to again?" Larry asked.

"My cousin Veronica's," I said. "Her mom, my aunt Mařenka, sold her house after she lost her husband Kuba last year. So, now we're going to her daughter's, Veronica's house.

Veronica is married to Tom, and they have two grown kids, Ivanka and Kája. I only met her husband and the kids once before.

"So you missed your uncle only by a few months," Larry said, sorting things out. "Is your Aunt living with Veronica now?"

"She lives nearby, like across the street or something."

In Horní Planá we turned left at the crossroads just like Veronica's son Kája had instructed us. We parked in front of the first house past the convenience store. In front of a new three-story villa with oversized windows, a woman was bent over a flowerpot. At the sound of the motor, she straightened up.

"Veronica!" I waved out the window. She looked the same. Her boyish haircut was as I remembered when we were kids.

"Why are you so late?" she hollered, wiping her hands on her jeans. "We were expecting you yesterday." Striding toward a low wire gate, she sounded ticked off, but her eyes danced and sparkled; crow's feet decorated the edges. "We already ate all the schnitzels and potato salad!"

Veronica and I embraced in a long, tight hug. Over her shoulder, I saw my Aunt Mařenka coming out of the house. When our eyes met, she stumbled, laying her hand on her heart. Her face tightened, and I couldn't tell if she was going to laugh or cry. We walked toward each other with open arms. My aunt's embrace said, you are still ours; all those decades apart didn't change a thing. I felt like a little girl again, and suddenly it was me who couldn't hold back tears. Mařenka took my face in her hands and grinned, displaying gaps of missing teeth. She used to welcome me with scolds of how skinny I was, and a promise to fatten me up during the summer. This time she stepped back, measured me up and down, and nodded approvingly.

"Yep, butt and hips. All there," I said and turned to introduce Larry, who stood by the gate, a slow smile hiding uncertainty.

In the spacious, bright kitchen on the second floor, Veronica showed Larry and me to a table draped by a neatly ironed tablecloth. Mařenka retired to the stool by the window. Veronica covered the table with platters of cold cuts, cheeses and three kinds of homemade pastries. Then she leaned against the cabinet, ready to assist, to keep our glasses and plates filled. I made a mental note to go beyond the customary vegetable dip, next time we have visitors from the Czech Republic.

"Aren't they going to eat with us?" Larry asked from a corner of his mouth.

I wished they would, but I knew that trying to make them join us would be a lost struggle. This was their way of honoring us. And so we ate while they watched.

The delectable cake slices spread with shiny, dark fudge were so good, I inhaled one after the other, not giving our hostess a chance for the customary encouragements — eat, help yourselves, eat more, don't be shy.

Veronica's husband Tom entered the kitchen, extending his hand to Larry.

"Speak Czech?"

Larry shook his head.

"German?"

Larry disappointed him again.

With no common language, the four of them were at a loss. My Aunt Mařenka, cousin Veronica, and her husband Tom measured Larry with uncertain smiles. Tom was the first to recover. He reached in the cabinet for an unmarked bottle of slivovitz.

"Homemade. From Moravia," he said with lustful pride and filled two shot glasses, handing one to Larry.

"*Na zdraví!*" Both men cheered, Larry exhausting half of his Czech vocabulary. The glasses clinked, and Tom expertly turned his shot bottom up. All eyes were on Larry who, I knew, didn't wish to follow in Tom's suicide act. But he did. Blushing, Larry gasped for air. He looked like his throat, chest, and even his eyeballs were on fire. Tom gave Larry a hardy slap on the back and then retreated into the living room where he turned on the TV.

"To divert attention from Larry, who needed a moment to recover, I stepped toward the Formica cabinet where a traditional Easter lamb cake was displayed on a silver oval platter in the glass cabinet. The chocolate-chip eyes inside the curls made with royal icing gave the sugar lamb the look of a real animal.

"I haven't seen one of those in years," I said in a soft affectionate voice.

"Oh, I should get rid of that old thing, but I just can't part with her," Veronica apologized.

"Do you bake the Easter lamb cakes in America?" Aunt Mařenka wanted to know.

"Not really," I said, and then corrected myself. "Once I did."

"They aren't easy to make," Veronica said. "You have to have the special cake form and the cake batter has to be heavy like cement. That's the only way they'll last. This one is over two years old."

"So they don't make these in America?" Mařenka repeated. "Wouldn't they like them?"

"Actually, they wouldn't," I said with confidence.

"When I was still new in America, my co-worker invited me to her house for Easter dinner. She said she wanted to impress her guests by having someone from such an exotic country like Czechoslovakia." Mocking my American friend made Veronica and Mařenka chuckle the same way I chuckled when I heard the word exotic in connection with Czechoslovakia.

"I wanted to bring something traditional from our country, so I wiped the dust off my lamb and brought her as a gift, glad she would spend her final hours as a glamorous center-piece. At the dinner table, while I was yakking with some American man sitting next to me, boasting about the Czecho-slovakian tradition of pastry making, we were interrupted by passing dessert plates. They'd sliced up my ancient lamb!"

"No!" Veronica cried burying her face in her hands. In the midst of horrifying laughter she asked, "Wouldn't they need a chainsaw?"

"I have no idea how they did it. It was hard as a brick, but they cut her up! All the people at that long table had a piece of my stale symbol of spring on fancy gold-rimmed dessert plates sitting in front of them."

"Oh, my gosh," Veronica squealed, "By the time I dump my lamb, not even chickens would peck at it. What did you do? You didn't let them eat it, did you?"

"It was too late, some of them were already gnawing on it. The man next to me was gesturing for more coffee, the chunk in his mouth stretching his cheek, ready to tear it. It was a nightmare! And it got worse! The hostess announced, 'This dessert was baked by my friend Lenka, the European pastry chef!'"

Mařenka's shoulders were bobbing with quiet laughter long after the topic steered away from my American Easter lamb disaster. Larry politely followed the conversation, appreciating the sparse bits of translations I tossed in his direction: "Kája will be home after the hockey game. Ivanka works in Prague and is coming home for the weekend. Mařenka lives in an old farmhouse converted into a pension." Larry accompanied his nods with an attentive "um, okay, I see."

The rays of the afternoon sun entered the kitchen through the lace curtains. Mařenka slowly got up from her stool, and Veronica took the empty glasses off the table. "My mom wants to show you guys where she lives now."

I welcomed the opportunity, keen to ask my aunt questions about her first years in Šumava during the turbulent post-war era.

The three of us walked a short distance on a grassy path toward the stone wall where my aunt pushed open a wooden gate. It was easy to imagine the spacious courtyard as the lively farmstead it once was: noisy with pigs, geese and barking dogs, the wooden wagons, wheelbarrows and farm machinery crowding the open-front barn, the fragrance of hay and manure lingering in the air.

This courtyard was strangely vacant and still; the neatly swept animal stalls were bare and odorless, not even a feather was tucked in the most remote corner. The only object that suggested movement was a garden swing dangling from a chain by the entrance to the main building, a testimony that this was no longer a working farm.

My aunt Mařenka unlocked the door of the house, pointing to the side walls. "Look how thick they are. The Germans who built this house brought each stone from the fields. Can you imagine?" My aunt's face scrunched in dismay.

"Not even a cannon ball would puncture it," Larry said appraisingly.

Recognizing the word cannon, Mařenka nodded, smiling shyly at Larry. "At first, I didn't know if I should be scared here. Except for the summer, when the German tourists come, I'm here alone."

We followed her through the furnished rooms, all equipped with flat screen TVs, private bathrooms, and modern kitchenettes.

At the other side of the long building, Mařenka opened up the final door. The front of the house faced the town square across from the Baroque church and the water fountain. Arm in arm we strolled along the empty plaza, Larry lagging behind. My aunt stopped in front of a store window.

"Vietnamese shop," she said, examining the cramped window display: the yellow silk tulips, cheap plastic sunglasses, a naked doll, paper cake doilies, hair clips. Her eyes rested on a little porcelain dish, no different from those sold in every Chinatown. "Oh, I like this," she said with a dreamy appreciation of someone who had lived her life deprived of knick-knacks, so essential to a woman's heart.

I recalled my British friend who, in the 1980's, traveled to Eastern Europe. He described perfectly the bare world behind the Iron Curtain: "As soon as we crossed the border from West Germany to Czechoslovakia, it was like a movie that suddenly switched from color to black and white."

When I was about 16, my friend lent me plastic red lips, a pin that her aunt had sent from Austria. The brooch on my green hand-knitted turtleneck transformed my world. I felt so unconventional and fashionable. I felt like I was no longer a part of the marching masses.

"Things sure changed, didn't they?" I said, slowly walking toward a bench beneath a linden tree. We sat down, and I finally asked, "Aunty, how was it when you first came here?"

As if caught doing something bad, my aunt forced a smile. Then, like a stubborn child, she looked away. After a while, she said, "It was a long time ago."

"I know," I pressed. "That's why it's so interesting."

Her face reddened, and her eyes filled with tears, the stifling silence lasted way too long, but she finally admitted the troublesome truth. "I don't remember," she whispered. Oh, how I hated myself at that moment, how I hated aging, that merciless thief. I only hoped it took away the painful stuff too. With my uncle no longer with us, and my aunt's memory gone, I'll never know.

I helped my aunt up, and we slowly walked back toward the pension.

31. Ivanka

Veronica had left the outside light on and the front door unlocked. Larry and I groped along the hallways toward our upstairs loft when we saw a thin strip of light under the kitchen door. Veronica's daughter Ivanka answered my soft knock. Fresh out of the shower, wrapped in a bulky housecoat, her short hair wet, she still looked stunning. Sophisticated. When Ivanka smiled and extended her slender hand to greet us, I saw her mom's brown eyes.

"Mom is working the night shift at the convalescent hospital. She left a few minutes after I got home."

Ivanka filled a tea-kettle with water and set three mugs on the kitchen table. I asked about her train ride home.

"I am tired of roaming between Prague and Šumava, always carrying a backpack full of laundry back and forth," she confessed. "But if I don't come home on the weekend, I get sick in Prague. The crowds, the air pollution, the rented flat with shared kitchen... Mom always said that education would open the doors, but sometimes I wonder if college was such a good thing for me."

I recalled my college-educated nieces — both in their 30s, both with great jobs, both still single.

Ivanka went on, "Most of my high school classmates didn't go to college, and they all found good work around here, earning years toward their retirements, raising their families." Ivanka placed both hands to the side of her mug and lifted the cup to her lips. After a few seconds she put the cup down without talking a sip. "I have a good job in Prague, but I don't want to commute forever."

My generation of women had fewer options. We walked down the aisle early. My sister was the last from her class to marry. She was 23. By my 30th birthday, the girls I knew had school-age children.

This generation of educated girls is balancing alone on the narrow steps of corporate ladders. One day their daughters may end up assisting a senile parent with one hand while rocking a baby in the other. If there will be a baby.

Ivanka brought a thick photo album and placed it on the kitchen table. We sipped our tea, slowly turning the stiff pages. In a flowery purple dress, Ivanka posed in front of Bangkok's Grand Palace. Her vibrant smile in the next picture made the blue domes of Santorini fade into the distance. The white sand of Florida's Clearwater Beach offset Ivanka's golden-brown tan. This charismatic young woman had traveled extensively, a trade-off for having foregone getting married and having a family. Ivanka pointed to a photograph where she sat on the roof of a Jeep, looking through binoculars. "The safari guide said that because of poaching, long-tusked elephants are starting to grow less valued smaller tusks."

"Nature's way of securing their survival," I said, wondering if nature would start prolonging women's fertile years.

Suddenly the kitchen door flew open, and a handsome young man stormed in. "Lenka! Larry!" Ivanka's younger brother shouted, extending his arms above his head, nearly touching the ceiling. "It's three to one! We just beat Russia! Three to one!" The nationalistic feeling comes through in the most popular Czech sport — hockey.

Kája smothered us in a bear hug, roaring into our ears, "and in two weeks we'll send you to third place." Larry and I find ourselves representing not just the U.S. hockey team, but the whole nation, which Kája hoped would be defeated by the Czech hockey players.

"Let's drink to that! What can I offer you, Larry? Budweiser? Staropramen?"

In stunned amusement, Ivanka watched her brother, "But we don't even have any beer," she said.

"In the 1968 World Cup, right after the Russian occupation, the Czechs beat Russia 4:0," I said. "I was ten-years-old then. After the televised match was over, I had to go to bed. It was hard to sleep with all the shouting and cheering outside. The next morning the walls were covered with riddles. I still remember this one:

Poslali jste na nás tanky —
dali jsme vám čtyři branky!

You send tanks on us — we gave you four goals. (It rhymes better in Czech.)

"That afternoon on my way home from school, most of the graffiti was already cleaned up, even my favorite pink-colored 4:0 on the front glass door of our apartment building. Later at dinner, Mom said, 'I sacrificed the only lipstick I had on it.' But there wasn't any regret in her voice."

Ivanka, Kája, Larry and I stayed up late, talking and laughing. We enjoyed every minute together. I don't think Kája even realized that Larry didn't speak Czech. Our stories were like tiny stitches, patching up the long tear of time.

32. The Western Side of *Lipno* Reservoir

I opened my eyes, wondering what I was doing in this loft just as Larry, wobbling from the restroom, smiling at the prospect of crawling back under the downy comforter, walked right into the low, slanted ceiling. Like an asteroid, his body crashed on top of mine. Both of us stared at the red dots dripping on the pillowcase. "Blood," Larry said, touching his forehead. Then he pressed a handkerchief to my split lip. That was the first time he banged his head that morning; half an hour later, he did it again.

"This is a freaking mystery spot," he cried, "You don't see the wall until you're in it."

We examined the white wall for blood marks left by previous visitors and were surprised to find none.

"Freshly painted, that's why," Larry said.

The forehead bruised, the lip swollen, we entered the sunny kitchen filled with the aroma of sweet bell pepper and sausage.

"Dobré ráno," my cousin Veronica said, pouring steaming tea in the mugs. "We could leave right after breakfast," Ivanka said from the counter where she was preparing sandwiches.

My aunt Mařenka nodded from her stool by the window, "Long walks aren't for me any more. I'll be happy right here." Then she stuck her head outside, waving toward her grandson Kája who was already clearing some wood pallets. "Put your shirt back on! The wind will give you muscle cramps." To my surprise, he obeyed immediately.

"He is so helpful around the house." Veronica uttered a sentence that in all my parenting years had never escaped my lips. These people could model for a Norman Rockwell painting. Mother, daughter and grandmother, three generations of women together in the kitchen on an ordinary Saturday morning. The moment so precious and so rare in my life.

Veronica and Ivanka, both Šumava natives, accompanied Larry and me on our hike to a lookout tower on the Austrian side. Our Škoda carried the four of us along the Lipno's shimmering water.

"One January, when the Lipno was frozen over, Kája and his friends drove by just as a speed-skating competition was going on," Ivanka said. "His friends dared Kája to enter, and he ended up winning the 1,000-meter race. His prize was a weekend in a pension. A half a block from our house!" Ivanka laughed with sibling-spite satisfaction.

"There are competitions in speed skating for moms pushing strollers too," Veronica added.

Suddenly Mařenka's old house came into view. The front looked exactly how I remembered, with its three deep-set windows and yellow-ochre colored walls. This time, though, scaffolding covered its side. "They are remodeling!" Ivanka exclaimed. We all leaned forward. "They are expanding, adding a floor." We twisted our necks as the house quickly shrunk in the rearview mirror.

"Since Mom sold the house, she has never gone back. She hasn't even driven by. And it's been nearly a year." Veronica paused, offering us the hard candy Hašlerky, and then, sucking noisily, she continued. "After the revolution, some Germans began reclaiming their properties. One afternoon, an elegant older lady knocked on Mom's door explaining in broken Czech that before the war this house belonged to her family. You can't imagine how terrified we were, sure she had come to reclaim her house. Mom lived there for over half a century and thought it was her turn to be kicked out now. The lady assured us she didn't want the house. She only wanted to visit her birthplace, the house her father had built. We walked her from room to room, and the next thing, all three of us were wiping tears. She stayed for tea and then she was gone."

The road ended at the banks of Lipno Reservoir. Larry drove slowly onto a ferry, parking behind another car. The four of us chatted on as if crossing the Lipno Reservoir to the Western side was the most ordinary, everyday thing. And today it was. In my time, walking on Mars would have been more likely.

In my first-grade reader, I remember a poem with a picture of a smiling Czech soldier, the red star on his cap, rifle across his shoulder and a friendly, almost smiling, German shepherd by his side. The poem talked about how we could sleep soundly now, unafraid of the enemy traitors because our brave soldiers were guarding the borders. Being afraid of enemy traitors had never occurred to me before I read that poem. I mostly worried about the boogeyman in the wolf skin which, I was sure, hid under my bed at night. But I liked that poem. It rhymed. One evening I recited it with prideful vigor to my parents, bowing deeply at the end. There was no applause, only two sets of worried eyes. Their brainwashed child was reciting Communist propaganda.

Now, I was on the forbidden Western side. The only indications that we were in Austria was the German road sign. No more barbed wire or border patrols. We drove through the woodsy cross-country ski area. Larry parked in front of a modern resort that now was closed for the season. We set off towards the observation tower Moldaublick. I looked forward to crossing the bubbly brooks and the wild meadows my sister described with such passion. After a couple of miles on the gravel road, Ivanka pulled out a sad excuse for a map. "We must have missed the trail someplace," she said, rotating the advertising pamphlet, trying to orient herself from the useless colorful diagram. Just then a work truck sped by, enveloping us in a cloud of dust, the gray powder settling on yellow petals of marsh marigolds.

I realized our nature experience in Šumava wouldn't include the soft mosses under our feet, or poetry-inspiring pastures. We were stuck on a dusty, gravel road, trying not to get run over by passing trucks.

Finally we found ourselves in an empty parking lot where a seemingly deserted wooden lodge stood. Beside it a five-story drilling tower had been converted into a lookout. Just as I thought there wasn't a living soul for miles, a head popped from the window, and an arm pointed to the fee board. On the climb to the top, Larry busied himself calculating, not the 137 steps, but converting euros into dollars, figuring how much this climb cost him. "Damn!" he exclaimed. I wasn't sure if he was referring to the dense woods or the pricey tickets.

At the top, Veronica turned around transfixed. "All those trees!"

Aren't those the same trees she had lived among all her life? I thought and asked Ivanka, "Have you hiked much around here with your parents?"

"Hike with my parents?" she repeated. "Do they strike you as hikers? They never took us anywhere, castles, towns, or woods. Never! We were lucky when they sent us to a Communist-run summer camp."

Back home in the kitchen, Veronica was getting ready for her night shift at the convalescent hospital. Mařenka asked if she bought her the seedless raspberry jam.

"For the fifth time, Mom! They were out but the grocer ordered it for you. How many times do I have to repeat it?"

Ivanka butted in, "Mom, you need to learn how to talk to old people."

"Did you hear that?" Veronica looked at me. "I need to learn how to talk to old people! I, who worked with them all my life."

Mother, daughter, and grandmother, three generations of women together in the kitchen, a moment blessedly rare in my life. Perhaps not Norman Rockwell, but Kandinsky or Picasso would be fitting artists for their family portrait.

33. The 90 Eggs in *Český Krumlov*

The next morning, as we waved goodbye from our slowly rolling Škoda, Mařenka yelled after us, "Wait!" and disappeared into the house. When she came back, she held three flats of eggs. "Take them home to your parents," she said. I couldn't break her heart by admitting that we weren't going straight home to Mom and Dad like good children would, so I accepted the gift. With 90 eggs on my lap, we headed north toward Český Krumlov, the second most-visited city in the Czech Republic. I hadn't realized how close it was to my aunt's house. Within minutes we parked the car in a spacious lot below the castle by the stone city wall.

"How about those eggs?" asked Larry. "It's too hot to leave them in the car."

Across the lot, a herd of tourists was getting off of a double-decker tour bus.

"We could ask someone to hold them for us and then run. I saw a reality show where a man with a sheep on a leash asked random businessmen on the street to watch her for just a second. It was hilarious how the good samaritan, briefcase in one hand, leashed sheep in the other, kept nervously checking his watch."

Since a vulnerable businessman was nowhere in sight, we left the eggs searing in the car and followed the crowd of Japanese visitors toward the city's historical center.

The wooden pedestrian bridge over the meandering Vltava river provided a glorious view. Tidy pastel-colored houses with steep red roofs nestled on one side of the river and from the opposing bedrock rose the castle with its unique pink and green tower. Clusters of flowering chestnut trees framed the view. Why hadn't I ever come here? I'd spent summers just a few minutes from this jewel of a town, and this was my first visit here.

Larry and I strolled happily past alluring outdoor restaurants, peeking into modern art galleries and funky coffee houses. The law that protects historical sites saved Český Krumlov from the monochromatic boxy architecture of the Communist era. Today, this tourist haven is a showcase of craftsmanship and ingenious, offbeat designs, from vaulted ceilings of cozy souvenir shops to the metal utility hole covers, stamped decoratively with the city's coat of arms: the five-petalled rose of the royal Rožmberk family.

We wandered over the curvy cobblestones toward the Regional Museum where we could enjoy a perfect view of the castle, once the home of a wealthy man. I told Larry how the legendary Petr Vok, a member of the Rožmberk family, saved the people around Český Krumlov from an army of misplaced mercenaries.

"Vok's story begins with one of the Habsburgs, the paranoid Czech King Rudolf who, in 1611, for a not entirely clear reason, invited 12,000 foreign mercenaries onto the Czech land. As was customary in those days, a small army of prostitutes, so-called brides of the regiment, lagged behind. In Prague, people fought ferociously against the trespassers."

"Wait, the King invited an army to Prague for no reason?" Larry asked.

"And on top of it he had no plan of how to pay for this craziness," I said. "Madness ran in the Habsburg family. They didn't know that marrying one's cousin wasn't good for them. They had that big bottom lip, making their mouth hang open all the time.

"Anyway, civilians poured boiling water from their windows and attacked the mercenaries with pitchforks and hoes. The mercenaries were defeated but refused to leave the Czech kingdom without getting paid. They set up camps in this area, robbing and vandalizing the country folks while King Rudolf insisted that his treasury was empty. The King's advisors, Habsburg's two-faced bureaucrats, were blamed for Rudolf's poor decision. Eventually, the Protestants threw those same advisors out of the window, initiating The Thirty Years War. But that's another story."

"The second defenestration," Larry nodded. "Czechs seem to have a bad habit of throwing people out of windows."

"Someone needed to stop the plundering. That's where good old Vok came in. He filled 16 wagons with silver from his family treasury and had it minted into coins in Kutná Hora, to pay off the troops. Financially exhausted, Vok was forced to sell this castle. He was a spoiled nobleman, but when it came down to it, he knew the right thing to do. He died a year later, as did the mad King Rudolf."

From the top of the hill, looking on Vok's castle, Larry said, "I don't think that Vok's deed was so noble. He was a feudal society man. He owned this land and the people; he approved or denied their marriages, their requests to move. His subordinates needed his written approval to visit relatives in neighboring towns. They had to work for free on his land. It was his responsibility to protect them. Imagine that some vagabonds take over your backyard, crapping all over the lawn. The police, due to budget cuts, wouldn't get involved. You too would run to Bank of America for your silver to pay them to leave."

Larry was dimming my bright picture of Vok, but he had a point.

We leaned against the short stone wall and did what everyone around was doing — taking dozens of selfies with the bubbling Vltava below and the looming castle above.

Before leaving Český Krumlov, we aired out the hot car. "For sure we can't eat those eggs. They're probably spoiled," I said, just as an idea struck me. I needed to figure out how to persuade Larry to execute it.

We were driving through the lowland of the Třeboň region known for its lakes filled with the celebrated carp. The flat waters were visible on both sides of the road. "This is where our Christmas carp came from!" I rejoiced at the memory of the snowy Christmas days when Dad would take my sister and me to buy our carp from a bundled-up street vendor who would net out the biggest, liveliest one from the barrel. For Czechs, it wouldn't be Christmas without the traditional fish soup and fried carp.

"Mom had the bathtub filled with water when we brought the carp home," I said.

"It was alive?"

"My sister and I would spend hours by the tub, hypnotized, watching the poor carp swim in tight ovals. His big round mouth was opening and closing as if sending us kisses."

I recalled the excitement of that special day. Images began to pop in my head: Mom, Dad, my sister and I wearing our best clothes. The kitchen table with the red embroidered tablecloth we had brought from Bulgaria. Candlelight illuminating our expectant faces. Mom passing the platter with breaded filets of fried carp. "Look under your plates," she would remind us. Everyone acted surprised discovering a few gold scales, the symbol of prosperity. Mom carried couple in her wallet for an entire year thereafter.

Our Christmas was as much about the carp as it was about the baby Jesus who placed presents underneath the Christmas tree. We ate carp once a year, on the holiest day of all, the day when even my sister and I knew not to bicker.

Continuing on the journey, our Škoda passed many brown signs pointing to special places of interest. At the next one, I couldn't stand it any longer and yelled, "Turn right here!"

Unlike in Český Krumlov, our car was the only one in the parking lot. I threw a sweater over the stack of eggs, a feeble attempt to keep them cool, and set out on a path beside a lake hemmed by stately oak trees. About 500 years ago some entrepreneurs began to transform local swamps into a lake district to grow fish for commerce. Hundreds of trees were planted to strengthen the embankments of these man-made lakes, creating an exquisite and rare harmony between economy and nature. Today this flat land full of lakes and gorgeous trees is a protected biosphere reservation registered by UNESCO.

The path led us to an impressive English garden crowned with a mini hexagonal-shaped white castle. The guide, an elderly man, sat on a chair outside the entrance, warming himself in the sun. "Welcome to the Schwarzenberg Tomb," he said formally, then added in a friendly tone, "Inside is too cold for my bones."

The man told us about the 2002 flood, when water from surrounding lakes overflowed and formed a sea around Třeboň, making the city look like an island. I wondered if the carp swam in the streets, but I didn't ask. The man was so happy to learn we were from California, where his nephew lives, that he snuck us in for free. "They are with me," he called out to the lady collecting the entrance fee. A poster by the entry door advertised a candlelight concert. Awesome! Violin echoing against the white sandstone, elegant marble, and bones of 26 members of the Schwarzenberg family.

"After the last Rožmberk, Petr Vok, died, the Schwarzenbergs were the next wealthiest Czech royals. They were big supporters of the Habsburgs, which made them unpopular.

"When the Communists confiscated the Schwarzenbergs' castles and land, even this tomb," the man said, "the royal family emigrated to Austria. After the 1989 revolution,

Duke Karel Schwarzenberg returned to the Czech Republic, his homeland, and became President Havel's adviser and later his Minister of Foreign Affairs. He is the current owner of this tomb and owns 300 of the 400 lakes in Třeboň. In 2012, the 75-year-old Schwarzenberg campaigned for the presidential office, but he lost to the social democrat Miloš Zeman."

"Schwarzenberg is a good guy, but he keeps falling asleep at the meetings," my dad told me later over the phone, quoting the minister: "What else is one to do while listening to bullshit?"

Leaving the tomb, the tour guide said, "You should go visit our castle. Compared with Český Krumlov, it's like his poor cousin, but it's the place where Petr Vok died."

I almost felt sorry for my favorite Rožmberk, but Larry said, "I have no pity for anyone who spends his final days in a castle."

We headed toward Jindřichův Hradec, the city that would become our favorite.

34. Folk Art — *Kraslice*

As we drove through a lush green tunnel of linden trees, I scanned the roadside for pensions and moto-rests. Jindřichův Hradec was highlighted in my auto atlas as an interesting tourist destination. The further from the city center, the cheaper the lodging, I figured. We needed a casual place where we wouldn't alarm the receptionist with our three flats of eggs. Every time I spotted a promising pension, Larry had already passed it. I didn't ask him to go back since maneuvering on Czech roads drove him to barely audible, but constant mumbling. Not a good time to introduce my plan for the eggs.

The women in my family have a peculiar connection to eggs. My mom, sister and I are linked to our ancestors by the ancient folk-art that Czechs call *kraslice*. Kraslice are hollowed, elaborately decorated eggshells. In olden times, eggs were associated with magical powers. Although most people were illiterate, they understood the engraved symbols on the egg shell. Decorated eggs were given when a child was born, a couple got married, as a get well wish, or when someone died. I call them prehistoric Hallmark cards.

All through the year I work on my eggs. My home in California looks like the Easter bunny's headquarters. First, two tiny holes have to be drilled into the shell to blow out the contents. That's where Larry comes in. I paint and etch the hollow shells in the traditional technique of southern Moravia, although with my own contemporary designs. Czechs can pinpoint the region, if not the exact village, by the pattern on the egg. My family's designs would confuse many, however. Years in California have inspired my designs, from California poppies and bright citrus to starfish, sea shells and sea otters. My mom's love for mushrooms and simple village cottages is evident from her kraslice. My sister adores children, so she decorates her eggs with little people. I am delighted that even my tech-savvy daughter and skateboarder son are familiar with the secretive ancient skill of egg decorating. When people say, that's a lot of work; we say — that's a lot of fun.

The 90 eggs on the back seat could supply hours of creative bliss and hundreds of dollars.

We drove by some nice lodgings, always noticing them too late. Next, Larry was asking where to park while circling the central plaza in Jindřichův Hradec. That didn't fit into my "further-the-cheaper" theory, but the city's charm had already wrapped us in its web.

We found parking and went to check out the lovely old hotel named Vajgar. Forty-three dollars for a room overlooking the plaza was a deal not even we could refuse.

Returning for our suitcases, Larry said, "I know what you're thinking." He lowered his voice, "You distract the receptionist, and I'll sneak in the eggs."

In the room, as soon as we closed the door behind us, Larry checked his Swiss army knife for a sharp needle. "Okay, where do you want to do it?" he asked, like a conspirator who was about to perform a kidney transplant on a drunk victim. Luckily, the entire hotel was vacant and we had the communal bathroom at the far end of the hallway to ourselves.

An hour later, Larry was still hovered over the toilet, blowing and flushing the contents of the shells while I drilled the holes. "That's what happens when you marry a Czech," he mumbled to himself. After the last egg was blown he moaned, "I need a beer."

I love this guy, I thought. But I'm not going to kiss him just yet.

35. Air Travel in *Jindřichův Hradec*

In the outdoor restaurant across from our hotel, oversized umbrellas sheltered us from the blinding mid-afternoon sun. Larry took a swig of chilled Pilsner-Urquell, then leaned back in his garden chair, looked around the town square and after a long moment said, "This is nice."

Hand in hand, couples with ice cream cones strolled up and down the plaza. In front of a bike shop, two elderly gentlemen exchanged greetings and paused for a chat. A young woman sitting on a bench rocked a stroller while absorbed in a book. Small groups of school children skipped and hopped, their backpacks bouncing. An unleashed dog followed his master who wore a checkered fedora. Encircling this oasis were pastel-colored, three-story Renaissance buildings, crisp with newness, like freshly ironed Easter dresses.

Refreshed, Larry called the waiter over and paid for the beer. With no destination in mind, we wandered the city's pedestrian zone, passing pubs with names like Golden Goose, Black Eagle, and White Ghost. Unhurried people went in and out of a bookstore, a flower shop, and a smoked-fish store. Women stopped to gaze at the fashion in store windows. This idyllic town of 23,000 contented residents seemed to be in perfect balance.

Larry and I entered a delicatessen which sold a single item — *tvaroh*. Behind the glass counter, rows of deep oval trays were filled with mountains of flavored farm cheese. Czechs love their open-face sandwiches smeared with whipped tvaroh spiced with a variety of flavors: salmon, chives, red paprika, chopped bell peppers, hard-boiled eggs, smoked fish, sardines, salami, green onion, garlic, dill, horse-radish, nuts, cocoa, and fresh or dried fruit. Overwhelmed by the array of choices, I stared and salivated, the same way I do in the 31 flavors ice-cream store back in the States. We finally decided on tvaroh with chunks of red bell peppers. Outside, sitting on a wooden bench, we took turns using our baked rolls to scoop out the creamy treat from a plastic deli container. We observed a community that seemed to have it all: a church with a lookout tower, a huge Renaissance castle, well-maintained parks, museums, art galleries, squares with water fountains, countless historical buildings, specialized shops and even a lake in the middle of the city with a winding mellow river that, like a silver ribbon, tied together the per-fect package.

"This is what life without a mall and Wal-Mart looks like," observed Larry.

At 4 p.m. the church bell rang and the streets emptied. Where did everyone go? Slightly freaked out, Larry and I looked at each other. Was the bell a signal for people to report to some underground shelter? If so, the residents went about it in an admiringly controlled fashion, without the slightest hint of panic. Poof! They just disappeared.

Minutes into our confusion, an outburst of cheers pen-etrated the silence. We followed the noise to a hospoda. The well-lit beer house was jammed. All eyes were set above the door to a flat screen TV. We could have walked in naked, and no one would have noticed, everyone focused on the U.S.–Czech ice-hockey match.

We settled at the last available table at a corner furthest from the TV screen. In one tense moment when a U.S. player took a shot on the Czech goalie, a yelp of encouragement escaped Larry's lips. I pressed my fingernails into his forearm, reminding him that we were outnumbered. "You're gonna get us beat up," I hissed. Soon the Czechs scored their second goal. With a thundering roar, everyone jumped to their feet, hands above their heads. Wouldn't it be polite, perhaps even safe, to fake a little enthusiasm? I wondered, unable to decide whose side I was on.

"To watch the U.S. getting whupped as the walls shake with encouragement is just wrong," Larry said, and we slinked toward the exit. The town was all ours. Outbursts of merriment blasted through the city twice more.

"Uh-oh, that can't be good," Larry said. "I think we lost 4-0." Throughout the city, cheers echoed from the open windows, confirming Larry's fear.

As the sun set, Larry and I ended up in front of our hotel. Unnoticed, from a bench across the now deserted plaza, we watched our waiter accompanied by our hotel receptionist closing the umbrellas in the vacated restaurant where we drank beer earlier. I heard the receptionist boast to the waiter, "I checked in two Americans today." His buddy told him that he also waited on two American customers.

"They are talking about us," I said to Larry, who, to my astonishment, got up and walked toward the two restaurant workers. I watched Larry as he held up four fingers on one hand and formed zero with the other. Then he gave both thumbs up. And then there was laughter and handshakes.

"Give credit where credit is due," Larry said with a grin when he returned.

The next morning, at the Jindřichův Hradec castle's ticket office, Larry and I were startled by the crowd of foreign visitors. We hadn't seen any tourists the previous day. As our group followed the guide, we learned that the castle was the third largest in the country and that it had been owned by Vilém Slavata, one of the three ass-kissing Habsburg bureaucrats who, in 1618, were thrown from a Prague castle window by angry Protestants.

Slavata felt obliged to the Virgin Mary for surviving his air travel and commissioned an artist to immortalize his flight through history. Larry and I studied the floor-to-ceiling painting where large angels were catching two petite men. Slavata was already enjoying the safety of the heavenly net. The painter left out the angry mob and the ignoble hands and feet flying wildly, nor did he show the horror in Slavata's eyes.

In a muffled voice, Larry leaned closer and said, "I don't know about you, but if people hate me enough to toss me out the window, and if I survive, I'd hide in a monk's habit and split."

Depending on the history book, Slavata wasn't always the bad guy. He loved the Czech people. If only the bastards had worshipped the Habsburgs' way, Catholic Europe would be in peace.

Tossing Slavata and his buddies out the window, an act known as the Second Defenestration of Prague, brought almost 400 years of systematic Germanization that nearly suffocated the Czech identity.

In Slavata's castle, visitors were passing by the painting of angels and the flying little men. The scene looked so playful, the divine beings catching men like butterflies. It didn't look like an event that triggered one of the darkest eras in European history.

36. The Spirit of *Slavonice*

From Jindřichův Hradec, we drove out of our way to visit Slavonice. I had always wanted to see that mystical southern

Bohemian town (or Moravian, depending on the pamphlet) located near the Austrian border.

"With only 2,500 people, isn't it a village?" Larry wondered aloud.

The city of Slavonice was established in the 12th century on one of the main roads to Vienna. When the road was relocated north, Slavonice's glory days were over. Not much good happened after that. During The Thirty Years War (1618-1648) the Swedish Army almost wiped out the city's population. A few decades later, in 1680, the Black Plague claimed more lives. A devastating fire swept through the city in 1750 destroying over 40 houses. Just another day in Slavonice. In 1939, the city fell into Hitler's Sudetenland sector and the Germans kicked out the Czechs. After WWII, the Czechs kicked out the Germans.

If the freshly painted buildings in Jindřichův Hradec resembled lacy Easter dresses, the Gothic and Renaissance buildings in Slavonice's main plaza looked like musty ballroom gowns forgotten in an old trunk.

Larry and I strolled the figure-eight plaza, deciphering the intricate etchings on the facades of the ancient walls: Here were Adam and Eve being chased out of the Garden of Eden, and there was a King signing an important document. Our favorite image was a townsman with his prized possession, a monstrous hog.

The absence of cars and pedestrians felt like the Black Death had just swept through the medieval town, orphaning the impressive houses. From one corner of my eye, I spotted movement. A girl with smudged cheeks, perhaps six-years-old, was following us. Whenever we stopped, she stopped. With piercing unfriendly eyes, she watched us from a distance. Each time I looked back, she was there, staring.

"Who is that girl?" I asked.

"What girl? I don't see any girl," said Larry.

A minute later, stiff, claw-like fingers touched my neck. I almost jumped out of my skin.

"What?" Larry asked, baffled.

American historian David McCullough, who says he doesn't believe in ghosts, testified to the spiritual presence of our Founding Fathers on the darkened streets of Philadelphia. "You can feel them," he said. In Slavonice, spirits don't wait for midnight. Those once terrorized by black boils, a blazing fire or the swords of the Swedes, those forced out of their houses or trapped there against their will, those spirits linger in Slavonice even in the hot afternoon sun.

"Let's ditch her," I said, and pulled Larry inside a buffet patronized by working men. The cafeteria-style dishes were listed on the blackboard above the counter: creamy sauerkraut soup, tripe soup, kale hamburger, fried cheese and of course the bramboráček (potato pancake). Nothing cost over five dollars. Larry and I ordered eggs baked inside meatloaf. We collected our plates and sat by the window. Across the street, in a doorway, I caught a glimpse of the strange girl. "There! You saw her?" But Larry was studying the hard-boiled yolk in his meatloaf. A few workers in blue overalls absentmindedly chewed their food, staring into space.

In 1961, the Conservation Act declared the city center a protected historical site, a cruel joke since Slavonice and its surroundings were also declared a border zone, and locals were encouraged to report to the police every new face in town. Any wrong step could lead a tourist to jail, and that was the best-case scenario. The border patrol was instructed to shoot to kill. In Communist times the city became isolated. Still, my newlywed parents had laced up their hiking boots, strapped on their rucksacks, and had gone to check out historical Slavonice. Just as they reached this plaza, the local policeman ordered them to clear out of town.

We finished our meal and stepped back onto the street. The doors where the girl had stood were slightly open.

Larry and I continued to explore the lower loop of the plaza. Inside a shop window, an array of mismatched items fought for the attention of passers-by. A chubby garden troll with green pants and a red peaked hat musingly eyeballed a four-foot statue of Michelangelo's David. A figure of Louis Armstrong was tucked between colorful beach towels. The reflection of the strange girl was also there. The three of us locked eyes. Larry grabbed my hand. Quickly walking away, we passed by two young children squatting on the cobblestone sidewalk, concentrating on ripping the wings off a live bug.

In silent agreement, we made a beeline toward our car.

After four weeks of traveling through the Bohemian region, we finally entered Moravia, the home of my people. Its poetic name — Morava — as we call it, never fails to envelop me in tenderness, just like my grandmother's embrace, so familiar and comforting, a precious gift that once I took for granted.

We were heading north, toward Pardubice to meet our friend Alena. Larry concentrated on the road while I leafed through the map.

In the long alphabetic index, I noticed a pattern created by the repetition of words.

"There are 23 towns name Sedlec," I marveled. "We'll never find Alena if we are to meet her in Sedlec."

I counted 24 towns named Podolí, 17 Ždár, 21 Újezd, and 31 Háje. One has to know the name of the nearest town to find the correct Podolí or Újezd.

My favorite town was named after *vůl*. Vůl is a popular Czech cuss word. On the harshness scale, it measures someplace between dude and shithead.

"There is one town named after the devil and six after angels."

"A small victory over evil," commented Larry.

"Sixty towns named after Peter!" I kept filling Larry in on the Czech town names as he drove past the green fields. I couldn't put the map down. There was Jealousy, Frogcarriers, Mushroomeaters, and two towns with names that had to do with farting. Thirty-two towns were named after wolves. But holding wolves in high regard didn't stop Czechs from hunting them to extinction. They honored the last one shot in Šumava, almost 150 years ago, with a monument.

Long columns of town names began with the adjective "Lower," and even more, I estimated about 400, began with the adjective "Upper." One town couldn't decide and called itself "Lower-Upper."

I was surprised to find four Amerikas. One Amerika was tucked in a restricted military zone. During the Cold War, the Commies must have been beside themselves with triumph.

There were gazillions of New Villages. The first picture that popped up online had a banner: New Village celebrates its 780th Birthday!

Seven villages were named Hospoda, the beer place. Wives don't like hospodas. It's hard to steer the wheelbarrow when hauling their drunken men home.

The most difficult name to pronounce for Larry was Předklášteří, where my sister used to live. On his first visit, Larry copied the name down and tucked the piece of paper in his wallet, "So I could show it to the policeman if you guys ditch me."

We were approaching Telč, the pearl of Moravia. I wanted to see the delight on Larry's face when the stunning beauty of the Telč plaza came into view. His eyes did brighten. He scanned the plaza, and said, "Oh, good, a coffee shop," and, oblivious to architectural wonders, marched toward it.

From the outdoor table at the top of the plaza, we had an unobstructed view of the colorful Renaissance and Baroque houses. "Which would you pick?" I asked.

"The pink gingerbread one," Larry pointed with his chin.

"I'll take the peach one with the cupcake crown," I said. "Better yet, the baby blue one, with the five-layer wedding cake roof." Like kids in a fancy pastry shop, we lusted over the ornate treasures.

When Larry finished his espresso, we strolled along the arcade that circled the perimeter of the large plaza. Passing two local men, I overheard their lament: "If a preservationist finds out you drilled a hole in the wall of your own house, they'll smack you with a fine. No shitting around."

In front of us, groups of teenagers on a school trip compared the knick-knacks they had bought in souvenir shops. Three girls, obliviously blocking the walkway, giggled and tugged on each other's arms. My thoughts raced back to when I was just like them, loud and self-absorbed, with my two best friends by my side. Fatima ended up marrying the boy I had a crush on. In her thirties, she fatally overdosed. Redheaded Olga always wore nerdy glasses. One day she shocked everyone when she showed up in school without them. When did she become such a beauty? Leukemia claimed Olga seven years after our last school trip. Once Fatima, Olga and I, drunk with youth, were just like these giggling girls, who hadn't yet tasted the stale tang of life's hangovers.

I looped my hand around Larry's arm, seeking to balance myself after the sorrowful time travel.

37. Cubism in the Spa Town *Bohdaneč*

We didn't mind driving out of the way to meet our friend Alena. It had been almost ten years since we last saw her. Because visits with our European friends and families are few and far between, Larry and I jumped at the opportunity when we learned Alena was traveling to Pardubice to see a dentist. In the Czech Republic she'd pay a third of what she would have paid in her adoptive home in Belgium, and probably a tenth of what she would have paid in the States.

I had met Alena in California at a dog park. Her baby, Catherina, was strapped to her chest. Alena's two Great Danes circled my dog Peggy; three long tails wagged vigorously. The dogs, baby Catherina, Alena and I became a tight pack right from the start.

Our sweet days in California ended four years later, when Alena returned from a visit to the Czech Republic. She had gone to say goodbye to her grandma, but arrived too late.

"We're moving back to Belgium," Alena dropped the bomb next time we walked together. Stunned, I stared at the ground like Catherina once did when her perfect strawberry ice-cream scoop dropped on the sun-baked sidewalk. "I need to be closer to my family," Alena added softly. "I never want to be late coming home again."

I saw the strawberry ice-cream melting away, leaving behind a long sticky streak.

Alena's husband went ahead. Two weeks later, Alena, Catherina, her new baby sister and the Great Danes were packed in my van, waiting for me to drive them to the airport. I just needed to lock up Peggy, who watched the commotion from the backyard.

"Peggy! Stay!" I ordered. But she squeezed through the gate and darted toward the van. She hopped in, her lean body stretching between the seats. She gave a quick face-lick to Catherina and her baby sister, then further back one kiss for each of her four-legged friends. Alena got her parting slobber last. Only then, did Peggy hop out of the car and run back home.

I wondered how close Alena was now, driving to Pardubice all the way from Belgium. I dialed her cell phone.

"Do you have a place to say?" I yelled over the static.

"No. Do you guys?"

"No."

"I have two dogs in the car with me. We could —," We lost connection. How were we going to find her?

Growing up in Brno, the second largest city after Prague, I had an arrogant notion that other Czech cities were just big villages, too small to get lost in. Pardubice proved me wrong. We did all we could to avoid berserk cars, buses and cable cars. The commotion abruptly ended and we found ourselves driving through dimming woods without phone reception. Twice we ended up on a dead-end road.

"Almost there!" Larry chirped with over-zealous confidence, attempting to revive my sinking spirits. We didn't even know where "there" was. I squinted at the road map. "Looks like we're approaching Bohdaneč, a spa town," I said, trying to sound optimistic. "They must have accommodations."

Spas in the Czech Republic have a strong tradition. My parents said it was the best thing about Communism. Every other year, workers were entitled to four weeks in one of the many fancy spa towns where they were treated to mud baths, massages, water therapies and great meals. Rumor had it that after evening dances, guests seldom returned to their rooms alone.

At the Bohdaneč health pavilion, the young receptionist welcomed us with a question, "What procedures are you going to sign up for? We specialize in the musculoskeletal system." She handed us a shiny brochure where a tan, silver-haired couple flashed their dentured smiles. When the receptionist saw our hesitation, she offered, "You may like to tour the grounds first."

"Impossible to sneak in Alena's dogs," I said to Larry as we walked out.

Back in the car, circling Bohdaneč's mini plaza adorned with water fountains, I saw what we were searching for. "A pension!" I yelped and pointed to a three-story building.

Mr. Škroup, the pension owner, gestured us in through a narrow alleyway leading to a yard where we could park. With no more than six inches on each side — Mr. Škroup yelling in Czech, I in English — Easy...more to the left... to the right ... Stop! Stop!

Larry whispered his mantra — "Almost there."

We followed Mr. Škroup up to the third floor, stepping on planks that covered the gutted floors. He neglected to tell us that his building was undergoing major construction. The three of us maneuvered through scaffolding, ladders, cans of paint, bags of cement and sand, empty buckets and scattered tools, leaving a trail of footprints on the dusty floor. On the third level, Mr. Škroup unlocked the door. With long faces we stared inside a tiny room.

"The terror of backing out of that narrow-ass alley is the only thing that's stopping me from walking away." Larry sighed.

"I'll show you an apartment on the main floor," Mr. Škroup said, "Same price." We retraced our dusty footprints.

Larry and I dumped our bags in the hallway of the spacious three-room apartment, paid Mr. Škroup 540 korunas, less then half of most Motel Six rates, and set out across the plaza. My mobile rang when we stepped into a restaurant.

"I'm in Pardubice, but with the dogs I can't find a room under 2,000 korunas," Alena said. I was ecstatic to invite the three of them to stay with us in the apartment.

"There is so much room! You could bring your horse, too."

Just as Larry and I washed down the first bramboráček with the black Kozel beer, my phone rang again.

"I'm circling the water fountains," Alena announced and I leaped to my feet sprinting out of the restaurant, barely registering Larry's caution, "Now, don't you two get in trouble."

"I see you!" I cried, swinging my arms over my head, directing Alena into the parking lot. In my excitement I was pointing the wrong way. Her car bounced up over the curb and on to the sidewalk.

"I think I just violated about eleven traffic rules!" Alena shouted. Hopping out of the car, her windblown blond hair bounced onto her shoulders. Two handsome albino German shepherds bounded out behind her. We laughed crazily; at that moment, even getting a traffic ticket would have seemed hilarious.

"Are you sure they'll let you in the restaurant with these polar bears?" I said, still hugging my friend.

"We are in Europe, girlie! They love dogs here," Alena said.

Minutes later the restaurant owner, not so courteously, showed us the exit. He didn't even let us finish the beer.

In the apartment, Alena looked over the worn linoleum. "Perfect!" she said, and unleashed her dogs. We couldn't have wished for a better place.

Alena and I flopped on the couch and Larry disappeared into the kitchen. Alena took a fancy box of Belgian chocolates out of her bag. Larry, the magician, returned with a bottle of champagne, three un-matched mugs, and a winning smile.

"We saw your girls on Facebook," he said, putting down the cups. "They look so grown up."

Drinking the champagne, we recalled our favorite memories: Alena cutting my hair while Peggy, in the next room licked baby Catherina, her cheeks wet and pink, her thin hair sticking straight up like shiny needles.

"And remember how Catherina didn't talk, but barked instead?" Alena said, "I was a little concerned. Well, she was just warming up. Now both girls are fluent in five languages. That's not uncommon in Europe. Belgium's official languages are Dutch, French, and German. The girls also speak English and Czech."

I tried to think if I knew any California kid who could speak an additional language. My neighbor once bragged that her six-year-old granddaughter could count to 20 in French.

At about one a.m., I got up to search the kitchen for some snacks. When I returned, Alena was slumped on the couch, gently snoring. No wonder. She had spent eight hours behind the wheel and her dental appointment was the first thing the next morning. Larry and I propped her head with a pillow and covered her with blanket.

I awoke to the sound of the water fountains. The sun shone through the lace curtains. I carefully lifted Larry's hand from my belly and reached for my watch. Jesus Maria! Ten o'clock! Alena and her dogs must have left two hours ago. Was she even here? Our reunion was like a tease granted by skimpy Grandfather Time, to whom, none-the-less, I was grateful. I wondered what dogs Alena would have the next time, and when would the next time be?

I scanned the mismatched décor in our room: the flamingo pink walls, the boxy armoire with chipped corners, the red worn-out carpet, the cheap plastic ceiling lamp. Despite the tackiness, I saw something I hadn't paid attention to the night before. The worn-out furniture couldn't conceal the old elegance of the deep arching doorways graced by half columns, and the round windows divided into geometric sections. These were elements of Cubist architecture, the avant-garde art movement of the early 20th century.

Even as a child, I was aware of the various architectures in my city. I admired the tall rocket-shaped stained glass windows, which represented the Gothic era. I was overwhelmed by the ornate, loud Baroque style, with its chubby angels and gold frescos — too busy, almost frightening. I always wondered how it would be to live in one of those Cubist style buildings where simplicity blended with luxury: the spacious balconies, round glass-brick corners and oversized, strangely shaped windows. Those wonderful extras contrasted with the panelák where I grew up.

Around the time of Czechoslovakia's birth in 1917, before the Communists took over, Picasso and Braque's new Cubist paintings influenced Czech architects. Banks, restaurants and luxury villas featured dramatic angles that suggested three or four dimensions simultaneously, challenging the customary linear perspective found in the functionalist architecture.

When I revealed my fondness for Cubism to Mr. Škroup, he invited Larry and me to his apartment located next to ours. He pointed toward his large unmade bed that stood on a stage between tall columns. "This stage used to hold an orchestra that played jazz for the high society guests of the Bohdaneč spa director. You see, this building was custom designed by the famous Czech architect Josef Gočár." Mr. Škroup studied my face for a spark of recognition. When he found none, he added, "The guy who built the Black Madonna building in Prague."

"Just a few weeks ago we had coffee there. In the upstairs Grand Cafe Orient," I said excitedly, recalling the crazy, complex stairway railings, seats with angled corners, bizarre chandeliers and the artsy coat-hooks.

Mr. Škroup jumped in. "Gočár's building in Prague is owned by the museum. The city has money and Praguers love how that modern gem fits in their old town.

"His building here isn't so lucky. When the Communists came to power, they subdivided the luxury apartments and moved in low-income tenants. After the 1989 revolution, when I bought the building, the tenants raised holy hell when their rents went up. But what could I do? I needed the money for renovation. No one had lifted a hammer here for over 40 years. What a struggle it was to move the renters out. Now, with my son's help, we are patching it the best we can." Mr. Škroup laughed to himself and went on. "Gočár didn't just design futuristic buildings. He took it a step further. He created so-called functional art, modernistic furniture to match the exterior. He said that furniture shouldn't just be tasteful — it should capture the essence of art." Mr. Škroup chuckled again. "Gočár would turn over in his grave if he could see the crap I'm forced to stuff these rooms with. After the revolution, the city of Bohdaneč wanted to declare the building a protected historical site, but that would have obligated them financially, so they backed off. However, it doesn't stop them from dictating what I can and can't do. I am sick and tired of arguing with the city all the time."

Mr. Škroup stepped closer to the wide glass door. Like a boy showing off his collection of autographed baseball cards, he pointed to the sectioned frosted glass. His eyes softened, "You see, they don't make these any more," and he brushed his fingers over the ornate glass.

38. The Gingerbread Town *Pardubice*

Before heading south to reunite with my family, we decided to make a brief stop in the historical center of Pardubice, a city famous for its gingerbread. I never much liked those aromatic cakes glued together with jam that Mom sometimes added to my school lunches. Before Christmas, she baked them at home. The aroma of cinnamon, cardamom, and nutmeg filled our kitchen as the dough needed weeks to ferment. I didn't want to hurt Mom's feelings, so when the gingerbread was ready, I choked it down.

In the tight space of the store dedicated solely to Pardubice's sweet tradition, Larry and I were the only customers. A lively saleslady welcomed the opportunity to educate us. "Gingerbread is older than yeast bread," she said, her eyes jumping from Larry to me as if asking — did you know that? Ain't that something? "The original recipe had just flour, pepper, and the essential gingerbread ingredient — wild bees' honey. In time, more spices were introduced. But because seasonings were still rare and expensive in the 15th century, gingerbread remained a luxury." She carried on, presenting each new nugget of information with the triumph of a winning card player.

"The master gingerbread makers pressed the dough into hand-carved wooden forms. After it was baked, they hand-decorated each piece with sugar icing. Pardubice made itself known to the world by exporting gingerbread in the shape of coats of arms decorated with the city's emblem — a white horse on red background. Other old world designs were saints, churches or noble men and women in fancy dresses."

The shelves behind the saleslady were lined with Smurfs coated in caustic-looking blue icing. In the special-order-book, there were even some X-rated scenes. The churches and saints in pure white were a thing of the past.

"Everyone's favorites are the hearts with love messages," the saleslady suggested. Seeing our indecision, she played her trump card, "Leaving Pardubice without gingerbread would seem like you were never even here."

We settled on a beer stein gingerbread cookie scripted "For Dad" and a heart that said "For Mom." Later my sister would say, "Don't you know they don't like gingerbread? Mom only made it because of you."

In the Perštýnské Náměstí, Pardubice's central plaza, Larry took photos of every building surrounding the gingerbread shop. The architectural details were as intricate as the old-fashioned gingerbread cookies themselves.

In the center of the plaza, a massive sculpture honored the Virgin Mary for sparing the town from the 1695 Black Plague. Lions, angels, and saints guarded the gold-plated Mary at the top.

The *Pizzeria Santa Maria* sign above a restaurant unleashed the devil in both of us.

"So, what would they call their signature dish?" I asked. "Something like Peter and Paul's Double Pepperoni Pizza?"

"Or Genuflecting Garlic," Larry offered as we sauntered, letting the winding side streets decide our path. "One side of the menu could list Madonna's toppings, and the plain pizza, the one with only cheese, could be The Topless Madonna with a choice of thin crust or Jesus crust."

I imagined our souls boiling in jalapeño sauce for eternity, a punishment for this blasphemy.

"For appetizers, they would serve The Angel Gabriel's hot wings, and the pizza for three would be named Father, Son, and Holy Bacon." Larry was on a roll.

"Of course the wine would be sold by the chalice," I said.

"Of course," Larry seconded.

The street had eased into a courtyard of an elegant white castle, the home of four free-range peacocks with imperial crowns and nasty, runny droppings.

The castle was built in the 14th century by Ernest of Pardubice, the archbishop of Prague who served as a diplomat and advisor to Emperor Charles IV, and the same guy whose statue I kept running into while lost in that shadowy monastery hallway the first night in Prague. We were visiting the hometown of an old buddy. Despite Ernest's enticing home, plus the rumor of a top-secret atomic fallout shelter hiding beneath it, both great incentives to stay and investigate. But I became homesick and impatient to see my parents. It was time to go home.

39. At Home in *Dolní Loučky*

I glanced at the digital clock on the dashboard. "Just another hour or so," I said and patted Larry on the arm. His eyes stayed fixed ahead on the narrow gray strip with no dividing line and no shoulder line.

With each passing motorist swishing by, Larry pressed his elbows together to appear narrower and to avoid a collision with a car or one of the plum trees that lined these back roads. Suddenly I heard him mutter between clenched teeth, "I am not gonna give him that satisfaction." The tension in his voice brought me to my highest alert. The car behind nearly touched our bumper. Larry downshifted and jammed the gas pedal to the floor. The pitch of the motor, like a desperate vocalist, soared to its crowning note. I pressed my fingernails into the vinyl door handle. The testosterone-saturated roads which seized these drivers had not spared Larry either.

"I can't believe he is going to squeeze 120 out of that Ford Fiesta," Larry hissed. "I'm not gonna let him!"

"I don't want to die less than an hour from my parents' house," I pleaded and propped my arms against the dashboard. With a huge relief, I felt the car slowing down.

"I have to alter my thinking," Larry said. This time his voice was soft, almost apologetic.

"That would be one sure way to reduce deaths on these god-forsaken roads." I leaned back, thankful that Larry let the death-defying idiot pass us without further challenge.

By the year 2020, the Czech government wants to lower the number of fatal accidents to match the European Union's average. The number needs to shrink by half. From what I've seen, even 3020 seems too ambitious. The national defiance of rules and regulations has made the highway patrol the butt of jokes, second only to blond adulteresses.

"Hey, Larry, do you want to hear a joke?

> *"The highway patrol pulls over a driver and says, 'Because you are driving at the speed limit, we are going to reward you with a cash prize.' The officer hands over an envelope with 10,000 korunas. 'I'm curious,' the officer says, 'what are you going to do with the money?' The driver thought about it for a while, 'I'll probably go to drivers' school and get my license.'*
>
> *'Don't listen to him officer,' his wife jumps in, 'he always jokes when he is drunk.' Then a guy in the back seat wakes up, sees the police uniform and says, 'I told you guys we're not gonna get far in a stolen car.'"*

"I bet it's a true story," Larry said dryly.

I had visited my family only twice since they moved to their new house in Dolní Loučky, a small village in the high country of Western Moravia. Now we passed the place where

Leoš, my brother-in-law, occasionally pulls over, gets out of the car, and in a moment of quiet appreciation scans the gently rolling hills blending into the haze. "Could there be a more beautiful place on this earth?" he whispers. Then he jumps into his car and drives off like a maniac.

I had put away the map and directed Larry through sleepy villages where pedestrians still pause to look after a moving vehicle. Soon we passed the grove of linden trees, then the house where mom sometimes, on very special occasions, orders pastries from Mrs. Novotná. The road descended between the white church my dad attends and the walled cemetery. At the fork we turned left onto the dead-end street where we stopped at the last house before the forest.

Through the apple trees along the short chain-link fence, I caught the first glimpse of my family. Up to their elbows in barbecue, everyone sat around the long, wooden table my dad had built. It was just like in the photographs my parents sometimes sent me: Mom's undulating hair whiter than snow, Dad in his flannel checkered shirt, more fragile than the last time I saw him, my pretty sister in her favorite flowery dress she calls her summer-skin, her muscular and tanned husband Leoš, their two blond long-haired daughters with their tall, handsome brother. They were all there. I used to study those family photographs, feeling sorry for myself for missing out.

Now, only a few steps separated Larry and me from being in that happy picture with them. I would have liked to watch them longer, but Amor's bark announced us.

"They're here!" my niece Laďka shouted when Larry and I got out of the car. The next moment Dad held my face in his hands. He looked blurry through my tears, although I could smell his barbecue fingers just fine. "Leničko!" he laughed, using my pet name. Then came mom's plump embrace scented with thyme.

"Jesus Maria, I made you greasy," my younger niece apologized. She wiped her hands on her jeans and went to embrace

Larry. When we were properly greased and seasoned, we all sat down at the garden table. Mom piled the crispy, reddish brown chicken thighs on Larry's plate and ordered, "Eat, Lerry!" Leoš passed around bottles of Starobrno, the local beer, and Hana refilled the glasses almost to the rim with red wine. Leoš cheered, "Na zdraví!"

"Na zdraví!" everyone yelled. The glasses clinked. Mom and Dad's eyes shone with happiness. I took a bite of the crunchy pickle my dad had cured with his delicious, spicy, sweet-and-sour brine. Each harvest he asks me, "Guess how many jars we canned this year?" My estimate is never high enough. I reached for a piece of rye bread seasoned with caraway seeds, a simple pleasure that no Czech emigrant ever stops dreaming of. Mom passed the jar with tiny white pickled onions. "From the garden," Dad said, and loaded a bunch on my plate.

A white box filled with pastries from Mrs. Novotná sat at the end of the table. It was like a dream. All that I missed now was a fork, knife, and a napkin. I knew better than to ask. They would laugh at two prissy Americans who needed utensils.

Late in the evening, after everyone retreated to their bedrooms, a soft knock got me out of bed. Dad, in pajamas, gestured for me to follow.

He quietly shut the kitchen door behind us and turned on the small light, motioning for me to sit next to him, handing me a book-sized mahogany box. On its lid, the gold metal plaque read: *Naší Leničce.* (To our Lenka). I had never seen my name engraved. In our family, gifts rarely exceeded the value of a chocolate bar or a mediocre bottle of wine. This was extraordinary.

"Oh, Dad..." I blinked, trying to read the rest of the engraving through the tears: *"Czech Saints Through the Work of Artists."* The box contained 12 large silver coins: Saint Ludmila, Saint Vít, Saint Václav, Anežka, Cyril... the whole gang was there. Stunned and guilty, I sat there with 12 Saints in my lap — months of Dad's savings.

Smiling, he whispered, "Don't tell Mom."

40. The Canyon *Trenkova Rokle*

Larry climbed over me to get out of bed. Outside it was still dark. "I need to pee," he whispered.

The thought of the cold hallway tiles made me snuggle deeper between the sheets, back to my dream.

When Larry crawled back into bed, it was already daylight.

"Where were you so long?"

"Your parents made me breakfast. Then they sat across the table, watching me eat it alone."

What a vision! Mom loading sausages and sliced tomatoes onto Larry's plate, ordering, "Eat, Lerrry!" as my polite husband shivered in his boxers and undershirt. I stifled my giggles into the pillow. Larry stared at the ceiling, the back of his hand resting on his forehead.

Later that morning, Mom suggested that my 25 year-old nephew Luboš could take Larry and me hiking in nearby Trenck's Canyon (Trenkova Rokle). We welcomed the opportunity to reconnect with Luboš who was being too shy to test his eight years of classroom English on us.

When Mom handed me brown paper bags with lunches, she pressed some money into my hand. Before I could object, she hissed, "Don't tell Dad." And since he stood within earshot, I, the compliant, accepted the money Mom had pinched away.

Under a cloudless sky, Luboš, Larry and I waved to my parents, who leaned out the window, each sending their conspiratorial winks.

From the back seat, Luboš said, "To je dnes krásně!"

"What did he say?" Larry asked.

"He said that we have a nice day today."

"To se nám to vydařilo!" Luboš said a minute later.

"What did he say?"

"He said that we have a really nice day today."

It's going to be a long one, I thought, but then Larry's eyes met Luboš' in the rearview mirror, "So, today, we'll do English, okay?"

Timidly, Luboš nodded, "Ve'll do."

Following Luboš' instructions, Larry parked the car beside a tourist information sign. We learned that the first written records about the surrounding villages dated back to the 12th century, and that the local hospoda was built in Baroque architecture. Interesting, but our attention was on a car sharing the same dirt parking lot. The two-door sedan without wheels sat on four logs.

"I guess someone needed new tires," Luboš said in English. Larry and I exchanged concerned looks, too worried about leaving our Škoda to rejoice over Luboš' accented, but comprehensible English.

From the parking lot we marched in single file amid curtains of conifer branches draping down on both sides. The muddy trail led to a vast, grassy meadow.

"The canyon vas named after Baron Trenck," Luboš said. "He vas a high ranking official in the Austrian Imperial Army. He hid here after being sentenced to death."

We stopped to unlace our boots before crossing the wide, but shallow river Loučka. At the sound of swishing wings we looked up. A white stork with long red legs glided low, casting a shadow over the silver water. As a child, I knew these "baby-messengers" only from my picture books, wondering if they were just mythical creatures like dragons and unicorns. In recent years, due to a conservation programs, the storks have made a comeback, their huge nests emerging on village chimneys again.

The trail on the far side of the river curved into the woods. Luboš gestured for us to follow him a short distance off the path to a spring. A handsome brown frog who sat by a red enamel mug took one impressive leap and disappeared into the ferns. Following Luboš' example, I filled up the cup and drank, feeling the icy sensation descending in my chest. We left the cup for the next thirsty hiker.

The mossy earth cushioned our steps as we continued through the woods. It was comfortable and pretty, and just when I thought I could hike on forever, the trail opened up. In the center of the forest clearing, stones the sizes of overgrown watermelons encircled a fire ring.

"Tramp settlement," Luboš said.

"Homeless people?" Larry asked.

Luboš and I traded looks, wondering how to explain. Tramps were not backpackers, hippies, drifters, or the homeless, but a distinctive subculture with nearly a century-long tradition, unique to Czech and Slovak peoples.

"It began with Scouting, just before WWI," Luboš said as our hike advanced to an ambitious rock climb along a trickling waterfall. "Some Scouts vere discouraged by rules and broke from the organization." Luboš paused for us to catch our breath. "But they loved nature and freedom, so they kept returning to the voods."

"I can see that," Larry, the enthusiastic outdoorsman concurred. Plastered to the vertical wall, his fingertips were white from gripping the crevices of the slippery rocks. Stretching his legs, he aimed for a boulder. Luboš and I stiffened, holding our breath. When Larry safely landed, Luboš continued. "It vas Jack London's stories from Vild Vest that inspired first tramps. They slept under stars. Just like that. Vithout tents, sleeping bags or raingear."

"Like hobos in the States," Larry stated.

"Not really," I said. "Tramps hold regular jobs. Only on weekends, they became characters from their favorite westerns, living by their unwritten rules."

"So tramps spend weekends sleeping in the woods, and on Monday morning they pull out a few ticks, clip on their ties and go to work," Larry concluded correctly.

"Their nicknames vere Americanized, too." Luboš thought for a second, "Like Gray Volf, Tornado, Billy-Boy — "

"No Larry?" my smart aleck husband suggested.

"Often tramps didn't even know their friends' real names. Their camps vere christened with Vestern names too, like Arizona or Last Chance. In the voods they got avay from conventional vorld."

"And the Communist bullshit," I added.

At the top of the falls, we rested on a sun-warmed log. I stretched my feet and with my bandana wiped sweat off my forehead.

"They renamed rivers to Big River, Old River, Snake River... They even vore certain clothes," Luboš chuckled, "like mismatched army uniforms. Some made old dress hats into cowboy hats. Most of them had cowhide rucksacks, and heavy hiking boots called "Canadas." Grandpa said the handy ones hammered out metal sheriff badges, and sewed leather knife pouches for bone-handled knives."

"No other movement attracted as many people as the free-spirited tramps did," I said, taking a sip from my water bottle.

"Vere you a tramp, Aunty?" Luboš asked with a teasing smile.

Bill Bryson's sentence from his book *A Walk in the Woods* came to mind — *Yeah, I've shit in the woods*. Instead, I said slowly, stretching my back, "In my day, whatever even remotely resembled the West was a threat to the government. Even scouting was illegal. But somehow — miraculously — train stations were always full of tramps on Friday afternoons. Sometimes the police harassed them and checked their documents until they missed their trains. The only organizations allowed then were the Socialist Youth Groups."

"So you vere afraid?" Luboš pressed.

"Well, my best friend and I vere lucky. Our favorite teacher introduced us to an unusual old man, nicknamed Dwarf. I didn't know his real name. Dwarf organized a group of 20 or so campers. My friend and I were the youngest ones."

"Your parents were okay with that?" Larry asked.

"Are you kidding? Dad even let me use his army canteen. My parents didn't hover over us; the only rule was to be home before dark. On weekends, I strapped on my rucksack and went to meet my group at the train station. I loved the sound of guitars and singing from every corner of the crowded train. There were two or three guitars in our group alone. It was so much fun; we never ran out of songs."

Luboš and Larry gave me that sympathetic, grandmother-tell-us-more look, and I complied, remembering how Dwarf taught us to start a fire by rubbing dry sticks, communicate by Morse Code and cook over the fire pit. He frowned on canned food; I loved his nettle goulash with wild artichokes. Dwarf taught us the names of trees, birds, and flowers. He showed us how to break down camp, so the only evidence of us having been there was the hum of our songs lingering in the crowns of the trees, and the promise given to the prayer rock by ecstatic kids who honored the sacred fire, friendship, and every bird, flower, and cloud.

"That explains it!" Larry exclaimed as if he had just cracked open a life mystery. "Now I understand why you prefer a sleeping bag in the woods to a king-size bed in the hotel."

"Some young people who dressed like tramps gave the movement a bad name," I continued. "Villagers sometimes missed a chicken or two after a group of tramps passed by their yards. On one of my summer vacations in Šumava, my uncle Kuba showed me an uprooted row of potato plants in his garden. Some so-called tramps had planned to help themselves to a dinner. 'How stupid they are,' my uncle vented, 'they don't even know that the potato plants produce in the fall after they finish blossoming.'"

Larry sat with his arms folded over his knees, studying a shiny green beetle tapping its antenna on a crease of his denim shirt. "Is tramping still popular with your friends?" he asked Luboš. "Did you do it?"

"It's not nearly as popular as during Communism vhen no one could leave the country, and the bit of freedom one got vas in voods. It still lives on, but not so much as Auntie remembers. Today's young generation of tramps has subgroups of festival tramps."

I recalled the video on Luboš' Facebook page where a bunch of his friends partied under purple laser lights synchronized with the sound of soaring decibels from large speakers. What a contrast to Dwarf's collection of pressed leaves and flowers with neatly written names underneath. A wave of nostalgia overtook me, and for a second I almost thought that I could smell the wood smoke of smoldering campfires from long ago.

"Should we?" Larry asked, slowly getting up. Our trio trekked on. We were rewarded by a bird's eye view of a boundless green vista unscarred by human hands. An enchanting tiny wooden cabin, hanging slightly over the rocky cliff, overlooked the fertile wilderness. I imagined volumes of beautiful poetry flowing from the pen of its inspired occupant. I took a deep breath, filling my lungs with the aroma of the pine-scented air, longing to spend the rest of my days gazing out of its window. I would call my cabin the Innisfree, after the William Butler Yeats' poem. Bits of the verses mingled in my head:

> I will arise and go now, and go to Innisfree
> And a small cabin build there.
> I shall have some peace there,
> For peace comes dropping slow,
> There midnight's all a glimmer,

And noon a purple glow,
I will arise and go now...

As Yeats would have done, while standing on "the road-way," or on "the pavement gray," I too would hold my Innis-free deep in my heart's core.

Or at least put its picture on my computer screen.

The shutters were closed, so we invited ourselves onto the miniature veranda and sat on a patched, scrub-wood bench. I wondered if our weight would tip the cabin and send us tumbling hundreds of feet to the valley below. As our feet dangled at the tips of the tallest conifers, we unpacked the lunch my mom had prepared — rye bread with wonderfully greasy schnitzels. Luboš reached in his backpack and sur-prised us with bottles of local beer named after the famous outlaw. "To Mom's schnitzels and Baron Trenck!" we cheered.

"Let's not romanticize him too much," I said. "He was sentenced to death for brutality in the age of witch-burn-ing." Larry and I stared ahead, our thoughts mingling with long stretches of happy stupor until Luboš, who had contin-ued exploring, yelled for us to come see what he had stum-bled upon. We found him inside a log cabin built into a rock. A bull's skull with mean-looking horns hung over the hinge-less doorframe. Inside the cabin were two wooden cots, a cast iron frying pan, a kettle, and a sealed jar of salt, evidence that tramps still roamed the woods.

Back in my parents' house, the hallway smelled of the nuttiness of sautéed flour.

"Ahh, Grandma's potato pancakes." Luboš' eyes sparkled. Our ravenous trio stormed into the kitchen where Mom's flour-covered fingers nimbly flipped the potato pancakes onto the hot cast-iron griddle. The simple recipe of boiled and grated potatoes, mixed with flour, had sustained Mom through the lean years of her childhood. But for us kids, it symbolized the romantic old world.

Dad sat at the kitchen table while my sister assisted Mom, but even two of them couldn't make the potato pancakes fast enough. Mouths full, the conversation stirred around Dwarf.

"How did he get away with organizing the campers in the midst of Communism?" Larry asked.

Mom and Dad took turns interrupting each other, but at the end, they gave us a good picture of what the history books refer to as the Prague Spring — the short-lived window of political freedom in the midst of the Communist regime. The sudden lack of restrictions, during the spring of 1968 brought unprecedented opportunity, and that's what Dwarf, the scout at heart, took advantage of.

"In the 50s, America and *Rusáci* aimed nuclear rockets at each other," my dad said in his unhurried way. Dad always referred to Russians as Rusáci, the synonym for cockroaches. Then he took a deep breath and wiped his glasses with his handkerchief.

"The later years were more laid back." From the stove, Mom took over what she feared would be Dad's long-winded explanation. "The world finally realized all those nuclear weapons could blow up the planet and the pressure between Russia and America eased up. In spring 1968, the new, more liberal Communist leader, Alexandr Dubček, made changes. The borders weren't so closely watched, and the — Radio Free Europe — was suddenly almost without static."

Dad corrected, "It was Voice of America we listened to."

"Everything changed in the spring of 68," Mom went on as if Dad hadn't spoken. "The boys grew long hair and girls started wearing skirts up to here," Mom jabbed her floury fingers above the edge of her apron. "We were in love with the Beatles, even though none of us knew what "lovemedo" meant. That's when Dwarf organized the campers. I liked that man," Mom said as Hana placed a plate with more hot pancakes on the table. I reached for one with golden, delicious blisters around its edge and with my mouth full said,

"The only thing I remember from Prague Spring were the pictures of naked ladies on the front pages of the magazines." I caught Luboš' raised eyebrows.

"Nudity in the media had been strictly forbidden before," Dad said.

"Unheard of," Mom nodded, stopping in the middle of the kitchen, a mischievous smile in her eyes. "During Prague Spring, Dad and I and some other textile factory workers were rewarded with a striptease show at a nightclub. Dad put on his suit; I wore my best dress, and, with our bosses and co-workers, we watched young girls undressing."

My jaw dropped.

"Only their tops," Dad murmured, setting off a round of laughter. Ready to change the subject, he said, "Of course Rusáci didn't like the liberal changes, and at night on August 21st, 1968, their tanks crossed our borders."

Mom passed the next round of steaming potato pancakes, replacing the empty plate in the middle of the table. Dad looked at me and gestured toward Larry, "Tell him." Then Dad wanted to know what Americans thought about the 1968 occupation.

Larry admitted that learning about the occupation was the first time he remembered hearing of Czechoslovakia. He had to open up an atlas to see where that country with the strange name had been hiding.

"The truth was," Larry said, "we had plenty of our own problems. In 1968, Robert Kennedy and Martin Luther King Jr. were both assassinated. But more relevant for me, that year I got two draft notices, one to fight in Vietnam, the other to marry my pregnant girlfriend. Lucky for me, the second notice canceled out the first." Larry didn't need to explain that the politics of some faraway place with an unpronounceable name was the least of his worries.

"I'll always remember that August morning," my sister said, holding up a spoon full of shiny *povidla*, the thick, black plum jam she liked to smear the pancakes with. "I woke up to pounding on the door and hysterical shouting. 'We are being occupied! Russians are everywhere!'" Hana mimicked our neighbor Mrs. Šrámková's high-pitched voice shouting through the panelák. "I can still see the horror on Dad's face, too. I was so scared; I thought we were at war. Dad ran to turn on the TV where the reporter, unshaven and exhausted-looking, kept repeating, *Staying calm and clear-headed is our only weapon.* So what did Dad do? He stood on the balcony and shook his fist toward the convoy of Russian tanks. Remember?" Hana nodded toward our dad. "Mom tried to pull you back in. You just grabbed the camera and ran out the door."

Dad shook his head. "They pulled out my film. I was lucky to get my camera back." With a tired smile, as if repeating some expired anecdote, he added, "They were just kids. Boys in uniforms driving tanks. Some of them thought they were on a military exercise someplace in Russia. I almost felt sorry for them."

"The last Russian soldier didn't leave until the 1989 Revolution," Mom said from the stove.

"That summer of 68," Dad continued, "440,000 people didn't come home from their vacations abroad when they found out that — our country — had become a barbed-wire cage again. After that miserable August, life returned to how it was before the Prague Spring."

"What are you saying?" Mom snapped in that spirited way old married couples sometimes save for each other. "Nothing was the same! Communists became stronger than ever! They didn't need to be as brutal as they were in the 50s, broadcasting orchestrated trials and hanging innocent people. After the occupation, we were crawling on our knees. We lost all hope." Mom wiped her hands on her apron and pulled a chair to the table. "Dwarf tried to keep the campers together under the Socialist Youth Association, but the Communists didn't trust him and forbade him working with the youngsters. I ran into him few times after that, but he just walked past me, head low, staring at the ground."

None of us could agree on exactly how long Dwarf ran the group but, no matter. By camping with him, he taught me how to find peace in nature, a precious gift that keeps on giving.

For a while, in silence, we just sat there. My belly stuffed with potato pancakes, my head stuffed with thoughts about that unique man. At last, I got up to do the dishes. Too bad Larry couldn't tell my dad that when the Soviets invaded, Americans had been up in arms protesting the occupation of our beloved homeland. How Dad would like to believe that the world cared. Be it in America or Czechoslovakia, political decisions end up right at our kitchen tables, I thought, as I watched the hot water slowly fill the sink.

41. At the Apartment in *Brno*

The next morning Larry and I climbed the steep hill from my parent's house to the train station. Six times a day, passenger trains stop at Dolni Loučky, heading for Brno. Soon the hum on the metal track forecast the train's arrival and, a minute later, with a thundering roar, the massive machine screeched to a halt in front of us.

Larry and I were traveling to the city that had witnessed my school days, my first cigarette and my first clumsy love. My Brno. I wanted to show Larry the panelák where I grew up.

About 40 minutes later we arrived at Brno's chaotic main train station. In the street, we faced the crazy pandemonium of colorful cable cars swallowing and spitting Brno's residents. The city has an excellent transportation system. Buses, trolleys, and cable cars run throughout the day. For a small fee one can travel through the city and beyond. I used to know those cable car routes like the hallways in my panelák.

In the refugee camp, during the first months of my emigration and aching with homesickness, I often played a virtual tour game. With eyes closed, I tried to find my way around Brno. I was quite good at that. Years later, in California, the familiar streets gradually began to blend in a haze. No matter how much I focused, the streets stubbornly dead-ended. Today, I felt ecstatic and once again confident about my way around Brno, as if I had never left.

Larry and I passed the four-story main post office adjacent to the train station. "I have to show you something cool," I said and grabbed Larry's hand. "As kids, my sister and I always begged Mom to take us here. Linda also brought her American husband to Brno's post office."

But the surprise was on me. Yellow construction tape blocked off the gutted elevator shaft. Due to reconstruction, the historical elevator was out of service.

"What are we looking at?" Larry asked.

"Paternoster," I said, unable to hide my disappointment.

"Pater – what?"

"Sort of an elevator. Think of the beads of the rosary: how one side goes up and the other down. Now, imagine that the beads are two-person cabins that keep on going up and down without stopping. And, here is the best part — the cabins have no doors. People have to leap in and out."

I recalled how this historical invention fascinated my 12-year-old friend Věra and me. With nervous giggles, we entertained ourselves by jumping on and off. Eventually, we began to wonder what would happen if we didn't hop out on the last floor. One day we dared to find out. As the last person at the top floor dove out, Věra and I stayed, missing the last chance to squeeze out through the narrowing opening. There was no turning back. Would some greasy mechanism shred us to pieces? Would the cabin flip upside down? Terrified, we anticipated our dismemberment. I whispered, "In Latin, paternoster means to pray."

"A sure sign we're gonna die," Věra whispered back, clinging to my arm. We held our breath as the dimming, screeching cabin shifted on a huge metal wheel and without skipping a beat, began its slow descent. Věra let go of my arm, and we both breathed a sigh of relief. I imagine many of Brno's kids tested their bravery on that mechanical wonder.

One post office worker told us that after about 70 years of service the paternoster became a fire hazard because of its oil-soaked rope. "Once the restoration is complete, the paternoster will be just like the old one," he said. "Historians make sure that every sign and every railing will be exactly like the original one. And the European Union, with all their safety laws, can't do diddly squat since, technically, our paternoster is not an elevator, but a historical machine protected by different sets of rules."

Across the street from the post office, cable car number four was ready to take off. My cable car. A thousand times before, in snow, rain, or in the hot summer, I had anticipated its arrival. Other times, just like Larry and I did now, I zigzagged through traffic and jumped aboard as its doors closed. With one hand, I held onto the overhead railing, and with the other, I clung to Larry. The car jerked abruptly, and we nearly lost our balance. "We may need to strap ourselves to the pole with my belt," Larry said, pulling me closer.

As we were without tickets, always a daring badge of honor for my friends and me, I was on the lookout for the controller disguised in plain clothing. My plan was to look him in the eye and chirp in broken Czech, sorry, no speak Czech. But, he might take out his walky-talky, and — my knees trembling and heart racing — I would hand over all our valuables, including our wedding rings. I was relieved when our stop came, and we exited the car. Riding without tickets had lost its appeal.

Walking down the street leading to my panelák, we passed the row of 19th century pre-Communist apartments where my friend Věra once lived. She didn't want our friends to know that she had come from one of those sad buildings of unidentifiable color. Now, it was restored, and looking like a polished emerald. The sleek, modern features offset its antiquity. I stared with my mouth ajar.

The sides of the solid cherry wood frames of Palladian windows were adorned with the oversize vases carved in relief. The decoration contrasted beautifully with the iron balconies that protruded like contemporary brooches on a custom tailored coat from Saks Fifth Avenue. When I used to visit Věra, it never occurred to me to look up at her building. I always felt sorry for her having to live there.

The transformation was stunning. I felt like I was in some time-travel science fiction movie. To ground myself I searched the faces of passersby, hoping to recognize someone.

We were now almost at the intersection leading to my panelák.

"My street isn't a typical street," I told Larry who still didn't fully forgive me for making him ride the cable car without a ticket.

"It's a hidden island of greenery right in the middle of the city. It has only five street numbers. From our windows, we could see a hillside covered with trees and flowering bushes, a park with a playground, benches and even a soccer field. In the winter, my dad and his friends hosed the field down, and overnight all the neighboring kids had an ice-skating rink."

The next turn revealed my childhood haven. Ahead of us, across from where boys forever kicked a soccer ball and where each summer I scraped my knees, rows of apartment windows stared back at us. "It may seem strange to have fuzzy feelings toward a gray mass of concrete, but the people behind those windows created my world. All 54 families. In the 19 years that I lived here, only one family moved out. I knew everyone's name, and they knew mine. I knew which kid won the spitting contest and which kid jumped all 12 steps between floors. I knew the kid who stuck a match into Mr. Habrman's door-bell so that it continuously rang."

We knew intimate things about each other, like Mrs. Voráčová who lived below us. She took her weekly bath on Saturday evening, letting the hot water run until there wasn't enough for us. Mrs. Voráčová did her laundry on the first Thursday of the month, reserving the laundry room on the schedule list by the entry door. We knew she wore flowery underwear. She hung them on a clothes line in the drying room. On Sundays, she fried schnitzels. The pounding of pork echoed through the panelák. We salivated over the delicious smell of fried bread crumbs.

Because we lived like sardines on top of each other, people protected what was left of their private lives by being reserved, almost cold. It was barely ideal living, but there were 20-year-long waiting lists.

The bench in front of the long apartment block had a missing back. The metal bar to which the wooden beam used to be attached stuck out like a middle finger. We sat on the backless bench. The courtyard didn't look as desirable as I had described it to Larry earlier. Some of the concrete square tiles on the sidewalk were cracked or missing altogether. The soccer field and even the apartment block looked smaller, but the white birch tree with heart-shaped leaves reached all the way to the sixth floor in front of the bedroom I once shared with my sister. It was a sapling when my dad had planted it.

I got up to check the names on the doorbells by entrance number three. My entrance. From the rows of last names, I recognized only two. On a doorbell that held my parent's name for 38 years, the name now read Mr. Hron.

"Maybe they will let us in," I said.

"You don't even know them. Come on, let's leave." Larry took a few uncertain steps back. I pushed the doorbell. On the intercom a woman's voice said "Yes?" and I clumsily explained who I was. "Just a second. I'll come down," she replied.

Through the glass door, we saw the elevator set in motion.

"We're gonna look like con artists. You said it was just you, and suddenly you have an accomplice. How would she know that my backpack isn't for the stuff we are planning to steal?"

An elderly lady unlocked the door. I said, "This is my husband," and gestured toward Larry whose weak smile revealed uneasiness. I was taken aback when she agreed to let both of us in.

"We appreciate your trust," I stuttered.

"I know good people when I see them," she said simply.

The old elevator had barely enough room for the three of us. In my nervousness, I felt like I needed to demonstrate my familiarity with the building, so I kept blabbing about the bomb shelter in the basement, the potato storages and the laundry room where mom used to rinse clothes in a deep stone basin with a wooden oar.

"People have washing machines now," the woman said.

At the sixth floor, she unlocked the door and, with an apologetic smile, asked us to take off our shoes. My brain searched for the familiar smell of a machine shop. During Communism, services were very poor to non-existent. Dad was forever performing favors: fixing our neighbors' televisions, vacuum cleaners or blenders. Once he created a blowdryer that was also used as a mixer. His tools and the disassembled small motors crowded our kitchen table. This apartment had no smell.

The lady gestured for us to enter the sun-warmed living room. A crystal vase on a crocheted doily had been placed in the middle of the cherrywood table. Not a speck of dust was visible on its shiny reddish surface. The walls were covered with original paintings of bucolic scenes in ornate frames. We also had walls covered in original oil paintings — all done by Mom. Dad salvaged the frame-wood from old parquet flooring. In our kitchen, he cut, sanded and lacquered the home-made frames.

Our three-room apartment felt more like an art studio or a wood shop. This apartment was an art collector's gallery.

A white-haired man appeared in the doorway. His long, light blue housecoat matched his eyes. He said that in the year 2000, he bought the apartment from my parents when he had returned from Canada where he had lived most of his life. "I'm 97 years old. I came home to die. But so far I'm not successful." His English was flawless. For once, Larry did not need a translator.

The couple gave us a tour around the apartment. The newly installed wall closets gave the rooms new, narrow shapes. Kitchen cabinets, a stove, and built-in table were all customized for the small space. How did we, our four-person family, ever fit in here?

Everything felt foreign. Even the thresholds were new. Suddenly I wasn't sure why we were getting the house tour by these two strangers. I could barely hide my impatience. I wasn't interested in their customized kitchen, or their art collection. I just wanted to find a single door knob that I could recognize.

The woman and the man looked genuinely disappointed when we declined their coffee invitation.

42. Museum Night in *Brno*

We strolled around Brno's busy main square. Light rain drummed softly on our yellow umbrella. The warm glow spilled over Larry's face. We still had a few minutes before meeting with my school friend Pepa.

After I had left Communist Czechoslovakia, Pepa supplied me with Czech books and music. First, he sent fairy-tales for my children, then the hard-to-find authors like Milan Kundera and Bohumil Hrabal. Once, he even sent me a poetry book autographed by Brno's famous poet, Oldřich

Mikulášek. Pepa wouldn't hesitate to spend his last koruna in a second-hand bookstore.

Something was happening now at the city square. The sound of trumpets and drums announced solders in light blue uniforms raising and lowering their shiny bayonets. It was the same band Larry and I had craned our necks to see four weeks earlier in front of Prague Castle where we were suffocating in the mass of tourists. Today, we got the prime view.

Soon the plaza was packed with spectators and the red cable cars had little room to pass through the crowd. No one was in a hurry to move out of the way even though the cable cars brushed against peoples' jackets. Larry found it unnerving. In the States, such an event would be roped off and there would be plenty of police officers on hand. Unlike Americans, for better or worse, Czechs have little need to legislate every civic function.

"Hurry up! You're missing the band!" Pepa yelled into my mobile at the exact moment I spotted him in the crowd. When we worked our way closer to each other, I noticed white streaks peeking through his once charcoal-colored curls. Without preamble, his voice cracking in excitement, he announced, "Tonight Brno celebrates the night of open museums. We'll get to see places that are normally closed to the public."

What good luck to be in Brno with Pepa, the expert historian, on a night like this. With his Beloved, the nickname for his metal detector, Pepa treasure-hunts around Brno, where both famous and forgotten battles have been fought. Two shoeboxes under his bed are filled with buttons from French uniforms dating to the Napoleonic Wars, as well as thin Roman coins, ornate bronze bracelets, and half-corroded buckles. He even has some thick gold coins and an ancient gold ring.

The three of us mingled among the scores of people strolling the streets. "How's your Beloved? Are you still in love?" I asked.

"I went today but didn't find much, some recently expired coins, one 18th century button and a small bronze knife from about 1500 BC."

Larry's eyes nearly popped out of his head when I translated. Pepa shrugged with a grin.

The celebratory mood on the streets reminded me of a progressive dinner party on a gigantic scale — locals sauntered from one historical building to another, with wonderful treats in store at each venue. Public transportation was free until midnight. Since Brno hosts 14 institutes of higher education, including Janáček's Academy of Music, the world famous Masaryk's University, and the Technical University established in 1849, the city was full of young people.

On the sidewalk, in front of us, a couple quarreled about where to go next. The girl rooted either for a puppet theater or the Historical Toy Museum. Her boyfriend wanted to see the submarine in the Technical Museum. I leafed through a booklet Pepa handed me and scanned the program of the various open houses: Arabic coffee roasting in hot sand, wine-tasting in a monastery, the evolution of furniture making, fashion show, laser show, wood carving, modeling of uniforms from different eras... So many great choices, and free on top of it.

I read out loud: *"Castle Špilberk presents Old World Fair with horseback riding, fencing, and fire dancers."*

On the next page were two pictures of Brno's largest theaters, one modern, built with glass and white granite, the other ornate with columns and angels holding gold trumpets up high. I had never set foot in either of them. Their splendor had intimidated me. I imagined the usher would identify the philistine hiding beneath my homemade dress and would send me on my way.

I read on: *"Accompanied by spine-chilling sound effects, visitors can explore the dressing rooms, perform with the actors, and in a one-of-a-kind project, the audience will watch the show while lying down."*

I wanted to see it all! Where to start? "Even the Red Church is open!"

Pepa pivoted into a side street: "Good choice. We're almost there, anyway."

Brno's residents refer to the brick church simply as the Red Church. During Communism, I had walked by it daily. Its massive front doors were always locked, and its dusty Gothic windows were like the lifeless eyes of a petrified beast. The bells in its tower remained mute. Now, bright light and the sound of a heavenly chorus accompanied by the pipe organ came from the open door. The scene looked surreal.

"The Germans were the ones who shoved Catholicism down our throats, persecuting the non-Catholics, yet they built this Lutheran church, the first Protestant cathedral in Central Europe," Pepa said as we walked up the front steps.

I knew that Protestants don't believe in decoration, but still, the contrast between the elaborate Catholic churches and the bare, whitewashed interior walls of the Red Church was striking.

Pepa, reading my mind, said, "It's not like Protestants don't like art, they just don't want to be distracted by it."

We joined the slow-moving queue. On display was a national treasure: the first Czech Bible translated directly from Hebrew, Greek, and the language Jesus spoke, Aramaic.

"The Protestant brethren were determined to finish the translation," Pepa said. "They hid their wooden printing press, moving it from place to place."

The large, 400-year-old Bible was displayed open-face in a glass box. The colorful typography reminded me of my son's elaborate, impressive, and completely illegible tattoos. The bold-lettered words quoting Jan Hus on the sign placed above the box were much easier to read.

"Seek the truth, hear the truth, learn the truth, love the truth, speak the truth, hold the truth, and defend the truth until death, because the truth will set you free."

No wonder the church was locked up during Communism.

"We could check out the christening chapel," Pepa suggested, but I was restless. There was so much more to see.

Outside, it was already dark. The street lamps spilled yellow light over the sidewalks. Droplets of mist shimmered in the air like gold dust, an enchanting side effect to this magical night.

"Since the Red Church was always closed, it became only a point of reference. You know, a place where you switch cable cars," I said. "I don't even know its real name."

"Czech Brethren's Evangelical Cathedral of Jan Ámos Komenský," Pepa said, adding with a raised brow, "Did you know Komenský was Moravian, like us?"

"I know that he made the first illustrated textbook," I defended myself. "And that he spoke against physical punishment in classrooms. Who wouldn't love him for that? Do you remember how our teacher nearly scalped that kid? What was his name?"

Pepa laughed. "Some teachers were slow to catch on to Komenský's philosophy. Three-hundred years before school attendance was mandatory, he wrote about the necessity of education for all, girls and the poor included. His books on educational reforms were translated into dozens of languages! That was during The Thirty Years War. Galileo Galilei, Shakespeare, and Rubens probably read his stuff."

Pepa, the self-taught archeologist/historian, chattered on about his favorite topic, gradually working himself into derangement.

"Komenský was the father of modern education. His nickname is the Teacher of the Nations." Pepa waved an invisible baton, reciting the big man's words:

The road to peace follows the footsteps of truth, and the road to truth follows the footsteps of knowledge. Not loving books means not loving wisdom. And not loving wisdom is to be a fool.

"The Catholic Habsburgs had a problem with Komenský's free spirit. They kicked him out of the country and burned down his library. Years later, in Polish exile, his books went up in flames once more, including the Czech dictionary he had been working on throughout his life."

Pepa began to stammer, his brain moving ahead of his words. "When I was a teenager my mother gave me a crash course in sex-ed, quoting Komenský: *'It's better to give your willy a good shake than to sleep with a strumpet.'*"

The three of us aimed toward the nearby Moravian Gallery, the second largest art gallery in the Czech Republic. Inside, the atmosphere vibrated with the exhilarating beat of hand drums. I associate drumming with sunsets at the Santa Barbara coast or the Berkeley flea market where dreadlocked musicians jam in a circle. I didn't expect to hear it under the high, gold-plated ceiling. The energy created by a dozen Slavic-featured men sent goose bumps down my spine.

The applied-art museum exhibition created a timeline of art movements from the Renaissance, Gothic, and Baroque era to modern Realism, Pop Art and everything in between. The eclectic displays were like the most wonderful garage sale. The three of us wandered separately, admiring the blue and yellow cube-shaped wine glasses with spiraling stems, an enormous wall tapestry and the bizarre shaped 19th century vases. Just when I was studying the night lamp in the shape of a cookie jar, I felt a hand on my shoulder. "You have to see this," Larry said, leading me to a Cubist wooden chair, a coffee table, and a lamp. I glanced at the tag: Architect Josef Gočár. I called out to Pepa who was wandering nearby. It was my turn to stammer, "Just a few days ago we stayed in a pension built by Gočár. I bet this furniture was designed for that very building!"

"I knew it was Gočár without even reading the tag," Larry said with pride.

Our treasure-hunter friend smiled patiently.

We left the museum feeling like children who were unable to consume all the desserts on the plate in front of them. On the sidewalk, groups of students shared tips on the best street performers. From the windows of Brno's central library, the rhythm of salsa flooded the street.

Across the ornate Mahen Theater, a luminous sculpture depicted four huge lightbulbs.

"Mahen's Theater was the first in Europe to have electricity," Pepa explained. "The rest of Brno was still lit by gas lamps so the theater had to build its own power plant inside. That happened three years after Thomas Edison had invented the lightbulb. Edison personally designed the electrical installation here. Before Mahen's Theater was built, three major European theaters had burned down due to the gas-lamp fires. Hundreds died."

Anxious to finally put my foot in Brno's most beautiful theater, I took the broad stairs two at a time. At the doorway, an usher gestured me to stop.

"But, but, can we just... for only a minute?" I felt the blood pumping in my head. My fear had come true; I have been turned away by an usher.

"Chill!" Pepa touched my elbow. "He can't let you in during the show. We have to wait for intermission."

Larry checked his watch, "The last train leaves in less than 20 minutes."

"What! We didn't even get to see — "

Larry grabbed my hand, pulling me in the direction of the train station, "We better hustle."

"I'll call you tomorrow!" Pepa yelled after us.

Rushing off in the middle of the best party, Cinderella couldn't have felt worse.

Coughing and wheezing, unlike the graceful princess, I collapsed into a fake leather seat next to Larry. With a tug, our train moved.

"So when will we see Pepa again?" Larry asked.

Head buried in the booklet, I read about artwork for the blind, a dance performance by the hearing impaired, and a photo presentation called "Talent and Mental Illness." I was glad my countrymen finally included the handicapped. With pretense of the 'perfect society,' Communists hid the disabled, denying their existence. I took a deep breath and turned the page. "Oh, no! We missed the egg-decorating demo. I would have loved to see how those metal wire eggs are done. And the midnight concert in Brno's landmark — Saint Peter's Cathedral — and — "

Larry grabbed the booklet. "Stop torturing yourself. A single evening can't fix three decades of Czech cultural deprivation."

I sank back into the seat, exhausted. "Thanks," I said. "Keep that away from me."

43. The Remedies

Larry woke up the next day with a headache and sore throat. In the kitchen, waiting for the tea water to boil, Mom shot me the evil eye. "No wonder he got sick. You're running him all over the place." Another endorsement of my suspicion that Mom prefers Larry.

Examining each lemon in the wicker basket, she cut the biggest one in half and squeezed the juice into Larry's teacup. Then she handed me a bottle of aspirin. "Make sure he takes two."

As I plumped Larry's checkered pillow, Dad poked his head in. He held up a small brown bottle like it was the elixir of life. He stepped in and carefully filled a teaspoon to its rim with thick, ghastly smelling syrup.

"Tell him to swallow it fast, without tasting."

To my protest, Dad said, "This is nothing compared to what my mom did when I was sick. She used to smear lard around my neck, binding it with a towel." Dad shook disgustedly at that memory. "In the morning I had to go to school with a greasy neck."

Leoš came to the sickroom next, carrying a bottle of slivovitz. "The best medicine!" he said with a wink. "Straight from our Moravian plums." He fished a shot glass from his back pocket and ordered, "Bottoms up!"

My nieces, too, came with their contributions: cough syrup and a numbing throat spray. Larry, with submissive acceptance, opened his mouth and let them deposit their offerings.

"They talk as if I wasn't here," he said sleepily.

My sister Hana arrived with a bowl of steaming chicken soup. A layer of yellow fat circled the rim, "This will cure him, but he needs to eat it hot." After just a few spoonfuls, Larry sank into a deep slumber, and I tiptoed out of the room.

In the hallway my sister pointed to her new slacks and lowered her voice, "I told Leoš that you bought them for me."

People in my family always play these games. Finding myself in the middle of intrigue is irritating, but who knows, if I still lived here, I too may deceive my husband about my spendings. Things are about four times more expensive for Czechs than they are for Americans. Hana might have had to pinch pennies to buy those pants. The least I could do was to play my part in the charade.

In the kitchen, Mom placed a bowl of goulash on the table in front of me. When I scooped up the last chunk of spicy sausage, Mom poured another ladle full of the red stew in my bowl before I could stop her.

"Mom! I can't — "

"Don't you like it?"

"It was good but who can eat that much?"

"Do you want something else? I have a chocolate cake. I could make you a cup of tea. Would you like rose hip or peppermint?"

"Mom, please! I can't eat all that!" I pushed the plate aside and reached for a magazine.

"Do you have enough light?" Dad asked from the sofa and jumped to his feet. He grabbed the side of the table and dragged it closer to the window.

"I'm fine! I have plenty of light!" I cried, playing a tug-of-war with the table. Realizing at once that Mom and Dad were only making up for those long years when we couldnt see each other, I released my grip. What an insensitive jerk I was being!

"Actually, Mom, I would love more goulash and a cup of tea. And the cake would be great."

Whistling, Dad began to fiddle with the radio dial — um-pam-pa, um-pam-pa — the sound of brass instruments filled the room. There were times when my sister and I would leave at the first strains of polka, the old folk's music. This time, I approached Dad with a slight bow. "May I?" Dad spun me across the kitchen floor to the fast rhythm of his beloved Czech tune. Three quick steps and a hop, three quick steps and a hop...clumsily I followed Dad's lead.

Dance classes were mandatory for students, even in the pastry chef school I attended. Once the dance instructor called on me (the girl with a serious rhythm-deficiency), to demonstrate some new steps. I would have rather scrubbed public restrooms. Here, in the safety of my parents' kitchen, it was different. Or was it? Mom was laughing pretty hard. Roll out the barrel — we'll have a barrel of fun... I panted, singing the English version of the Czech song, as dad and I lost our slippers, hopping on the linoleum floor in our socks. Dad's embrace was firm, yet gentle. I felt his thin arm through his flannel shirt.

Dad used to be strong and fast. When I was a little girl I would yell, "Let's race to that tree!" Dad always let me win. At the finish line, out of breath, he would spin me in circles, holding me by an ankle and a wrist. With limbs spread, my body flew up and down like a car on the roller coaster until the grass underneath became a blur.

When the song ended, dizzy and breathless, we sank onto the sofa next to Mom, spending the afternoon listening to the radio and gorging on the chocolate cake. Every half hour, Mom dispatched me to check on Larry. Ever vigilant, she had a tray of food ready for him. But he was out until the next morning.

In the evening, Leoš and Hana joined us in the kitchen where Dad kept refilling our wine glasses. After the third round, Leoš raised his arm and, in his melodious baritone, began to sing. Dad joined in, followed by the rest of us. The absence of musical talent never stops people in my family. When the notes were too high, we sang louder. When we especially liked the song, we sang it twice. For me, being reunited with familiar melodies was like finding the lost beads of my precious necklace. Where had they been hiding all these years? I didn't even know I had so many songs in my head. Next, my sister chose a song that celebrated the soft rolling hills of Moravia. Trying to conceal the lump in my throat, I turned my head toward the window where I saw a reflection of people who pretend, argue and smother. People who I wouldn't change for the world.

"I am feeling much better," Larry said when he woke up the next morning.

"Really? You don't want a few more drops of Dad's secret medicine?"

Larry shuddered, "I've never been better."

209

44. Mushrooms

When Mom told me at breakfast that the previous week had brought rain, I stopped smearing gooseberry jam on my bread. Our eyes met and I lowered my voice. "Do you think they're growing?" With a sparkle in her eye, Mom gave me a collaborative nod.

Czechs are nuts about the wild mushrooms that pop up from the saturated forest floor. Young and old grab their baskets and scamper into the woods.

I shared the good news with Larry.

"Nice!" he called out. Like most Americans, he had not always been enthusiastic about mushrooms. With names like Destroying Angel, Death Cap, Satan or my favorite — Dead Man's Foot, who could blame him?

While Americans view wild mushrooms with concern or downright repulsion, Czechs find them delicious, even inspirational. My sister and I didn't grow up on American superheroes; our first picture books were filled with illustrations of plump mushrooms. They housed beautiful fairies and benevolent elves. Being in the forest was like being in a fairytale. We imagined playful goblins sliding off Slippery Jack caps onto cushiony mosses, feasting on sweet forest strawberries. We built miniature houses for imaginary trolls, cushioning their teeny beds with leaves. Above all, we collected mushrooms. Every new find was a reason for happy whooping and howling. As easily as one could point out a friend in the crowd, Hana and I, like many other Czech preschoolers, could identify a dozen or so species. A postage stamp with the picture of the most deadly mushroom, the pale green Death Cap, exposed the lethal villains. In the woods, Hana and I left them for the mean-spirited witches to add to their stews.

Before the sun peeked out of the morning fog, Mom, Larry and I were scanning the lush woods behind the house — pocketknives in our baskets. The soil was blackened with nourishment, and the air was freshened with pine scent. It felt as if we were inhaling directly from earth's oxygen tank.

There are more mushrooms than there are names. Some mushrooms can reach the size of a coffee table. Edible Giant Puff Balls can grow almost 60 inches in diameter and weigh over 40 pounds, while others have stalks as thin as a spider's web and a cap that is barely the size of a pin. Some mushrooms have an almond extract fragrance. Candy Caps, button-size rust-color mushrooms, smell like maple syrup, great for flavoring ice cream, cookies and bread pudding. I adore the eccentric shapes, colors and strange and various qualities mushrooms possess, such as the delicious young Shaggy Mane that drips black ink when mature. Some mushrooms are used for dying wool or coloring hair. Others are said to lower cholesterol, cure food allergies, diabetes and even cancer. A small group is known for their hallucinogenic effects. There are mushrooms that remind me of fat clowns, elegant brides and grooms, or gracious ballerinas. Parrot mushrooms' glassy green caps look like the creations of a glass-blowing artist. All those colors and shapes are like daring fashion statements of an experimental milliner.

"Did you know there are mushrooms that glow in the dark?" I asked Larry who was examining some Turkey Tails growing from a tree stump. "But only at the peak of their maturity, when they are releasing their spores."

Larry wiggled his eyebrows and asked, "Do you want to see me glowing?"

Names like Jack O' Lantern or Witch's Butter perfectly capture their mythical quality. Once in the depth of the Northern California woods, I stumbled upon the white cups of Fairy Ring mushrooms. They created a circle about 15 feet in diameter. I imagined that a person who stepped in its center would disappear with a sudden swoosh and a puff of purple smoke. I didn't dare test it.

California woods are more forbidding than Czech forests where even the privately owned ones are accessible to the public. The old growth is regularly thinned out, so it's easy to explore off the main path. Most importantly, unlike in California, in the Czech Republic no one gets fined or is thrown in jail for picking mushrooms. Even when conditions are dry, and the picking is thin, the forest is my muse, be it in California or my native country. I always find something special. It could be a creaking tree that snores like a sleeping giant, a mysterious single white orchid, or a lizard that has made its home inside a deer skull. Where some find solace in a church, I find my inspiration in the splendor and mystery of the woods.

We heard Mom's two short whistles, a signal that she had stumbled upon something good. Larry and I found her kneeling on the fluffy moss among conifers. With her pocketknife she was cleaning a beautiful King Bolete, the most sought-after of all mushrooms. With its plump white stalk and chocolate brown cap, it looked as if it had been molded out of chocolate and marzipan. In the States, dehydrated King Boletes sell for $100 per pound.

"Look next to your foot," Mom said. I leaped to reach another of those perfect beauties. Then Larry spotted one too, and another. With serious concentration, he examined the ground, measuring his steps, determined not to miss any.

Mom winked at me. "I think he's caught our fever." She held up the flawless specimen for closer examination, her eyes reflected joyful satisfaction. "Do you remember how I made you and Hana mushroom costumes for the carnival?"

I recalled a black-and-white photograph of two little girls in boyish haircuts wearing white shirts, short crépe paper skirts and matching bell-shaped, polka-dotted paper hats. We represented the most decorative mushroom of the woods, the fiery red hallucinogenic specimen known by its Latin name "*Amanita Muscarias*."

In the adjacent meadow, I spotted my favorite edibles. The Shaggy Parasols stood erect on their long thin legs. I counted eight. For many, fried Shaggy Parasols are an ultimate culinary delight. Larry likes to set the fried bite-size pieces on crackers smeared with goat cheese and chopped arugula. Mom, on the other hand, fries the steak-like caps in duck fat, seasons them with caraway seeds and salt and serves them on thick slices of rye bread.

The cups of the Shaggy Parasols were too fragile to carry in the baskets, so Mom pinched off their stems, which are not edible anyway, and strung the caps on a long young branch. Tired and enormously happy, we carried them home like donuts on a stick.

"Doesn't the forest floor remind you of the sea floor?" Larry asked. "All those orange and purple mushrooms are as brilliant as tropical fish. If Jacques Cousteau had been born in this country, he would certainly have become a mycologist."

Just as I was making a mental list of aquatic names of mushrooms — Oysters, Lobsters, Shrimps, Corals — Larry put down his basket and squatted. "Look at this!" he said in amazement. Leaning against the base of a tree stood a miniature twig house, about three-inches tall. It even had a tiny twig garden.

"A home of trolls!" I exclaimed, pleased that the children keep taking care of the magical woodsy creatures for me.

Mom smiled and said, "I always told you they live here."

After the evening news, when our stomachs were full of fried Shaggy Parasols, dumplings and Alfredo mushroom sauce, we watched an interview with the director of the Czech atomic power plant. She talked about the years following the 1986 disastrous explosion of the Chernobyl atomic power plant in the former Soviet Union. Czechs, concerned that radioactive fallout had contaminated their mushrooms, brought buckets of healthy looking edibles to be tested.

"After our analysis proved negative, we had to follow the rules and dispose of the constituent elements," the director said, then added with a wicked grin, "We devoured them."

Gobbling down the constituent elements and bragging about it on national TV... That would never fly in the States.

At the commercial break, as Dad was refilling everyone's beer, Larry said, "To get the flavor of America, one has to spend an afternoon watching a baseball game in a big league park. To understand the Czechs, one has to experience the bliss of leaning back with a belly-full of personally picked wild mushrooms washed down with world-class Czech beer."

We all cheered to that.

45. Gypsies

On a weekday morning, as people rushed about their business through downtown Brno, Larry and I savored the luxury of a lazy stroll. Underneath my contentment, however, I continued to have the feeling of being an odd ball. I wanted to shout: I used to live here, and I haven't been here for a really long time!

There was no one to say hi to. No one to exchange smiles with. Unlike in America, where strangers greet each other with wide grins, Czechs save their smiles only for their buddies.

I watched a woman in smart city clothes running into a friend, casually arranging a date for afternoon coffee. They parted with a wave, calling out a joyous, "Ahoj!" For many years after I had emigrated, a simple thing like having a date with a friend became wishful thinking, my penalty for leaving home. I imagined a fairy godmother holding a wand over my cradle, her words falling upon me like stardust: *"I'm blessing you with an opportunity to leave your barbed wire homeland."* Then, a wicked fairy elbowed her aside, spitting words dark like ashes: *"If you leave, you'll never be home again."*

A fast-approaching rumpus jerked me back to the present. Pedestrians jumped left and right on the sloping cobblestone sidewalk to make way for two daredevils on roller skates. Oh, what a thrill! We're-flying-and-no-one-can-stop-us! their shining eyes cried.

"Jesus Maria!" an elderly woman cursed after the boys, whose coal-black curls bounced on ahead.

"Damn Gypsies !" someone else yelled.

"They weren't more than eight-years old," Larry said, amused.

"Congratulations on your first encounter with Czech Gypsies."

"How do you know they were Gypsies?"

"What do you mean how do I know?" I replied, incredulously. "Didn't you see them? They stuck out like a sore thumb."

Shaped by California liberalism, my sweet husband tried hard to view humans for the individual spirits they possess. We spent a good portion of our stroll arguing about whether one can identify a Gypsy just by looking at him. I worried that for the sake of humanistic correctness, Larry had stopped trusting his eyes.

Further ahead, the pedestrian zone merged into a plaza; we saw the same boys in an eatery. Like a pair of curious puppies, they were crawling between people's feet, scouring the dusty tile floor for change that might have fallen out of the pockets of the diners. Their grins alternated with conspiratorial whispers. It took a moment for the woman behind the counter to spot them. "Get out of here!" She shouted, shaking her meaty pink arm. "Aren't you supposed to be in school?" They scampered away, but not without their prizes, each clutching a few coins.

We continued walking toward the Cabbage Marketplace (Zelný Trh), a nearby farmers market where, for over 700 years, Brno's residents have come to buy their produce. At the lower section of the market, rising above the vendors' yellow umbrellas, stood the 17th century Baroque water fountain, an artistic reproduction of a tall rocky cave with strange mystical creatures including a three-headed dog and a winged lion.

Larry and I sat on the steps encircling the fountain. It felt nice to be a part of this busy outdoor scene, but my memory chose to replay a scratched black-and-white movie instead:

Mom and I are holding hands. We're walking around mostly empty stalls. Mom is pointing to a pile of shriveled gray cauliflowers on one of the chipped plywood tables. We are taking a place in line. She gives me a happy squeeze. We're going to have fried cauliflower for dinner tonight!

Another movie clip:

Mom and I are waiting in a line for some spotted bananas. There isn't enough for everyone so the merchant allows just a kilo per person. Luck is on our side. The man hands us the last two bananas. The woman behind us sobs, "Please, I have a sick child." "Everybody could say that," the merchant barks. "We're sold out."

At home Mom gives one banana to my sister and one to me, insisting she doesn't like them. But when she finally accepts a nibble, she chews slow, closing her eyes.

In today's vibrant market, people pass mountains of yellow bananas without special notice.

Like actors on a stage, everyone played a part here: a vendor smashed a walnut with one hit of his bear-like palm, another was building a pyramid display out of shiny green, yellow and red peppers, an older woman listened with skepticism to the sweet spiel of the tomato merchant. A kaleidoscope of colorful patterns accompanied lively sounds and sweet smells.

Something prompted me to look up at the fountain. At the very top, next to the stone dragon, unnoticed, sat two little Gypsy girls in grubby dresses. In unison, they began to sing, swaying and clapping, mirroring each other's performances. Larry, with a wistful smile on his face, said, "They have the best seats."

Yes, indeed. Unlike the kids who pester their parents to provide their entertainment, those Gypsy girls created high times of their own, realizing what most wouldn't even dream of.

Centuries ago, Cabbage Marketplace was where public punishments took place. A person who had been convicted of a crime was tied to a post and left to the mercy of citizens. Some cast stones, some spat at the poor devil while others jeered. Cabbage Marketplace was also Brno's first supermarket where locals shopped for produce, pottery, poultry, and tools. Farmers, together with wealthy city merchants, displayed their goods and competed for sales. At night, the watchman kept an eye on the property. The more expensive or perishable merchandise was moved into refrigerators, the deep, cool underground cellars located directly below the market. Some cellars were so large that wagons could fit inside. Surrounding buildings linked their cellars to those directly below the market, creating a labyrinth of mysterious catacombs. When the underground cellars were no longer used, the various entrances were blocked off and forgotten.

"Larry, let me show you something!" I said, leaping to my feet, heading toward the upper end of the market. "When I was a teenager, I found Baker Street, which I walked on daily, roped off. That was unusual. In those days nothing, I mean nothing out of the ordinary ever happened... or so I thought. Communists created a sense of security by not reporting crimes or accidents." I recounted to Larry how a hidden cavity had weakened beneath the cobblestones and the sidewalk opened up and swallowed a woman and a man who tried to rescue her. We didn't find out from the media, but word-of-mouth traveled just as fast as news on the Internet does today. Soon the whole country was shocked by the horrifying fate of a woman who, on her way to work, had disappeared into the underground labyrinth. It took 16 years before sewer workers recovered some of her remains blocks from where she had fallen — they had been carried by the sewer and rats.

We stopped in front of historical St. Anna's Hospital, the place where the unfortunate woman sold flowers. After the Velvet Revolution a memorial plaque was installed on its wall. A woman with shoulder-length hair was smiling at us from a photograph. I translated for Larry the city's acknowledgment:

In this area, on 15.2.1976 died forty-year-old Marie Bartošová. Brno's city chancellors declare their partaking in this tragic event. It occurred unexpectedly due to human carelessness.

The incident prompted archeological research of Brno's underground. They found tunnels, wells and historical cellars shaped in elegant circular portals — several dating all the way to the 12th century. An ossuary with 50,000 skulls, second only to the famous one in Paris, was located not far from the Cabbage Marketplace. It is now open to the public.

Larry studied the uneven sidewalk, avoiding stepping on cracks, mindful not to disturb the underground spirits.

"No one knows all the secrets of Brno's underground," I said, "except maybe the Gypsy kids. Do you want to see the Gypsy museum?"

"Is there such a thing? How did we miss it on the Museum Night?"

"Some places you just don't go after dark. The museum is located in the neighborhood nicknamed Brno's Bronx."

I called our friend Pepa for directions.

"Hop on cable car number two, and don't even bother with tickets, the controllers never go to Bronx. The museum is near French Street. You'll recognize it. It gets pretty dark there."

In Czech culture, Gypsies are viewed as a drain on society. Everyone seems to have some personal experience with Gypsies, whom they regard as villains. People watch their pockets when in sight of them, not hiding their unflattering perceptions. How strange it seems that even in pre-school we used to sing *...home from a trip, dirty like Gypsies...*

"Who is going to see the first Gypsy?" I goaded when we exited the cable car and turned into French Street lined with neglected four-story 19th century apartment buildings. In the middle of a road ahead stood a group of dark, long-haired women, children in arms, speaking loudly among themselves. "Do you see what I see?" I victoriously singsonged the Christmas carol.

"I see women and children." Larry's answer was willful and definite, a caution for me to drop it. There were no trees or flowers, only dusty, cracked windows testifying to poverty and indifference. I began to feel the colorless beat-up buildings closing in on me. A car drove by, nearly striking two Gypsy men who were crossing the street. In a raspy voice that lacked the slightest trace of anger, the shorter of the two pointed out the irony, "They have a car and still are in a hurry."

A banner was hanging from the Museum of Roma Culture (Muzeum Romské Kultůry), the only freshly painted building around. A lively mural covered the three-story museum wall; it depicted mustached musicians in white shirts and black vests playing bass, fiddle, and accordion. The women's flowery skirts twirled.

We entered the building. The soft yellow light illuminated the kind of gift shop one expects to find in a modern museum. From a barstool in the cafeteria, a Gypsy man, the only visitor, shot us curious looks. We purchased two tickets and, while waiting for the curator, Larry and I leafed through some books. Memoirs with gloomy titles like *After Jews go Gypsies*, *Long Road*, or *Stolen Children*, chronicled struggles and hardships. Most were contemporary publications since Gypsies had not documented their lives in writing until the 20th century. I picked up a children's book. Its title was written in Romany, the language used by Gypsies, but I noticed the word *school* was in Czech. I wondered if the Romany language didn't have a word for school.

"Why don't Roma parents like to send their children to school?" I asked the jet-black-haired beauty behind the counter, hoping I wasn't rude.

"The parents believe their children won't succeed. They don't want to torture them," she said.

My mind flashed back to my first day of school:

Little boys and girls in ironed shirts seated in rows of short wooden desks, moms grouped in front of the blackboard. The teacher giving a welcome speech. Then, a Roma mother enters the room. Her son hides behind her. The last empty seat is next to me. I run to my mother. In my short life, I had heard countless times: if you don't behave, the Gypsies will get you.

"This classroom is full," the teacher says with authority. The mother and her son leave and I return to my seat.

Today, I cringed at the memory.

On the gift shop counter, I brushed my fingertips over some political buttons: *Racism isn't cool; I don't sleep with racists; Racism isn't sexy.* I wished they would have one saying, *All children deserve a chance.*

The curator, a slim woman with dark circles under her eyes, directed us upstairs to where the exhibition began.

"I came from Romania in 2000 to help establish this museum," the woman said in heavily accented Czech. "The Roma here didn't have any history or culture left. They didn't know any Romany songs. No ancestors' stories. In my country, some Romas are still wandering in horse-drawn wagons. Same in Bulgaria and the Balkans. We know the old ways." The woman unlocked the door and invited Larry and me on the journey of her people that began in Northern India hundreds of years ago. Through the velvety black museum halls, we followed. Beams of recessed lights pointed to colorful costumes, beaded jewelry, wooden dolls, paper flowers, photographs, and historical documents.

A diorama of a Gypsy camp took over one entire hall. It included a horse-drawn wagon adorned with sparkling trinkets, women in colorful skirts cooking in a pot darkened by the smoke, and the patriarch of the family opening his portable blacksmith workshop.

"Blacksmithing was the oldest and the most common trade of Gypsy men, holding as much respect as our musicians. We have a saying — *'Stay where there is music. Devils don't know how to sing.'* Building wooden puppets and toys represented another traditional occupation. More common ones were cobblers, tinkers, basket weavers and horsehair brush makers."

Just as I was about to compliment their resourcefulness in using natural materials, the guide said, "There were also professions like poultry thieves, fortune tellers, deceitful horse traders and circus animal trainers."

The three of us entered the Holocaust exposition, the Romengro Murda Ripen. In concentration camps, Hitler killed a staggering 95 percent of Czech and Slovak Gypsy men, women and children. I translated for Larry a poem written by an anonymous Roma:

In Auschwitz is a big house
Where Roma are locked up
Their children are being murdered there
Oh, Mothers are crying
Don't want to let go of their children
Mothers are ripping their hair
Oh, they are not going to see their little children again.

My throat tightened as I read the last two lines. Trying to control my emotions, I inhaled deeply.

The curator brought our attention to a blue, green, and red flag which is recognized around the world by the country-less Gypsies. She explained that the upper half represents the sky, the green is for the open country and the red wheel in the middle, as it is on the flag of India, symbolizes the Roma's itinerant way of life. The lyrics of their anthem, called *Gelem*, complement the symbols on the flag, telling a tale of happy wandering tribes.

In 1958, Communists outlawed the nomadic lifestyle and moved many Roma to paneláks.

The guide stepped toward photographs in which rows of multiple-story paneláks looked like giant overflowing garbage bins. Some Gypsies moved horses into their new residences and continued the tradition of having open fires. The constricted nomads made me think of American Indians who were forced by the U.S. government to live on reservations where many ended up ruined by cheap liquor.

In the visitors' book, words like *"excellent"* and *"great"* jumped off every page. Larry wrote below the signatures of guests from Italy, Philadelphia, Wisconsin, and London: *"Be proud of who you are."* Then, he signed our names.

To fill a couple of hours before the evening train would take us to my parents' house in Dolní Loučky, we decided to walk to the train station.

"The word Gypsy sounds romantic, like the swish of a dancer's skirt, its scent like a campfire crackling with dry pine needles," I said. "It almost burns the tip of the tongue with smoked red paprika. It crowds the imagination with hot-blooded, dark-haired lovers and tales of faraway places."

"But what about that little boy who didn't get to go to his first grade, mothers and children gassed in concentration camps, and the prejudice and unemployment that still affects their lives today?" Larry asked.

"As if centuries ago, in some faraway corner of India, wicked fairies swung their wands with curses. '*Wherever you go, you'll never be at home.*'"

The romance in the word Gypsy is deceiving.

46. The Church Bells of *Olomouc*

Larry and I didn't anticipate any difficulties getting to Pepa and his wife Jitka's apartment. Blue sky, MapQuest directions, it should have been smooth sailing, right? Wrong! We weren't even out of Dolní Loučky, and nothing on the instructions correlated with what we saw out the window. Suddenly we were on the freeway, and all we knew for sure was that my parents' village was behind us. Soon the green road sign pointed toward our final destination — Olomouc. That would have been great if we had not needed to first pick up our friends from their high-rise apartment in one of the massive neighborhoods that had sprouted around Brno in the late 70s. Pepa and Jitka were planning to join us for a couple of days on our travels through Central Moravia and Olomouc.

From the freeway, my city looked foreign and big. The approaching split required a quick decision.

"Which way?" Larry screeched.

"It doesn't matter," I shrugged. "I'm so disoriented; it makes no difference if we're going to be lost on the right or on the left."

"You can't expect me to know where to go," Larry yelled. "It's all I can do to fight off these Grand Prix racers."

After some aimless circling, Larry said in that cheery way he reserves for desperate situations, "We passed that blue panelák a few times. Now we've got a point of reference."

"Reference to what? That we're driving in circles? We need to get off the freeway and call Pepa."

"Are you lost?" Pepa shouted into the phone moments later.

I couldn't adequately describe our location. It all looked the same, paneláks and more paneláks.

"So, what did he say?"

"He told me to ask someone."

I didn't have much faith in the lonely pedestrian shuffling behind a walker. The man seemed more disoriented than we were. Plus, he was hard of hearing. Our exchange proved useless, and I didn't have the nerve to tell Larry.

"He said to go straight," I lied, and dialed Pepa's number again.

"Do you see a cable car or a bus?" he asked.

"A red bus number 78."

"Okay, that's good. Stay behind. Don't let him get away."

And so we didn't. With Pepa on the phone, Larry stopped each time the bus did. Glued to its rear, we inhaled the fumes while pretending not to see the driver gesturing for us to go around. Finally, Pepa ordered us to turn before the overpass.

"We're on a dirt road in the woods," I soon reported.

"What do you mean? I told you to turn at the restaurant, before the woods!"

Jitka, his wife, grabbed the phone. "Stay there. Don't move. Just stay there."

In a few minutes, we spotted a little figure jogging up the road toward our car. It was Jitka, a trim, lean, surgical nurse who once stitched up a three-inch-long cut on her own calf when backpacking in the French Alps. This superwoman never broke a sweat. Not then, not now.

She climbed in the car, and within a few turns, we parked in front of their building. On the seventh floor Jitka, Larry and I got off the elevator. Across the hall Pepa leaned against the doorway, grinning.

"Amazing precision," he said. "Eleven o'clock right on the dot. Coffee anyone?"

Hanging on the walls in their living room were glass displays with ancient coins, pieces of Neolithic ceramics, antiquated books, and yellowing lithographs. On the coffee table rested an old harmonica next to a carving of an Indonesian fisherman. I could see myself parked on Jitka and Pepa's couch, taking time to examine each treasure. With the four of us, their place felt congested. I stepped toward the sunny balcony. All those paneláks out there! But I also saw patches of woods and football field-sized lawns.

Pepa said, "When we moved here, all this was a huge construction site. No grass. But our kids were happy. They loved building castles from mud." Laughing, Pepa added, "Scrubbing the dirt off them forever jammed the drain pipes."

I remembered the Mudville around my own newly built panelák, adults chasing us kids off the sprouting lawn.

"When I moved to California, not far from my apartment, I discovered the most immaculate lawn," I said. "The sea of greenery went on forever. I had never seen anything like it. Linda had just begun to crawl and I thought the soft green carpet would feel nice on her chubby knees. I packed a picnic and a blanket, and off we went. I sunbathed for less than a minute when in the distance three men appeared, yelling and swinging sticks at me. That was my first introduction to the American golf course."

Sitting on the sofa, sipping coffee, Larry asked Pepa how they liked living here.

"No complaints. Grocery store, art gallery, hospoda, all within walking distance. All kinds of classes, concerts, plays, right here in the cultural center. Every ten minutes a cable car takes off for Brno. What else could we ask for?"

"And there's a great new fitness center, too," shouted Jitka from the kitchen where she was preparing some snacks. Just as I began to think that I, too, could happily live here, the sound of the neighbor's flushing toilet behind a thin wall brought me back to my senses.

On the freeway toward Olomouc, Pepa mumbled about the advantages of trains: "You don't have to worry about getting lost, you have plenty of room, no stress, no crazy drivers, no freeway toll stickers..." Jitka told us about an exemption from freeway tolls for parents with children who suffer from cancer.

Even though the historical core of Olomouc is second only to Prague, none of us had been there before. Our collective knowledge of the city boiled down to two facts:

1- Olomouc once had more hospodas than Prague — a matter any self-respecting Moravian wouldn't dispute;

2 - Olomouc cheese, called *Tvarůžky*, is the stinkiest edible in the country, possibly in the world. We were exceedingly proud of it.

I had not yet recovered from the tangle of Brno's streets and feared the same scenario would play out in Olomouc. Luckily Jitka, always calm in severe circumstances, guided us right toward the historical center.

Backpacks over our shoulders, ready to explore the city on foot, we spotted two pretty, young policewomen taking seductive photos of each other as they stuck parking violations behind the windshield wipers of cars parked near ours. I never thought getting a parking ticket could be sexy.

"Excuse us," I cooed, "Can we park here?"

"With a parking permit," one of them said and then added, "Or you could park in front of the Billa grocery store. That's what I always do."

Moments later, near the sign — *Parking for Billa's shoppers only* — Larry turned off the engine and mumbled, "I wouldn't expect anything less from Czech authorities — instructing us how to game the system."

We had grown accustomed to seeing Holy Trinity monuments in Czech cities, But the colossal Baroque monstrosity in Olomouc's Upper Square was unparalleled not only throughout the Czech Republic, but also the Austro-Hungarian Empire.

Reaching 35 meters high, the monument looked like a giant dusty wedding cake. The saints, like grooms ready for a collective wedding ceremony, lined its edges. In the hidden chapel beneath, a volunteer told us how once the invading Prussian army used the tower as a target for their cannonballs. When the Prussian general complied with the pleas of Olomouc's residents to spare their shrine, locals memorialized the event by fitting a gold-plated cannon ball into the column. In 2000, the Holy Trinity Monument was placed on the UNESCO list.

A few steps from the monument, the setting sun created a copper glare over a pool set in the cobblestones. Among the city's ten historical fountains, this one celebrated the tale of Arion, a musician lost at sea who was rescued by dolphins. Pepa, Jitka, Larry and I took off our shoes, rolled up our pants and together stepped in the comfortably chilly water. Like playful kids, we discovered all kinds of bronze turtles, dolphins and shells. The Beatles' song *Octopus's Garden* played in my mind ... *I'd like to be under the sea... in an octopus' garden in the shade...*

There were times I hadn't allowed myself to dream of being together with my friends because the impossibility of it hurt too much. The dreadful separation, I believed, was permanent. But now we were here, together in Olomouc plaza, the laser-beam sun rays tickling land and sea creatures alike. At moments like these, it was easy to believe that everything is possible. Perhaps one day, the four of us would wade in low tide just as the sun set over the Pacific, finding real starfish and seashells. We're now free to do what once was impossible. We just have to remember to dream.

The next morning Larry could hardly lift his eyelids. Disoriented, he gazed sleepily around the room, his eyes resting on my face. Dry mouths and throbbing heads reminded us of the previous night in the garden pub. The stinky Tvarůžky melted over fried garlic bread washed down with a river of local dark beer seemed like a good idea at the time.

"Where am I?" Larry croaked.

"Army dormitory. The best deal in Olomouc," I mimicked Pepa.

Mercifully, our patroness of severities knocked on our door holding two cups of steaming coffee. Jitka reminded us that the astronomical clock chimes only once a day, at noon. She added, "If we hustle, we can still make it."

Just like the Old Town in Prague, Olomouc too has its Orloj, and I didn't want to miss it.

A small group of tourists had gathered in front of the town hall, expectantly looking up at the tall clock, waiting for a hidden mechanism to set in motion the painted wooden figurines. In the background, the life-size mosaic of a factory worker holding a crowbar hinted that the statuettes may not be what one would expect of a 15th century astronomical clock. Promptly at noon, the factory worker's mechanical comrades moved out of the clock's depth — the milkmaid, chemist, athlete, mechanic, office worker, steel worker... then came a rooster's sickly crow and all came to a halt.

"That's it?" I shot Pepa a questioning look.

He shrugged and said, "In the 50s, the socialists replaced the saints and angels with the working class figurines."

"What would you expect from Bolsheviks who once named this town square after Stalin?" added Jitka.

To celebrate socialism, Marxists destroyed the clock's historical value. Now, the figurines spinning in endless circles were like workers trapped in the atrocious wheel of the totalitarian regime, performing useless routines, representing mountains of inefficiency, lies, and hopelessness.

The four of us shuffled behind a group of bemused tourists into the visitor center at the town hall. From behind the counter, a woman pointed out that today was Monday, the day tourist attractions are closed.

"I totally forgot," said Pepa.

The poster on the wall advertised Olomouc Castle — *an attraction you simply can't miss*. Like kids discovering a *closed* sign at the entry to Disneyland, we just gaped: no visit to Archbishop Palace, the Jesuit monastery, or the 800-year-old town hall, among other Olomouc' jewels.

"Go to some churches," suggested the lady behind the counter. "Olomouc has more churches per person than any other city in central Europe. Open even on Mondays."

We loaded up on glossy brochures with photos of places we would only see from the outside. In the hallway, I rushed toward a vending machine, eager for some comforting junk food, perhaps a bag of M&M's and another cup of coffee, but instead, the machine offered Olomouc's famous Tvarůžky. Truly cheesy souvenirs, as Larry put it.

In the quiet pedestrian zone, where red and pink geraniums decorated the windowsills, Pepa pointed out the ceramic emblems above the doorways — a white rose, blue star, or green tree. "That's how they marked houses before they used numbers. A butcher would have ceramic sausages or a pig's head above his door, a pharmacist would have scales and so on."

Soon we stumbled on St. Michael's church. The four of us climbed the stairs to the tower to see a new bell which had replaced the one that had been stolen. All Olomouc's bells were stolen — some during WWI, the rest during WWII. Germans melted them to make cannons and other war hardware. Communists had no interest in church restorations, so the towers stayed silent, some for nearly a century.

The sound of a church bell is like the clear voice of a brave messenger calling people together to rejoice and to grieve. In times of sorrow, people find strength in togetherness. On the other hand, when joy isn't shared with neighbors, communities lose their cohesiveness and strength. Communists viewed gatherings as threats. I remember times when even a small crowd gave police a reason to intimidate citizens by asking for their identification.

Just recently, thanks to donations, new bells, some approaching 5,000 kilos, found their way back to the towers.

"It's a big boy," Larry said, testing the acoustics with his knuckles.

The bronze bell had donors' names cast around its diameter.

"Wouldn't you prefer to be immortalized by having your name cast on a bell rather than a tombstone?" I asked. Larry just raised his eyebrow.

Before we left the tower, I stroked the cool bronze bell with my fingers, looked out over the pointy red roofs, then up towards the fluffy white clouds, and made a wish: Don't let anyone silence you again.

Back on the street, we passed a house where movers were dumping a worn carpet and broken chairs into an overflowing metal trash bin. Pepa, eyeing the pile like an expert antique hunter, gestured for us to go on ahead. When he caught up with us, he held a carved wooden frame, grumbling that he didn't have room in his backpack for all the other good stuff.

We spent much of the afternoon sprawled on a blanket underneath a shady tree by the wall surrounding Olomouc Castle, taking turns holding up Pepa's antique frame, viewing the evidence of the majestic medieval past. Each new angle created a fabulous picture — from the dainty white daisies scattered in the grass to the 1,000-year-old cathedral where in the portal above the main entrance the marble Virgin Mary is holding her dying son.

With pamphlet in hand, Pepa pointed toward the castle. "King Wenceslas III was murdered here in 1306. He was the last Czech King. He was 16 when he died."

The death of King Wenceslas III ended the over 400-year-long Přemyslid dynasty during which the Bohemian kingdom stretched to its largest size.

The glorified stories of Czech Kings, told by my father, made me feel both proud and confused. What happened to all that glory, I wondered. From our living room window, the rows of houses with peeling stucco looked like wounded veterans returning from a lost battle. After Wenceslas' death,

Bohemia shrank back to its core size and the vacant throne was filled with a succession of foreign kings.

Fanning ourselves with the castle brochures, we lay on our backs. I stared at slow moving clouds, thinking about that pivotal moment in Czech history, which took place just a few feet from where we were now nursing our hangovers.

"King Wenceslas II died suddenly, and the young Wenceslas found himself with a triple crown and loads of enemies," Pepa said, turning on his side, propping his head with his arm. "Imagine the scenario. A hormonal teenager left home alone. What would you do?"

"Party. Of course," I said. "And with unlimited finances... What a party that would be!"

"That's it," said Pepa. "Wenceslas completely neglected his royal duties. In a drunken stupor, a regular kid might neglect watering begonias, and perhaps even starve the canary. But Wenceslas wasn't a regular kid. He was the new king of Bohemia, Poland, and Hungary. He came to his senses only when the canary began to smell." Pepa combed his hair with his fingers and continued, "His Polish rival reclaimed one of Wenceslas' castles, so in a hurry, Wenceslas put together an army and rushed toward Poland. The last stop he made on his home turf was right here in the Olomouc Castle. They never found who stabbed him."

Jitka, picking up the aged frame, squinted her eyes, framing the white towers of the castle. "If he'd not been assassinated, perhaps we would be a superpower today."

"It never fails to amaze me how Czechs talk about the ancient past as if it was yesterday," Larry said, slowly getting up.

"How can't we?" Pepa said. "Every other village has a castle that reminds us of our history. All you have to do is to look up. Wouldn't you want to know about the guy that used to live there? Our kids dream about kings and queens."

Olomouc is so rich with history, that even on Monday, the day when most museums and historical sites are closed, we had plenty to do. Pepa wanted to see two other national treasures. We drove to a hospital located on the outskirts of Olomouc. Established in 1077 as a monastery, the complex has served for the past 200 years as a hospital. Plastic directory signs on the gold-plated fresco walls pointed to neurology and ear and eye doctors. Chubby cherubs showed the ways to internal medicine, and to a festive auditorium rented out for weddings.

"So I could get a colonoscopy and get married at the same place," Larry said, his voice echoing under the ornate, high ceiling.

"Yeah, but you'd only want a photographer for one of those," Jitka suggested. The cost of the procedures were astonishing. The colonoscopy cost $50, a night in the hospital $15. Bikini hair removal was also on the hospital price list, surely causing the monks to spin in their graves.

The last place we toured was the nearby monumental Basilica Minor of the Blessed Virgin Mary. With mouths agape, we attempted to jam the massive decorated dome ceiling into our camera viewfinders.

Since it was time for Larry and me to think about where to spend the night, and since the Basilica was a pilgrimage site, I rang a bell at the priest's residence, hoping for the holy man's arms to fly open, welcoming his long lost lambs. Instead, a voice from the intercom barked, "This isn't a hotel." Luckily, in the Czech Republic, one is never far from one. We found a home with a pension sign in the window just up the hill, in a town called Samotišky. A lovely lady escorted us to the back of her property where rows of fruit trees hid a wooden cabin that faced the vast Olomouc valley below. There, on a secluded patio, our hostess supplied the four of us with cold beer and golden crisp potato pancakes (bramboráček). The setting sun cast smudges of red, orange and purple over the sky. Just when I thought that not even heaven could be more divine, we had to tear ourselves away because Jitka and Pepa had a train to catch. They had to go to work the next day, and we had to give them a ride to the train station.

It was late when Larry and I felt our way up the wooden ladder to the attic of that romantic dollhouse. We weren't asleep for five minutes when an ear-shattering scream came from just outside the window. We bolted upright. The darkness revealed the whites in Larry's bulging eyes.

"What the hell... " he whispered.

I held up my hand to shush him. We were breathless and terrified. A spine-chilling roar answered another high-pitched inhuman shriek someplace near.

"It's a jungle out there," I whispered. Larry put his arms around me, and we drifted off into an uneasy sleep.

In the morning we discovered a note attached to our front door:

Please feel free to use these passes to the zoo next door.

Funny how fast getting something gratis can placate ruffled nerves. We decided to see what had awakened us the night before.

In the zoo, from a rope bridge over a forested canyon we met our noisy neighbors. The monkeys swinging from tree to tree were too adorable to hold grudges against.

Later, the pension hostess told us about two monkeys who escaped from the zoo earlier that year. For months it was front-page news. One of the monkeys was eventually found hiding in a nearby barn. The other was believed to be dead. Larry and I weren't convinced. We think the second monkey is thriving in the lovely lady's yard, living off her berries and, after dark, tantalizing her caged buddies and serenading the pension guests.

47. The Stone Window in *Jesenîk* Moutains

On the way towards Jeseník, Moravia's highest mountain range and the natural border between the Czech Republic and Poland, we stopped in the city of Šternberk. At the information center, we picked up a self-guided walking map. Dots on the map showed multi-language audio machines that described various points of interest throughout the town center.

"Cool! Metal tour guides!" Larry said and practically ran to the plaza where he eagerly hand-cranked the first parking meter-like device. That was the end of the exciting part. A monotone voice lectured about the ornate building across the street. We tried to appear interested for the benefit of a local passerby, when an older man came out of the same house wearing a t-shirt, flip-flops and a Speedo. He unlocked a car parked in front, grabbed a briefcase, and then went back inside.

"What's up with those Czechs and their Speedos?" Larry said genuinely amused.

An American friend of mine, who lived in the Czech Republic for a few years, told me that, while there, her son begged her to buy him a Speedo. "At the pool, he didn't want to stand out like a preacher with his baggy, knee-length American swim trunks," she said.

"Sweetie, would you like me to buy you a Speedo so you would blend in?" I looked Larry in the eye, trying to appear sincere.

My husband searched my face. "I'd rather go naked!" he proclaimed and then marched toward the next point of interest.

We cranked a few more of the guided-tour meters, but we weren't patient students. After visiting historical Olomouc, any city was at a disadvantage. Plus, we were ready to put some mileage on our car.

"Keep going straight." I instructed and folded the map. By the roadside, long-stem daisies and fiery red poppies brightened the lacy grasses. Tiny towns here and there peeked from the lush vegetation. I sank into my thoughts.

While back in my parents' house, Leoš had eyed my Birkenstocks with a smirk, "You're going out in slippers?" Earlier Hana had pointed out that only school kids wore canvas backpacks like the one I had, my plain white t-shirt was better suited for a physical education class, and my jeans were out of fashion by at least a decade. Were my clothes really that embarrassing? Or was it something else? There was a time when my bakery salary in the States topped Leoš' and Hana's, both college-educated professionals. As the Czech Republic entered its capitalistic stride, the gap between American and Czech wages isn't so huge. Hana and Leoš, a Czech middle class couple, owned two cars and a comfortable house surrounded by a beautiful garden. Same as the middle class in the States, they worked hard for what they have. These days, owning a wine cellar, swimming pool, and a curious piece of original art is no longer a rarity. On the outside, people's lives looked pretty darn good. So was it really my clothes? I didn't know. All I knew was that my ways were irritating and for that I was sorry. In a perfect world, the miles and years between us would provide rich material for fascinating conversations. In this world, though, I kept on guessing.

"We're low on gas." Larry interrupted my thoughts.

"Why are we on a gravel road?" I asked. I couldn't even find the tiny village we'd just passed in the road map. I studied it closer, searching for a gas station symbol. For the next 20 kilometers, there wasn't any.

"Not to worry, we aren't even on reserve yet."

Larry's cheerfulness alarmed me. I leaned over to check the gas needle. It was touching the red.

"There isn't a gas station until Šumperk." I tried to sound calm, but the blame seeped through. Hadn't I told him to fill up in Šternberk?

The surrounding woods darkened as if reflecting the atmosphere in the car. There hadn't been a single road marker or other sign of civilization for a while. The bubbling creek kept mockingly appearing and disappearing. At least, we'll have water if we have to camp.

After a lengthy silence, Larry defended himself, "I wasn't counting on this detour."

"Why not? When have we ever stayed on the right path? It makes perfect sense to count on a detour every time we sit in this car." I also wanted to ask if he enjoyed driving through every single pothole, but I bit my tongue.

"I just don't understand how we got off the main road," Larry said.

I once heard about an Australian community where instead of greeting "How are you?" they would say "Which direction are you going?" They always knew their way, answering southwest, northeast and so on. Even inside windowless buildings, they knew. How I longed to be married to one of those tribesmen now.

"We should ask someone," I said.

"Ask someone? Like when they told us to turn left... but didn't say which one of the threefold lefts they had in mind, and we ended up in someone's driveway? Like when they told us to turn at the traffic light and didn't say if it was the first one that didn't work or the second, that actually did? Or when they told us to turn at the roundabout that was triangular — who makes triangular roundabouts? Everyone is eager to help — go more or less straight, turn right but not all the way..."

Larry ranted on while I envisioned the dry, dusty walls inside our gas tank. I held my breath as if it would help to save every last drop. Our car climbed the increasingly hilly landscape. At last, in the valley below, the city of Šumperk came into view. Larry turned off the motor and shifted into neutral. We coasted quietly into town.

With the gas tank full once again, the motor labored happily up the steep hairpin curves. The mountain air felt fresh and cool. The 18 wheelers' brakes squeaked and screeched as skillful truck drivers maneuvered their monstrous vehicles laden with timber from the Jeseník mountains.

We started our hike from Červenohorské Sedlo, a world-class ski resort. At 1,164 meters above sea level, its peak is slightly higher than the top of Mt. Diablo, the mountain Larry and I see from our kitchen window. Out of season, the large parking lot was deserted, and the ski lifts stood motionless on this weekday afternoon. A man was repainting the ski-rental sign.

A well-worn Škoda parked next to ours and an elderly couple climbed out.

"Dobrý den," I greeted them. "Do you know this area?"

"We used to hike every trail here," said the man, heavily relying on his cane. The woman with melancholy blue eyes added, "Now we are here for the memories."

"If you follow the red sign it will take you to Praděd," the man pointed out the direction. "The TV tower is the highest spot in the Czech Republic. It has a lookout, too. On a clear day like today, you can see the flat land of southern Poland, the peaks of Slovakia's Tatra Mountains, and maybe even the Austrian Alps. But if you like easier hiking, you should go to — "

"Honey," his wife patted him on his hand, "let them be. They are young; they'll find their own way."

We watched the couple support one another as they shuffled away. It felt like we were looking at our future selves.

Once upon a time my mom and dad hiked these mountains too. Mom had said that when God divided blessings in this country, by the time he made it to the Jeseník mountains, his pockets were empty, so he gave the people here only rocks. The locals were poor, but the tips of their mountains boasted stunning rock formations.

At a tree trunk post that looked like a crooked letter Y, Larry and I studied the colorful arrows pointing to various destinations. A small plaque informed us that since 1888, over 40,000 kilometers of marked trail had helped tourists reach their targets. The European Union recognized the Czech Tourist Club for creating this excellent system — a leading example in creating reliable trail markers. Larry and I decided to follow the yellow markings up to something called Stone Window.

The forest floor on both sides of the path was covered with low blueberry bushes full of green, unripe berries. We stopped frequently to enjoy the minty air and the rolling hills covered by healthy pines stretching toward the blue horizon. John Muir, the Scottish-born American naturalist best described our feelings: *"We are now in the mountains and they are in us, kindling enthusiasm, making every nerve quiver, filling every pore and cell of us."*

Whenever our trail intersected with another, a short yellow stripe painted on a stone or a trunk of a tree pointed the way. We didn't know what we were looking for and didn't much care if we found it. We were just happy to have the mountains to ourselves on that perfect sunny day — not a small triumph in a country where a steel-colored sky could hover over land for weeks at a time. Locals joke: *"What's your favorite season? That one sunny day called summer."*

The average temperature in the Jesenik mountains is one degree Celsius, a single degree over the freezing point. Today, though, we tied our jackets around our waists and happily skipped up the mountain. A distant coo-coo sound stopped Larry in his tracks.

"That's a real bird?" he asked. "I always thought it was just made up for cuckoo clock."

"Shh..., count the coo-coos," I whispered. "She'll tell us how many years we have left. Five, six, seven... twenty-nine, thirty, thirty-one ... " we listened for more, but there was silence. With a triumphant grin I announced, "Thirty-one coo-coos means we'll have thirty-one more years together."

Behind the next turn, gray boulders blocked our way. Tall stones leaning against each other created a tall, church-like window that framed a view of Poland.

"The Stone Window! We've actually found it," we cheered.

Back in our car, Larry sighed as he turned the key in the ignition, "If only the road-sign guys had taken lessons from the volunteers who put up those trail markers."

🐾 🐾 🐾

48. St. Christopher

Our plan was to find dinner and lodging in Velké Losiny, a tourist town known for its healing spa, the oldest in the country.

Larry, trying to make a U-turn on a dead-end street, maneuvered around a man who was pushing a wheeled cart. "There is absolutely no room, but you can always count on being stuck behind a tractor, or at least a wheelbarrow. I don't even know where we are right now."

"Maybe St. Christopher is leading us to a very specific place tonight," I suggested.

"Tell your St. Christopher to — "

"I have an idea!" I jumped in my seat, "Let's go back toward the mountains. There was a pub open. We'll have a beer or two, a nice dinner and then we'll decide what's next."

The men in the tavern looked up from their steins through a thick cloud of cigarette smoke when Larry and I made our way between the wooden benches.

Not wanting to attract any more attention, I headed toward a table in the corner, but a shaggy black dog beat us to it, claiming the bench for himself. I expected someone would call the beady-eyed creature off with apologies, but instead, I felt the cold stares jabbing our backs. Larry and I found another bench beneath a raggedy witch puppet hanging from the ceiling, the only decoration in the tavern. The waiter, in rolled-up sleeves and ash-smudged trousers, placed a stein in front of a man at the next table. Then, with his wet hand,the waiter smacked the back of the guy's neck. In a flash, the man retaliated, grabbing the waiter's crotch. Laughter roared through the tavern. The mechanical witch above our heads, obviously activated by noises, let go of a raspy chortle, her red eyes blinking.

When the waiter made it to our table, Larry, doing his best to sound tough, ordered Pilsner.

"Don't have it," said the waiter in Czech, and after a silence that clarified who was in charge, added, "Only local stuff."

"Okay," I said, "give us the local stuff then."

"That's the only thing we have."

The waiter cleared the empty steins left by previous guests off our table. The coasters beneath advertised *Holba — since 1874 — the beer from the mountains*. Heading toward the counter through rambunctious company, he dumped the beer dregs down the collar of an unsuspecting guest. Hearty cheers and applause resonated through the room. The witches' red eyes flashed gleefully.

We dined on greasy garlic bread, the single offering on the tavern's menu, washing it down with Holba, pretty good stuff, as Larry repeated, all the while nodding approvingly in an attempt not to anger our waiter, for neither of us wanted dregs dripping down our necks.

Even though there wasn't a pension sign, we rang the doorbell of a house recommended to us by the waiter. A middle-aged man answered the door, releasing the aroma of pan-fried steak. He showed us up the tiled staircase, assuring us that he didn't mind having his dinner interrupted. A young boy of about six, peeking behind the man, measured us with curious eyes.

"After my wife's accident, my son and I moved to this house." The man opened the door to a spacious bedroom.

The boy's and the man's expectant eyes were fixed on us. I saw the dusty bed frame and carpet that needed vacuuming. I saw streaky windows. I saw a hastily made bed. And yet I said okay, we'd take it. Later, when Larry softly snored next to me, I tried not to think about the body odor coming from the pillowcases. Why couldn't I just say no thanks, this wouldn't work for us, like a normal person would. As soon as I heard about his wife's accident, it became my responsibility to improve these people's lives by sleeping in their unwashed bed and brushing our teeth in their toothpaste-smudged sink. Damned do-gooder!

The sun was up when I ran into our landlord and his sweet son in the hallway.

"Going to school?" I asked.

"A school trip," the boy answered, unable to contain his excitement. "First my dad said I couldn't go because we don't have any money, but yesterday Mama sent us angels, and now I can go."

The man lowered his eyes, urging the boy out the door. Then he turned and said, "If you stay another night, I'll give you a discount."

Sure, we'll stay — I almost said. But just then Larry came out of the bedroom, our bags hanging over his shoulders, ready to hit the road.

"Oh... Sorry..." I said, unsure that I meant it.

Later in the car, Larry said, "St. Christopher did good. I left an extra $20."

49. The Crucible of *Velké Losiny*

Back in touristy Velké Losiny, we walked into a visitor information office where another cute witch swung on a broom from the ceiling. Ever since we drove through Šumperk, the big-nosed, wart-faced characters dangled from store windows or drivers' rearview mirrors, showing their toothless grins.

"What's up with those witches?" I asked the lady behind the counter.

"Don't you know our region is infamous for witch trials?" she said, handing me a pamphlet. The drawing on the front cover showed a woman tied to a stake engulfed by smoke.

"In the 17th century hundreds of people were convicted of practicing witchcraft," the woman said, adjusting her half-rimmed glasses and leaning forward. "You should see the movie *Witch Hunt, Malleus Maleficarum*. It's historically accurate, based on documented trials. Absolutely unforgettable."

Across the street in a coffee shop, we ordered two macchiato lattes. The tall glasses along with our laptop crowded the round table. The black-and-white movie began to play on You Tube. Grim music matched lyrics like *"fury, black cloud, a grim reaper on a black horse, bloodthirsty killer ripping into flesh, funerals without coffins..."*

The opening scene portrayed an old beggar woman caught stealing a communion wafer at Sunday mass. When questioned by the priest, she confessed she was going to feed it to an old cow so it would produce milk again. That single superstitious act unleashed a witch hunt, an insanely brutal chapter in Moravian history.

The imperial inquisitor was an evil character with the pompous name Heinrich Franz Bobling von Edelstadt. I'll refer to him as FB. The F isn't for Franz though.

The money-hungry FB first ordered the jailer to shave the victim's head. Then the tribunal examined his or her naked body for birthmarks or scars. A single wart was enough to prove association with the devil.

"Admit that you engaged in an orgy with the devil disguised as a black goat!" FB would shout. "Admit that you and others like you met on Peter's Rocks at midnight!" (The area Larry and I had hiked the day before.) "Admit that you stomped on Holy Communion wafers!"

FB correctly calculated that by accusing prosperous people of witchcraft, their confiscated possessions would bring him wealth and power.

When the next victim's thumbs were smashed and her shinbones crushed, Larry got up. "I've had enough of this creepiness."

While he strolled around town, I forced myself to watch the crazed victims reveal the names of their wealthy neighbors. My eyes were glued to the screen. I chewed my knuckles. The milk foam on my latte flattened. Oh God, what would I have done? Bald and naked in front of six male examiners, who would have known me from childhood. Would that have been enough to break my spirit? Would I have given the names of innocent people at the first glimpse of spikes on a torture chair?

I watched the trials to the end of the film when a local priest, the single brave critic of the inquisitors' practices, ended up in the torture chamber himself. Even though he was forced to confess his alliance with the devil, the good priest managed to break the chain of nearly two decades of orchestrated finger-pointing by making up a lie about being too drunk to identify others who partied at Peter's Rocks. The trials finally ended in 1686.

Before meeting Larry in the spa garden, I searched the Internet for additional information on sorcery. I found more evil stuff than I could digest in one afternoon.

The garden where Larry and I walked reminded me of California artist Thomas Kinkade's paintings. Through filtered canopies of greenery, sunbeams danced over exploding pink and lavender rhododendrons. The trees must have been hundreds of years old. It was all very pretty, but I couldn't shake off the eerie residue of the movie.

"Witch hunts happened in America too," Larry said. "In 1692, in Salem, Massachusetts, judges sent over 30 people accused of witchcraft to their deaths by hanging. In the 1950s Arthur Miller wrote a play called 'The Crucible,' comparing the hysteria of Protestant New England to the Cold War America obsessed about. That was a crazy time. At elementary school, we practiced hiding under our desks in case the Russians decided to send us an atomic bomb. Meanwhile, Hollywood stars and other prominent Americans were accused of being Communists and were brought before the House Unamerican Activities Committee created by Senator Joseph McCarthy. Some people were sent to jail but even more were blacklisted and lost jobs."

Larry pulled from his pocket a pamphlet with a picture of a cute little witch riding a velocipede.

"Look, I got this map. That's a bike trail following the witch path."

Ahead of us, a young mother held hands with a little boy. Will she someday take him up to the hill where people were burned alive? Will she caution him about superior righteousness?

Larry moved his index finger along the red line on the map. "Here is the church where it all started, here is the castle where the accused were held and tortured, and this is where the executions took place. There's even a witch museum."

"I read about it," I said. "That museum used to be the home of a wealthy merchant and his family."

"Bobling probably had his eye on their house," Larry guessed correctly.

"FB attempted to squeeze confessions out of the couple. The wife tried hard to save her husband." I said in a thin voice. "She didn't give his name even after they crushed her bones and stretched her on a wooden rack. But she still ended up in flames. Bobling said that some witches would rather be torn to pieces than give up their accomplices. She left behind four young children."

"What about the husband?"

"He died in prison after eleven years of torture. The evil bastard, FB, on the other hand, died at age 85. In his featherbed."

"I hope all the witches he created escorted the old geezer to hell," Larry said, adding, "Thank God those times are over."

"The latest witch execution was in 2014. Saudi Arabia." I said.

"Holy Jesus!" Larry stopped in the middle of a trail. "You always say that to understand a historical event one needs to know what happened before. So what happened in Bohemia before the witch trials?"

I counted on my fingers, "An exodus of educated Protestants, the Thirty Years War and the Black Plague."

"In another words, ignorance, violence and poverty," Larry said. "The perfect malicious trio."

Suddenly I was tired. We sat on a bench to watch the woman and her son. The boy filled his little fist with pebbles and threw them into a pond. He observed the ripples as they died away, then he ran toward his mother, past the picture of a witch grinning from the bike trail post.

50. Paper Mill in *Velké Losiny*

It was late afternoon when Larry pulled into a parking lot adjacent to a green building with a large steep roof. "Lodging at the Mill" announced the sign on its front.

I asked to see the cheapest room, feeling like a disgrace to the affluent American image. In Czech, the adjective "rich" automatically precedes the word "American." However, the Polish couple, who owned the pension, without a blink escorted us behind the building where a 70s era two-wheeled trailer balanced on raised wooden beams.

"The refrigerator doesn't work, and the windows don't open," the man said as I examined the crinkled mattress on the metal frame, more of a yoga mat than a cot.

"We could lend you more blankets," the woman said.

Larry replaced his customary *"It's up to you, Hon,"* with a very definite *"No."*

We followed the couple back into the main building up tall narrow stairs.

"This used to be a mill?" I asked.

"It's a residential home, built over 200 years ago," the man said.

His wife added, "The large white building you must have passed is the paper mill. Czech presidents get their stationery from there."

The deluxe room with rough-hewn ceiling beams made us feel the drift of centuries. More importantly, the mattress was nice and thick. We dumped our bags and went to see what we could see.

Passing the reception desk where our hosts drank coffee, the man asked if we were heading for a swim. "You can't miss the hot outdoor pool. That's the reason people come to Velké Losiny. You didn't bring your swimsuits? Big mistake! The Vietnamese shop around the corner may still be open. The healing water comes from a depth of 1,000 meters. You won't have such an opportunity again!"

Out of their sight, we entered the first restaurant in our path, a very modern and very expensive one. We ordered the regional specialties. Smelly local cheese melted in garlic soup, and a pork pocket filled with even smellier local cheese.

"Are you heading for a swim?" the waiter asked when pocketing our crisp 1,000 koruna bill.

"What else is there to do here?" I replied.

"The paper factory is a National Monument, registered with UNESCO."

What do I know about paper making? My grade school teachers pushed kids in my class to participate in paper recycling competitions. The prospect of hauling heavy stacks across town to the recycling centers, where we got petty cash, wasn't appealing to me. A diploma and a handshake from my teacher, should our class win the competition, wasn't attractive either. My friend Pepa, on the other hand, didn't miss an opportunity to sell his stacks of papers to the recycling centers. Each with a stolen brick in the middle.

Pepa cheated, and I couldn't be persuaded to participate. Karl Marx should have tested his social theory on school kids before going ahead with his common ownership experiment on a large scale.

I couldn't picture how paper was made or recycled until I saw the paper artisan at the Renaissance Faire fish the dripping paper mass from a barrel. After the pulp had dried in the sun, he pressed it between two sheets of thick felt material. I was already in my 40s when I finally understood the principles of papermaking and recycling.

The hand-made paper factory was a remarkable building with an imposing five-tier mansard shingle roof. The red geraniums in the windows contrasted with thick-whitewashed walls. If all factories were this attractive, I wouldn't mind if our house was surrounded by them.

We were just in time for the last afternoon tour. Our guide, an elderly lady with swollen ankles, rushed us, the only visitors, from the paper history room to the European paper production displays. Her eyes focused someplace past us, her inner audio was on fast-forward:

"The paper mill was founded in 1596 and without interruption is still operating. Handmade paper is manufactured today the same way by mixing cotton, flax fibers and water. Our paper lasts hundreds of years, unlike paper made in modern factories."

I pointed to a wooden wheel attached to a metal tub. "What is this for?"

"I told you that already," the woman said and marched to the next exhibit.

"How do they use — "

"You'll see that in the movie," she snapped and trooped out of the room.

Instead of following her, I walked across the room. The clicks of my heels bravely echoed through space, declaring... *screw-you-screw-you*... A window exposed the lower floor where, in a long production room, steel knives cut the cotton balls, and paddles in three large tubs mixed the fibers. Our guide was going to bypass this essential part of the hand-made paper operation! I reached to open the window for a better look, but I froze when the thundering voice behind me ordered, "Don't you open our windows!" With slouched shoulders and a contrite grin, I tiptoed back across the room.

"I tried to warn you," Larry mouthed behind the woman's back.

Among my favorite exhibitions, possibly because it was self-explanatory, was an original floor-to-ceiling 1720 map of Bohemia and Moravia. The tiny colorful lights represented the timeline of the hand-made paper factories as they spread throughout the Czech lands. The light first blinked near Prague. The year was 1499. The 17th and 18th centuries were the peak of hand-made paper production — tiny red lights covered the map like measles. With the industrial revolution, the lights disappeared. Now, in the 21st century, a single glow came from Velké Losiny, the last operating hand-made paper factory not just in the Czech Republic, but in all of Central Europe. The National Monument status was its saving grace.

Outside, in the factory's courtyard, our guide recited her final account: "When the witch trials and the Black Plague epidemic swept through Velké Losiny, many factory workers and their families were caught in the middle. A journeyman's wife, Barbora, was among the first accused of witchcraft and in 1680 was burned at the stake. Two months later her four children died of the plague, along with four paper mill workers."

On that happy note, with no goodbye, no thank you or kiss-my-ass, the woman, an exceptionally well-preserved relic of superior mentality, turned on her heels and was gone, possibly getting ready for her prison guard reunion.

In the gift shop, a very pleasant lady sold us ten sheets of the handmade, uneven-edged paper.

"If you look at the paper through the light, you'll see the watermark, a lion standing on a triple-crested mountain," she said with a smile.

She was so nice. I wanted to kiss her on both cheeks.

51. Cemetery in *Horní Loučky*

Through the chain-link fence, we saw Dad working in the vegetable garden. Beside the rows of strawberries and sprouting garlic, the garden was still bare. With his flat shovel, Dad turned the fluffy black soil, which by the end of summer would provide my family with mountains of cucumbers, sweet tomatoes, and yellow, green and red peppers. At age 80, dad's repetitive movements seemed effortless. He looked up at the sound of the motor, joy spilling over his face. "Finally you're back!" He rammed the shovel and hurried to open up the gate.

Dad, the homebody, is happiest to have all of us home. I dreaded telling him that in the morning we were leaving again, and taking Mom with us on top of it. I could think of only one thing to appease him. The cemetery!

"Would you like to go for a walk in the cemetery?" I asked later in the kitchen. Mom just rolled her eyes. "Ever since he bought that plot he is pestering Luboš to take his portrait for the new tombstone," she said.

Dad, possessed with the anticipation of departing this world, stood by the front door, ready. When I told him that

Larry's mom is well at age 92, he sighed like a weary traveler who just learned that his train might not arrive anytime soon.

The cemetery was a short, uphill walk from the house. If Dad had a tail, it would have wagged all the way. Today two visitors were joining him on his favorite walk.

I translated dad's affectionate words to Larry. "I don't know why Mom never wants to come with me. Our cemetery is so pretty; even the wall is newly painted."

The cemetery was well kept; the black iron gate didn't even squeak. That wasn't a surprise, though. In the Czech Republic, grave sites look like immaculate miniature gardens. In the spring and summer, they're adorned with bright marigolds, violets, begonias or low flowering shrubs. In cold months candles continue to burn next to silk flower arrangements. Surviving family members dutifully weed and replant, if not for the devotion to their loved one, then to safeguard their own reputation. What would the neighbors think?

Dad, standing in front of his shiny gray stone, looked like a kid showing off his first airplane model. "What do you say?"

"It's great," I nodded, relieved that the tombstone wasn't towering over the surrounding monuments like the sculpture in the center of the cemetery, the blacksmith statue with his hammer frozen in mid-air like Thor the superhero.

"Will you take a picture of the tombstone?" Dad said. "And make sure you get our house in the background, and then one picture with me too, okay?"

"In the meantime, I'll look around," Larry announced.

After the photo session was over, Dad started digging with his fingers in the ground between his and the neighboring plot, mumbling to himself, "I have to level the ground here. Otherwise, the rainwater will run inside my grave." And then, he said matter-of-factly, "I found the lady who purchased the plot next to ours."

"What for?"

"In the City Hall, they told me her name."

"And then what?"

"And then I called to introduce myself. 'We're going to be neighbors,' I said.

"Dad!"

"She said that we could play cards if the time drags for us down there," Dad chuckled.

When Larry returned, he shared an observation, "Rodina sure is a popular name. It's engraved on every other stone."

"Rodina is the Czech word for family," I burst out laughing, pointing to our stone, "Rodina Forejtníková means Family Forejtník."

While the rest of my family avoids the uncomfortable topic of dying, Dad's attitude toward mortality is pragmatic, although a bit eager. His mindset was formed on a farm where his parents took good care of animals, but when holidays came, that cute fuzzy bunny, plump goose or colorful chicken ended up in a roasting pot. If something on the farm died prematurely, the remains ended up in the ground, the productive, welcoming ground Dad wasn't afraid to touch. There is no mystery for him: The earth gives and to the earth all returns. Dad's comfort with death taught me comfort in living.

52. The Hospitality in *Hodonín*

The next day, Mom, Larry and I drove to Hodonín, the southern Moravian city which was once located in the center of Czechoslovakia. After the Czechs and Slovaks split, Hodonín became a border town. At one point, passports were needed among Moravian and Slovakian friends and relatives. Now though, since both countries are members of the European Union, both groups travel freely, although the currency differs.

The three of us waited in the light drizzle in front of Zdena's panelák to be buzzed in. Larry and I were curious to meet Mom's good friend since the two of them would soon be visiting California and staying in our house for two months.

The renovated yellow and green panelák with vinyl windows glowed with cleanliness, but the foul smelling, graffiti-covered elevator was a reminder of not-so-flourishing times.

"Stinks like a wet dog in dirty socks," Larry joked, not suspecting that soon the language barrier mixed with Moravian hospitality would put his humor to the test.

"We're getting a new elevator," Zdena's voice had echoed through the building before the cage stopped on the fourth floor. We stepped into a hallway.

Zdena, the welcoming committee, beamed in the doorway, extending a platter with a saltshaker, two slices of bread, and two shot glasses of slivovitz. Mom, feeling at home, stepped beside her apple-cheeked friend. Welcoming visitors with bread and salt is an ancient Slavic tradition reserved for honored guests from far away. Slivovitz is a Moravian improvement of the ritual. I was humbled. Tears crept into my eyes.

"Made from our plums," Zdena winked. "My great-grandfather planted the trees, and when his son was born, he buried a bottle of his homemade slivovitz in the garden. On my grandfather's 18th birthday, together they dug it up. My grandfather did the same for my father, and he did it for my brother, who did it for his son."

The custom required slamming down the fiery plum brandy on the spot. The heat spread through my chest. I blamed my tears on the high-octane slivovitz. Larry tried to breathe out the burning sensation that closed up his windpipe. Zdena and Mom found his hacking and sputtering to be as entertaining as my sister had the previous day when Larry twisted his tongue trying to pronounce common Czech words like švec (shoemaker) and zmrzlina (ice-cream). "I'm here to amuse you," he said simply.

Not all foreign visitors are such entertainers though. In 2008, on Queen Elizabeth's first trip to Slovakia, she managed to insult the Slovak people the minute she stepped onto their soil. She didn't taste the bread and salt with which the delegation, dressed in traditional costumes, welcomed her at Bratislava airport. I'm not sure that the Slovaks have fully forgiven her.

"Please excuse my humble home." Zdena gestured toward the tiny kitchen where a small table was set for two.

The light from the large window brightened the modern, smartly designed kitchen. The top of the washing machine was an extension of the Formica counter, a dish rack was installed above the sink, and the table could be folded and stored on the side of the refrigerator.

"Sit, sit," Zdena ordered, "food is coming."

Larry and I reluctantly assumed our privileged positions at the table, letting Zdena and Mom play the hostesses. We would have been happy with a slice of bread and cheese, knowing that Zdena has to subsidize her retirement by harvesting grapes for the local winery. But I knew, for Zdena and Mom, the legendary Moravian hospitality was a matter of pride.

The mountain of buttery potatoes and crisp golden chicken that Zdena and Mom placed in front of us would intimidate even the biggest eater. Although steam rose from the plates, Zdena asked, "Is it warm enough?"

When Larry gave a thumbs up, she took a half-step back looking thoughtfully, before exclaiming, "Beer! Mister sure would like beer." Mom jumped toward the refrigerator, filled two glasses and placed them in front of us.

"Is it cold enough?" Mom had asked before we had a chance to have a sip.

"Eat! You're not eating," Zdena called out. "It's not much, I know, but please eat."

Mom looked pleased, smiling a bit.

"Cake, or some wine — " Zdena was thinking out loud, the smile never leaving her face. Solving her dilemma, she took charge, addressing my mom by her nickname, "Mílo, two wine glasses!" How comfortable they were with each other,

I thought, glad Mom had such a close friend. Mom stopped washing the lettuce, grabbed a kitchen towel and polished the crystal goblets. Our tiny table was crowded with eight glasses filled with various refreshments, and more were on the way. They treated us like royalty. I wondered how many glasses Queen Elizabeth had at her banquet.

"More chicken coming up!" Zdena threatened.

I looked toward Mom for salvation, but she still busied herself with the lettuce. Even though the food was delicious, we couldn't finish it.

"You didn't like it?" Zdena panicked. "Was it salty enough?"

I began to worry that I wasn't playing my part correctly in this cultural dance. Should I be saying over and over how good the food was? I didn't want to screw up like the Queen.

When I finally persuaded Zdena that we were full and didn't need any more wine, beer, slivovitz or orange soda, she showed Larry and me to her combined living room/bedroom suite while she and Mom took their turns eating.

"Please sit down," Zdena gestured toward the couch. And then, before Larry knew what hit him, she lifted his feet and placed them on the coffee table, "Like in America," she said, "let's stretch those legs."

When she grabbed my ankles, I squeaked, "I like my legs bent please." It sounded like placing an order to a short order cook, I like my eggs soft, please.

"How about some Becherovka?" Zdena asked, and without receiving the answer, she shouted toward the kitchen, "Mílo, two Becherovkas!" Then she scrutinized Larry again. "Would Mister prefer to take a nap?" And with a swift motion, she threw all the couch cushions to the side and propped up Larry's head with pillows. Finally satisfied, Zdena left the room. Larry stared straight ahead with a strange expression on his face, a shot of Becherovka in one hand, a glass of orange soda in the other, feet stretched on the coffee table, neck cranked to a weird angle, head propped with two pillows. He looked like the camel must have looked seconds before the last straw broke his back. I recognized the danger just as Zdena poked her head in the door. "Would you like –"

"Please. No!" I jumped on Larry's lap and wrapped my arms around him. I was determined to protect him from whatever else Moravian etiquette dictated.

"I'll leave you two lovers alone," she said and, with a knowing smile, left the room for good.

After a long moment, Larry said, "how long are they going to stay in our house?"

53. The Wine Cellar in *Prušánky*

The windshield wipers swished and squeaked in Zdena's small Peugeot. Neither the poor visibility nor the perpetual drizzle kept her from accelerating through the curves of rolling hills covered with grapevines. The car's defroster didn't work, so at regular intervals Mom would reach over and wipe the fogged-up front window with a rag, momentarily obstructing Zdena's view.

"This is unnerving," Larry whimpered on the back seat next to me. "I'd better keep my head between my knees. Tell me when it's over."

Zdena parked the car at the outskirts of the village named Prušánky. A row of tightly squeezed adorable buildings with arched doorways that lined the narrow street reminded me of a food court at a county fair. The signs advertising curly fries and turkey drumsticks were replaced with primary colored grapevines, roses, pomegranates, hearts, and roosters. Unlike the temporary food court, these sturdy dollhouses had occupied the same place for centuries.

"They're wine cellars," Zdena said when we opened our umbrellas and began strolling along the deserted alleyway.

"Southern Moravia has countless wine cellars, many registered as world heritage sites," Zdena informed us with pride.

In front of one pretty painted entrance, a man invited us in. We followed him into the deep, wine-scented dimness. The cellar had a vaulted brick ceiling and walls lined with bottled wine stored in ornate metal wine racks crafted by a skillful blacksmith. In the alcove at the back stood a statue of St. Urban, the patron of viticulture. The center of the cellar was filled by two benches alongside a marble table.

"Nice," said Zdena, stroking the cool, shiny top.

"I'm a stone mason. I make tombstones. I got into wine making by helping my father," said the man while filling our wine glasses almost to the rim. The absence of a spit bucket worried me. The bland, store-bought Czech wines Larry and I have tasted in the past always awoke the same unenthusiastic thoughts: *stick with what you know — beer making is your thing.* We're not objective judges though; our taste buds are spoiled by the famous sun-warmed Napa Valley grapes grown practically in our backyard. Southern Moravia, on the other hand, is Europe's most northern wine-producing region. Further north, farmers grow only cold-tolerant crops like beets and potatoes.

Larry and I lifted our glasses. Smiles camouflaged our skepticism. After the first sip, Larry announced, "The best Cabernet in the Czech Republic."

It wasn't about the wine. It was about the joy that radiated from Mom's and Zdena's faces. It was about the traditions that make my people who they are. It was about belonging. Sure, the Napa Valley region produces superb wines. In a sleek, air-conditioned tasting room, for ten dollars, one can lick a drop from a Riedel wine glass, but would the California winemaker raise his arm and lead the visitors in familiar songs honoring their land, like our winemaker did? The first folk song celebrated white wine, a gift from a sweetheart, then red wine, a gift from another sweetheart, and a promise of faithful love to them both. Mom, Zdena and I joined in. The first sip of wine reincarnated all those dusty melodies in my head. The beat of my heart aligned to the beat of my people.

After our umpteenth song and second or third glass, the conversation stirred to rich Moravian traditions. "The *bass fiddle burial* takes place before Lent," the winemaker's jovial eyes twinkled. He lifted his glass, took a mouthful, and continued, "The three-day festivities start with brass musicians and a dressed-up parade strolling through the village, inviting everyone to a dance. A man in a woman's dress carries a dummy on his back, poking fun at wives dragging home their drunken husbands. People dress up as fairy tale characters. Like *Vodník*. Does Mister know about Vodník? The green man sits in a willow tree by the lake and collects souls of drowned humans in his clay pot. Some Vodníks are nice, others like to trick people. But the moment the tail of his green tux dries, Vodník loses his power," the winemaker chuckled and refilled our glasses.

Larry looked a bit confused but reassured us that our animated faces were plenty entertaining.

"On the third day, the drinking and dancing end with a fake funeral procession," Zdena took over. "The mourners walk through the village behind six pallbearers carrying a bass fiddle on their shoulders like a coffin. They're burying happy times before the beginning of Lent. A guy in a priest robe and a sexton in a long white shirt recite rhyming litanies, recalling the previous year's sins of their neighbors." Here Zdena stood up, spread her arms and began her weepy performance, *"Oh, Bass have mercy and point out the ass among us who disposed of the motor oil in our planting soil."*

"Moravian festivities can't go on without music and wine," the winemaker stated, proposing another toast.

"To the Moravian Mardi Gras roast!" Larry cheered.

"To the carnivores and their Carnivals!" Said the winemaker. Glasses rang, sparkles danced in everyone's eyes.

"Does Lerrry know about the chimney sweep, the good-luck mascot?" Mom asked, eager to fill him in. "On New

Year's Day he goes around giving away calendars. People treat him to slivovitz. Girls rush to rub off some lucky ashes from his jacket."

This anecdote reminded me of my American Mormon friend. "She was new to Czech," I shared the story. "On the first day of the year, two chimney sweeps on unsteady feet rang her doorbell, gesturing bottoms up. So she brought them two glasses of water!"

"Oh no!" Mom burst out laughing. "I haven't seen your father drink water in the 60 years we've been married!"

"Water is for fish," the winemaker declared and popped the cork of another bottle. "There is no way around it. Traditions can't go on without fermentation," he said, checking the wine clarity against the light. "You should be here at the harvest festival!"

Not until we parted and the cool air hit my face, did I panic. "Who is going to drive? We're all drunk!"

"Don't worry," Mom said. "Zdena didn't have a sip."

Who could be that boisterous without booze? She sure fooled me.

54. Music Competition in *Velké Bílovice*

Zdena had already gathered speed on the wet roads in the lush Moravian countryside when I discovered that my seat belt wouldn't lock.

"Oh, don't worry, we're almost there. The music competition is in the neighboring village, Velké Bílovice," Zdena stated, adjusted her rearview mirror, and returned to the topic of festivities. "Do you celebrate St. Nicholas in America?" Neither Mom nor Zdena trusted me when I said no, and wanted me to ask Larry. Of course, I'm just an American wannabe. Mister would know.

"St. Nicholas comes on December seventh. Tell Lerrry," Mom said. "Bringing goodies to little kids. Tell him."

I envisioned the procession of neighbors dressed as devils and angels following St. Nicholas from door-to-door with his fake cotton beard, a tall bishop's hat, and a curving gold crutch. My sister and I believed the devils and angels were real. "You and Dad made us kneel and pray in front of them. We hated that." I said. "Once the devil shoved me in his bag and told me I was going with them. You and Dad just laughed, slamming down slivovitz with the good old Nick and his gang. That's when I first realized something was out of whack."

Mom paid no heed to my comment and offered everyone Hašlerky instead. I savored the licorice flavor, thinking about St. Nick who brought my sister and me treats that my parents had secretly bought: two delicious smelling Jonathan apples, unlike those shriveled ones in our pantry, some peanuts, gingerbread with a St. Nicholas sticker, and some dried, cellophane-wrapped figs. Hana and I sniffed the juicy apples before taking huge bites. Mom always declined when we offered her a bite. Hana and I chewed on that Jonathan apple until only the seeds and the stems were left. I was puzzled about the figs. Why would St. Nicholas bring us these leathery-skinned, dried up things, about as appealing to me as a farmer's cracked heels?

Nibbling on those bizarre figs, Mom studied the world atlas, her forefinger circling Italy, Spain, Greece. The faraway lands were so desperately unattainable then, sealed from us by the Iron Curtain. Was Mom dreaming of sunny, happy places, where children eat all the fruit they want, and their mothers don't have to pretend they don't like sweet aromatic apples?

Zdena's car squealed and screeched on a back road lined with thick-trunked cherry trees. I recalled how, near my house in California, I once stumbled on a strange, old tree with little sacks hanging from the branches. Ripe with stretch marks, purple on the outside, ruby red inside with many tiny seeds, I recognized the luscious fruit of my mom's dreams. I called her as soon as I got home.

"A real fig tree with fresh figs?" Mom gasped in the receiver. "How do they taste?"

Zdena cut the wheel hard, attempting to pass a pickup. Larry grabbed on to the seat in front of him. I clutched onto a door handle, holding my breath until Zdena got back on her side of the road just in time for the uncoming car to swish by. Mom, oblivious to this little road drama, just commented on how the cherries are turning color early this year. When did she become so calm? And when did her scalp become visible through her once thick and wavy hair? I resisted the urge to reach and pat her thin, white hair.

"Mom, do you remember when I called you from California when I found the fig tree?"

Mom's blue eyes met mine. "You said they were sweet and delicious."

Like your hugs, I wanted to add. Damn, why is it so hard for me to say what's really important?

The competition was in progress. Men and women in traditional costumes — colorful ribbons, starchy laces, fringes, tassels — crowded the stuffy cultural hall. The four of us were lucky to find seats, although not next to each other. The spectators at the long tables covered with white table-cloths drank wine, but the contest was a serious business. The audience's scrutinizing eyes judged every jump, clap, and squat of the dancer on the stage. The young man's shiny black boots kicked and swirled, chasing after the frenzied rhythm of the fiddles. The dancer's own whistles and yelps cheered him on. Jump, squat, turn, clap quicker and quicker. He spun and whirled. At the end, his hard heels stamped the wooden stage with triumph. Breathtaking, mesmerizing, thrilling! That was *slovácký verbuňk*, an old Moravian dance without rules, an improvisation, the recruited soldier's celebration of his last day of freedom. With daring jumps and intricate steps, the young man showed off strength to reassure his sweetheart and his mother of the nimbleness that will save him from an enemies' sword.

After a short break, during which I went to buy some local wine for us and *kofola* for Zdena, a musician came on the stage carrying an instrument that looked like a seven-foot long walking stick. The *fujara*, a three-finger-hole flute of Slovak sheepherders that is little known outside of Slovakia. The standing musician positioned his fujara between his legs and the wind-like melancholy tones filled the hall. I wondered if the acoustics of the room did justice to this unique instrument. I made a mental addition to my bucket list — to hear the fujara's deep tones reverberating against the dramatic walls of the Carpathians, the expansive mountain range where the flute was first born as a communication device between shepherds.

Even though the two performers couldn't differ more, one devilishly spirited, the other angelically calm, UNESCO registered both crafts as masterpieces of an oral and intangible heritage of humanity.

The performances were fantastic, but my favorite was yet to come, the dance called *odzemek*. A young dancer holding an ax wore light-brown fleece pants with a wide leather belt, a white puffy-sleeved shirt, and soft leather shoes; he looked like a lumberjack in ballet slippers. In front of a wooden log placed at center stage, his movements began gradually, like the stretching of a tightrope walker, warming up, balancing on some invisible line. But soon all hell broke loose. The folk dancer, under the quickening beats of hammered dulcimer and fiddles, turned into a break-dancer on crank. His ax, not the Mickey-Mouse-one Larry keeps in his camping box, but a serious tree-chopping, long-handled weapon swished above his head, ears, and by his legs. It looked like he wanted to chop them off right at the shin, but couldn't decide which one to start with. Should he lose his grip, the audience seated diagonally across the room would lose their scalps, up to the last guy by the back door. The deadly weapon swooshing in the crowded room... How fast can I duck? If the other people were thinking the same, their faces didn't show it. At the end, with a powerful swing, the dancer slammed the ax into the log. The small hairs on my neck stood up. The hall vibrated with roaring applause. I turned, and sent Larry, who sat a few rows behind me, the *can you believe it* look. I was proud of my culture. Those dances belonged to me too. Funny how one feels an association, even a claim to something he has nothing to do with. It wasn't like my grandparents swung axes at our family gatherings. The same as Larry, I had never seen those dances before. Yet, they were mine.

In the car, Larry commented, "Damn! That was better than Pete Townshend smashing his electric guitar! And not even a sneeze guard. The lawyers in America would have a field day."

Our bedroom with two slanted windows used to be the attic of an administrative building in the village named Milotice. Here, 17th century bureaucrats kept up with the finances of the royal family who lived in a nearby Baroque castle nicknamed the Pearl of South-Eastern Moravia. After WWII, the royals abandoned their castle. The new Czechoslovakian government confiscated their majestic residence and converted the castle's administrative building into a post office. After the 1989 revolution, the town of Milotice renovated the post office into a pension. There, Larry and I were falling asleep under a light green Ikea comforter. Mom was spending the night at Zdena's. In the morning, the four of us would go to one of the largest Southern Moravian celebrations, called The Ride of Kings.

"Can't wait for tomorrow," I whispered.

"Do these people ever *not* celebrate?" Larry murmured and rolled over.

Life in the Moravian wine country wasn't always about music and dancing. The locals have had more than their share of hardships. For example, Svatobořice, the village we had just driven through, was burned to the ground three times by passing armies. In WWI, local men were drafted and many were buried in unmarked graves far from home. The mourners built three monuments throughout the village. It surprised me when Mom said that my grandfather's regiment fought in Italy during WWI and he was wounded. I had no idea.

"The bullet damaged his spine, and they had to wheel him home. He never walked again," she said. "He died years later from complications. But he died in his own bed. He was lucky."

I began to bombard Mom with questions, but she couldn't answer any of them. "I don't remember," she said simply. "I was four when he died."

Like rivers carve new landscape, the tears of my people shaped stones into monuments. WWI monuments suddenly became personal.

Another Svatobořice's commemorative plaque reminded us of a WWII internment camp where Nazis had imprisoned parents, brothers and sisters of the brave souls who escaped occupied Czechoslovakia to fight Hitler abroad. Prisoners who violated the camp rules, like those who dared to remind captive children of their last names, were locked up in the morgue for days. Hitler's message was clear: you dare to work against us; we'll torture your loved ones.

No wonder people here live as if a day of freedom is a day worth celebrating. Oh, how I would like to believe that the scale between joy and sadness would stay tipped toward happy times.

55. The Ride of the King in *Vlčnov*

The flawless scene of blue skies with puffy cotton clouds floating above tall green weeds adorned with red poppies looked like the perfect kitsch painting. Parked cars crowded both sides of the narrow country road, some dangerously close to a ditch. Larry wasn't yet parked behind Zdena's Peugeot, and more cars already lined up behind us. Moms pushed strollers, dads carried children on their shoulders, striding down toward Vlčnov, the village where the famous festivity will take place.

"Why do they call it 'The Ride of the King?'" I asked Zdena who was pushing a Coca-Cola can in my face.

"Oh, no one knows where the tradition came from," she said. "It's a tradition. Have a sip. You'll be thirsty."

"People don't care how or why it started," Mom said, panting. "They are celebrating because their grandfathers and their grandfathers' grandfathers did the same. The celebration even survived Communism. Now it's so popular that we have to park a good three kilometers from the village. But that's okay. Traditions are important. They help us remember who we are."

"May they protect us in the world of McDonalds and Wal-Marts," I said.

Once we reached the first village houses, I grabbed Larry's hand and we wiggled through the crowd toward the tones of cymbals and fiddles. On the sidewalk by the brick wall, about a dozen gray-haired musicians were performing. White rooster feathers swung from their black fedoras. Their black vests and knee-high shiny boots accented white puffy-sleeved shirts and pants. Daisies, red poppies, and blue corn-flowers were embroidered on the long and wide ribbons tied around their waists. The ribbons were like cutout strips from the surrounding countryside. Some singers placed their arms affectionately over each other's shoulders, others with their arms wide open embraced the audience who sang along on a beloved folk song. One performer passed a demijohn, refill-ing wine into shot glasses that hung like medals in knitted pouches around the necks of his fellow entertainers. Being part of what felt like a spontaneous gathering of old friends was as satisfying as biting into a hot thick slice of bread spread with freshly churned butter. I would have stayed there forever if Zdena hadn't tugged on my sleeve.

"There is more. Come on." We followed her to a nearby plank stage where girls in knee-high, dark-blue batik skirts and white blouses spun in a circle, red ribbons flowing around their braided hair. Their happiness spilled over in spontaneous yelps. The joyful high-spirited energy vibrated in my bones; these girls were bound to their land through their dance.

Larry leaned closer. "Mike's daughter has taken dancing classes for more than half of her life. Wants to become professional. For these girls dancing seems to be a part of who they are, not who they want to become."

"Judging by their simple costumes, they're from the mountains." I said. The dancers spun faster and faster, their skirts revolving like flat plates; short white petticoats revealed youthful legs. "The richer the soil, the wealthier the region, and the more elaborate the costumes. The Southern Moravian wine regions have some crazy ornate ones," I shouted in Larry's ear over the audience's quickening applause. "The headdresses, the way they tie their scarves, the colors and length of their skirts, all of that tells where they're from. You can tell whether they're married or single by their head covering or by how the lace on their sleeves is ironed."

"Like in the US," Larry said. "I can tell where a guy is from by his baseball cap."

"Yeah. No." I elbowed him in the ribs.

According to Zdena, the prettiest costumes were from the rich agricultural land around Olomouc, but my favorites were always going to be from my grandmother's village, Dambořice, a small southern Moravian community north of Hodonín. We used to go to Dambořice with my parents for the three-day harvest festival called Hody, the yearly tribute to the village patron, Saint Martin.

Girls and boys in traditional costumes would meet in the Dambořice church on Sunday morning. After mass, the procession, accompanied by brass musicians, walked through the village. And what a show that was! Richly embroidered red vests accented the starched, puffed-up, lacy sleeves of the cheery young people. The girls were crowned with tall flowery wreaths and embroidered ribbons. Laces and garlands adorned layer upon layer of wide skirts. In those drab Communist years, under the bleak November sky, the procession provided glitter to offset the grayness.

As a girl I would stare in wonder at their intricate lacy collars, the most distinguishing feature of Dambořice's ceremonial costume. Starched and ironed straight up, the collars encircled the young women's heads, hiding half their faces. I was split between jealous admiration and pity for those fancy dolls. The stiff, tall collars prevented them from eating. How could they pass on the sweet farm-cheese filled koláče baked especially for the occasion? In the puffy skirts they couldn't sit, not even to rest their arms by their sides. They just smiled and looked beautiful, embroidered handkerchiefs covering their folded hands.

In the afternoon they would change into simpler costumes, better suited for dancing around the Májka, the slim young tree-trunk stripped of its bark, its top decorated with a wreath. Throughout our trip, Larry had been pointing out Májkas nearly as tall as the church towers, colorful ribbons flowing off the top wreath which had to be closely guarded. If the boys from rival villages steal the wreath, the locals would have to buy it back with a barrel of wine. A spirited fistfight would break out should the thieves get caught in the act. The Májka tradition was alive and well, but the traditional costumes my grandmother wore had become special-occasion showpieces.

"Where is everybody going?" Larry looked around as people abandoned the show and rushed toward the road.

"The King's procession is on the way!" someone called out.

The horses' clip-clops got lost among the men's shouts. Dressed in elaborate traditional costumes, their rhymes were formulated on the spot, as they requested donations. One addressed a bosomy lady:

"Look at that pretty aunty
Showing her bosom bounty.
Thank you for your donation
For our King's salvation!"

The lady dropped some coins in the horseman's boot. I slipped a bill in the passing rider's boot before he could call on me.

In the center of the Kings entourage rode three girls dressed in especially fancy costumes. The middle girl's white horse was almost concealed by festoons of colorful paper flowers and beads.

"But wait! Those are boys!"

"Yes, the King is a 12-year-old boy dressed in girl's clothing. The guards by his side too." Mom acted as if there was nothing unusual about boys dressed in fancy womens' dresses.

"And why is the King holding a rose in his mouth?"

"That's a tradition," Mom said, "He can't talk."

"And no one knows why?"

A woman standing near us, possibly exasperated by my questions, took pity on me. "Some say that during one of the many ancient wars, the King of the losing army was saved by people from the village. They hid him in a girl's dress, ordered him not to talk so his voice wouldn't give him away, and led him to safety." The lady smiled. "Who knows what really happened? It's a legend."

But a good one, I thought. Czech folklore, songs and dances, are like chronicles, reenacting everyday life, from sowing to harvesting, from weddings to military drafts, poking fun at betrayals and drunkenness. So why can't the Ride of the King celebration be rooted in real life too?

"Historians need to investigate," I said.

Something about the way Mom and Zdena looked at each other — that split second of charitable compassion ignited the light in my head. Facts and dates recorded in text-books can't compete with the way traditions and customs bind people. On those festive occasions when girls and boys put on immaculately ironed blouses embroidered by their grandmothers, and hear that first tone of a fiddle that makes their feet tap, they know who they are. They feel the great blessing of belonging.

When Larry wanted to know what I found out about the dressed-up boys, I said, "It's a tradition, that's all."

"We'll see you in San Francisco," I called out to Zdena from the moving car. Mom and the rest of my family would meet in a few days in Damboříce, my grandparent's village.

56. The Striking Landscape of *Lednice*

Near the chateau Lednice, one of the most visited of the Moravian castles, I negotiated the price at a contemporary bed and breakfast from $68 per night, the most expensive place we had stayed so far, down to $43. Larry thought $68 was a great deal, but he seemed to forget that this is a country where one could treat six people to dinner for 50 bucks, beer included.

The nosy proprietor snooped on everyone's comings and goings from his strategically located desk. The moment the door squeaked, his inquisitive eyes rose above his bifo-cals. Although he gave us a discount, I didn't like him much, so when the hot water from our door-less shower ran into our room, spilling over the new veneer flooring, I only cared because the soap bubbles got into my suitcase.

After the shower, I relaxed outside in a garden chair and waited for Larry. The manicured lawn used to be a fruit orchard surrounding a farmhouse. Located close to the Austrian border, this hot tourist destination used to be the forbidden end of the world for Czechoslovaks. Tin markers with the red Soviet star over the Czech lion's head posted a chilling warning: *State Border — Watch Out!* The weathered relic was displayed among trendy garden decor, a restored oak wagon wheel, and a trough filled with purple petunias.

I stretched my legs and leafed through some pamphlets, *"Welcome to Lednice — Valtice Cultural Landscape."*

"What's a cultural landscape?" I asked when Larry came out.

"Landscape with culture?"

The World Heritage List described it like this:

Between the 17th and 20th centuries, the ruling dukes of Lichtenstein transformed their domains in southern Moravia into a striking landscape. Their castles Lednice and Valtice sit in the country-side fashioned according to English romantic principles of landscape architecture.

At 200 square kilometers, it is one of the largest artificial landscapes in Europe, larger than the current Principality of Lichtenstein squeezed between Switzerland and Austria.

When a Czech King first invited the Duke of Lichtenstein to Southern Moravia in 1322, he couldn't have predicted that through strong vision and smart marriages, the Lichtenstein dynasty's wealth would grow into amazing proportions.

Hand in hand, Larry and I strolled the few blocks toward the castle Lednice, eager to see how Lichtenstein's green thumb and unlimited resources redirected the river, built lakes, islands, and bridges, replanted fully grown trees, built a minaret, a hunting lodge, chapel, chateau, temple, arch, antique colonnade, Turkish spa, Chinese palace... all elements that transformed the area into an Anglo-Chinese garden reflecting the British colonial empire.

We gawked at the grand yellow castle, bright and majestic like the sun in mid-summer. This Gothic palace used to be a princely family summerhouse. We walked past the equally ornate one-of-a-kind greenhouse which, in 1843, was filled with the world's largest orchid collection. In addition, the Lichtensteins sent expeditions across the Pacific to bring back thousands of new plants unknown to Europe and opened the first gardening school in the monarchy, the European mecca of horticulture. Through the greenhouse frosted glass, Larry and I saw outlines of tall palm trees.

We walked through shadowy forests and sunny open spaces. In the words of poet Johan Wolfgang von Goethe — *"...trails became mute guides through the garden."*

The afternoon sun shimmered in the long pool. In the distance, a Moorish-style minaret crowned with a crescent moon looked out of place here in Roman Catholic Southern Moravia.

Larry scanned the brochure, *"...302 steps to the top. The oldest lookout tower in the country."*

Further on, three black and white storks with thin red legs feasted in the grass, a scene straight from some bucolic landscape painting. Decades ago my mom, the visual artist with a poetic heart, decided to come here alone. I imagine rays of sunlight peeking through the crowns of exotic trees luring her deeper in the garden. The birds, her personal orchestra, accompanying her elated spirit. Just what the garden architects intended. The only problem — it was 1983. A shrieking motor and angry shouts slammed her off her cloud, back into Communist Czechoslovakia.

"Stop! What are you doing here?" Three uniformed border patrolmen took my mom, the suspicious character, all five-feet-two-inches of her, to the police station.

"If you wish to have true joy, you must always search for the simplest ways and find amusement which comes from nature, because those pleasures are the only ones that are true and lasting." The Father of the French Garden, Rene de Girardin, may have stated the obvious, but in those days, his words may have gotten my mom locked up for insubordination.

After hours of interrogation, the police officer told Mom that it would be up to the director of her factory to punish her for roaming so close to the border. The Communist gang was either too lazy or too disorganized because Mom's employer didn't find out. Still, she never told Dad about her adventure.

Something was off about the castle ruins even from afar. Although its walls were built with stones salvaged from true medieval ruins, and the remains of the four main towers looked like they were blasted by a cannon, the glass in the windows shone with cleanliness, and the cinnamon colored shutters were newly painted. These pseudo-Gothic ruins, when built in 1810, were designed to look like a medieval wreck. The structure served as a hunting lodge.

We continued our stroll through the forested park. Larry sighed when a bicyclist passed us. "That's the way to do it. This place is too big to see on foot."

According to the literature, the Roman-styled temple, the tomb, the arch, and all the other garden structures blend perfectly with the surrounding nature, *"...Impressive columns mixed effortlessly with the tall trunks of Scotch pines."*

To me, this cultural landscape looked as if a large ivory comb had brushed nature's free flowing hair into a stiff, elaborate hairdo. The fancy structures emerging from the woods continually took me by surprise.

Since the previous day, Larry had not shared my sentiment on negotiating the price of our room, I didn't inform him that our new discounted price didn't include the all-you-can-eat breakfast. "I'm not hungry," I said in the morning, taking my suitcase to the car. Passing the dining room on the way back, I found Larry happily piling fresh sliced pineapple and strawberries over his yogurt.

The proprietor's eyes darted between the two of us. "I'll wait outside," I mouthed to Larry.

Driving through a green tunnel of trees leading toward Valtice, the Lichtenstein family's primary residence, Larry said, "It felt like the guy was tallying all that went into my mouth."

"The all-you-can-eat premise is still new here," I squeaked and changed the subject.

🐌 🐌 🐌

57. The Lichtenstein Home in *Valtice*

Inside the castle, the Lichtenstein family home, a local guide handed out felt booties to the small group of visitors. We slipped them over our shoes to protect the shiny hardwood floor and clumsily skated behind.

"After the Lichtenstein family was thrown out in 1945, the Communist government confiscated their estates," she said. "Because this castle was too close to the border and the government didn't want to attract the attention of tourists, they closed the place down. The adjoining garden, established in 1727, almost disappeared during those years. When I was a little girl, there was only an overgrown mess. At that time, my father worked in the vineyard under the watchful eyes of armed guards, their rifles at the ready."

The bastards managed to hide the entire castle from the nation! Again, I was stunned by what the Communists were capable of.

I committed a major error when I asked the guide if her family lived in the village for many generations. "Valtice is a city," she informed me coldly, her eyes asking, "What kind of feeble-minded idiot are you?" Czechs are edgy about this kind of thing.

"The Lichtensteins got the best of the best," the guide said when she walked underneath the chandelier with gold-nosed, antlered fish driven by angels. "They had modern, often better things than their friend and frequent visitor Empress Marie Theresa had in her Viennese palace." The Lichtensteins got heated rooms, although the maximum was 18 Celsius,

(65F), the same temperature Larry sets the thermostat in our house. The royal ladies in their low-cut dresses would envy my thick sweat pants, flannel shirt, and long-sleeved thermal.

"They had flush toilets, an elevator, a large silver dish collection, furniture made of rare woods, ivory chairs, the best Arabian horses, and their famous gold carriages, the Rolls-Royce of those days. Still, they conserved drinking water and flushed their toilets with collected rainwater."

As the guide talked about the best of the best, I noticed the cheesy faux marble wall-coverings. "Imitation marble was a new invention then," she explained. "The Lichtensteins showed off the innovative, warmer and lighter material."

Next, the guide pointed to a bullet stuck in the gold frame of an oversized mirror. "Russian soldiers who were once housed here did more damage than war and all the years of Communism put together. They burned paintings for heating material."

Larry touched my elbow, whispering excitedly, "Look at this hallway!" The shiny hardwood floor passing eleven rooms was straight and wide. "The kids must have held sliding championships wearing only their socks. I can see them speeding past the countess's room, past the library, slowing to a stop before crashing through the bay window and plummeting to the courtyard below." Larry prodded me to ask if children were allowed to slide down the hallway. What was one more stupid question?

"Absolutely not!" The woman said. "The children were taught family history, horsemanship, piano... They spoke five languages."

"If we could get the horse to sit on the piano and slide him down the hallway..."

Oh, Larry, I thought. The too-many-castles-syndrome.

The Lichtenstein forefathers designed their will to protect future generations so no one could gamble their estates away. The Lichtensteins could use their properties, but couldn't own it. Still, the family lost it all. After WWII, the

Czechoslovakian government declared them German and ruled: Go away — leave us all your stuff — we're not playing with you anymore. During the Communist years, the Lichtensteins, even the Crown Prince, could see the castle only with binoculars from the safety of Austria.

If living 800 years in the same place doesn't secure one's citizenship, I don't know what does. Czechs have a strange attitude toward new settlers, even the likes of the Lichtensteins.

In 2009, after 60 years of sanctions, the Czechs finally restored diplomatic relations with the Lichtenstein monarchy. Naturally, the royals wanted their castles and properties back and presented their case to the European Court of Human Rights. Czech lawyers were quick to point out that in 1621, after losing the White Mountain Battle, Karl I, Prince of Lichtenstein, sent 27 leaders of the Bohemian revolts to death, cashing in on the tragedy that sent the Czech nation spiraling downward. That happened 400 years ago. Czech people are big on holding grudges. The court rejected the Lichtenstein claim.

"Today, the royal Lichtenstein family members come visit the castle regularly," the guide said. With a flame in her eyes, she added, "they buy tickets with other tourists at the kiosk, and I take them on tour."

I swear I heard her laughter echo through the hallways.

The day was still young, and I decided to show Larry the border crossing where 33 years ago my life took an unexpected turn. Our Škoda followed the same road the bus had taken my boyfriend and me, both 19 and naïve, for a visit to Austria in 1978, our first peek into the Western world. The Communist government wasn't issuing exit visas, so getting a permit for a one-day visit to Vienna was nothing short of a miracle, which explained why we were the only passengers on that bus. I was giggly with nervous anticipation. It was just before Christmas and I planned to return home with a special present for my parents and my sister. When the bus crossed the border I glued my nose to the window, watching my gray world gaining exciting new colors.

How the Christmas season in Vienna contrasted with the dullness of my city! The elegant shop windows glittered with abundance. My head spun over the panoply of striking choices. In the bakery, marzipan trolls sledded on chocolate logs, and magnificent gingerbread houses took me straight into a beautiful fairy tale. A deli shop displayed pyramids of fresh red strawberries. Strawberries! In December! I had never seen such a thing. In a famous Czech fable, the evil stepmother tries to get rid of her stepdaughter by ordering her to bring strawberries in the middle of winter, the most ridiculous wish of all. Every Czech child knew there are no strawberries in December. But we were wrong. In Vienna, I saw it with my own eyes.

Next to the strawberries was an amazing cornucopia of cascading cheeses and deli meats. And there it was, the perfect Christmas present. A long, smoked, beef tongue. My dad would love it!

The magical day was fast coming to an end. Tired, and with no money left, it was time to return to the bus station. Once there, my boyfriend proclaimed the chilling, life-altering sentence, "I'm not going back." Something in his eyes told me he meant it. Our bus was scheduled to leave in ten minutes. Not returning on time from a Western country was a crime punishable by a minimum of a two year prison sentence. I had ten minutes to decide the rest of my life.

"If we don't get on that bus now, we can never go home. Ever." My words were coming out thick as if fighting a massive slug plugging my throat. "Never see our parents, our families, my dog — " The slug was choking me. I couldn't talk. I knew that I couldn't change my boyfriend's mind and I couldn't stop the bus from leaving. I grabbed his forearms, but he just repeated, "I'm not going back." One more minute... and then it was too late. The bus revved its engine and left without us.

What had I done? Now we would go straight to jail if we ever returned. That was the Communist law.

From a teenager lost in a fairytale, I became a woman lost in guilt, responsible for my family's worst Christmas. Did my boyfriend even ask me to stay with him? Avoiding eye contact, we wandered the streets, now oblivious to the luster of Vienna, with no clue of what to do next. It was surreal. Perhaps I'd wake up back home, lying in my bed. But the blisters on my heels verified my new reality. It was well after midnight when I remembered what my grandmother once told me: If you ever find yourself in a desperate situation, go to a convent or a church. They'll help you.

The Catholic priest wearing a clerical collar drove us 20 kilometers south of Vienna to the Traiskirchen refugee camp.

"It's a violent place," he said in a quiet, even, voice. "Just last month I buried a Czechoslovakian, an ex-foreign legionnaire. His roommates, also Czechoslovakian refugees, threw him out the window."

A passing truck splashed brown slush on our windshield. I watched the wipers smearing the mud over the glass.

"The legionnaire was a brute, bullying his countrymen," the priest continued in the same monotone voice. "When they complained, the Austrian police told them to solve their own problems. So one evening, when the legionnaire threatened to beat them, his roommates unscrewed the metal bars from their beds and attacked him. Then they threw his body out the fourth-floor window. The police found him in the morning."

In the refugee camp, the Austrian policeman locked me in a large unoccupied room full of metal-framed beds with spotted mattresses. He handed me a pillow, a sheet, and an itchy green army blanket.

"Remember the signal," he said, tapping at the door: knock, knock — knock, knock. Don't open if the knock is different. You're the only woman on this floor full of men we can't trust." He explained that they had to keep the newcomers under quarantine until it was confirmed that we were not on Interpol's most wanted list. The door closed behind him, and the key turned in the lock. I was alone. My boyfriend was held a few doors down the hallway, sharing a room with some of the same guys that had thrown their countryman out the window.

There wasn't a wastebasket in my room, so on the third day I opened up the window and threw out the beef tongue. With a soft thump, it sank in the snow. Perhaps a German shepherd would sniff it out in the morning. I lay on the bed staring at the smudged wall illuminated by a feeble yellow light-bulb.

Seven months later, an organization called American Fund for Czechoslovakian Refugees sponsored my boyfriend and me in coming to the U.S. After three years, my boyfriend and I went our separate ways.

Larry and I were traveling now toward the Czech-Austrian border crossing. The road used to be dead because almost no one was allowed in and out of the country. Today it was dead because a new expressway was built to carry the heavy traffic. The old road has become a seldom-used bicycle path. A section of the 12-foot barbed wire fence was still standing. We parked by the border crossing headquarters, a lone sad-looking building, the same one my boyfriend and I passed on the bus with much trepidation over three decades ago. It appeared abandoned, ill-fitting in the beautiful countryside among rows of grapevines, budding wild roses, chirping birds, and buzzing insects. The peaceful surroundings contrasted with the drama that had taken place here in the not-so-distant past; so many wasted lives, so many families separated.

Larry and I walked around the guardhouse. The upstairs windows were cracked or broken. Larry's shoulders jerked when a rock smashed through the glass. With wide eyes, he looked at me, and then at the shattered glass on the pavement.

I don't know which was more satisfying, my primeval yell, or the throw itself.

On the other side of the building, we discovered a colorful banner announcing The Museum of the Iron Curtain. I'll be darned! The bottom level had been converted into a museum. It was open only on weekends. I was determined to get in and dialed the number listed on the front door. A woman's voice informed me what I already knew; the museum was currently closed. "The director is working at his vineyard, trimming the vines."

"We'll trim them for him if he'll let us in," I blurted.

Within half an hour the energetic, dark-haired man parked his car by the entrance, keys rattling in his hand. He seemed genuinely glad about our interest, waving off my apologies.

The inside of the museum looked as if the captain of the border guard had just stepped away from his office, and the bulky, black dial phone on his desk would ring at any second. An old, massive typewriter, an ashtray, a Communist newspaper, radio, a wall map and a chair, it all seemed so ordinary. A family — mom, dad and a child — were locked up in a cell. It would have had a chilling effect if the mannequins hadn't been taken from the window display of a fashion store: tall, full-lipped, trim people with high cheekbones, mom with long fluffy movie star hair. The child with hands on his hips, modeling for the beginning-of-school sale.

The day our bus stopped here, a bored soldier asked my boyfriend and me for our visas and passports. Would he have locked us up in this cell if he found the undeclared $20 taped to my boyfriend's heel? He just stamped our documents and waved the bus driver on. That was it, the final minutes on our native soil. Later, in the refugee camp, I was embarrassed to tell our fellow emigrants, many of whom climbed mountains, swam across rivers, or hid underneath moving trains, that we had a bus all to ourselves.

Shiny weapons used by the border guards were on display in the glass case. Other devices were too large to fit: lookout towers, trained German shepherds, high-voltage electric wires, motion-detector lights, mines, or the long, wide strip of perfectly raked ground to show footsteps. In the next room, the names of those whose dreams were ended by a bullet as they attempted to cross the border were lined in rows from floor to ceiling.

"There are as many, if not more, young border guards who committed suicide, or stepped on a mine, or got caught in the line of fire," the director said. "They were 19 year-old kids under tremendous pressure, submitted to systematic ideological brainwashing. Ordered to shoot to kill. They were expected to fill certain quotas during their two-year military service."

At the end of our short, mostly self-guided tour, the director refused both our help in his vineyard and our money. But he welcomed our donation to a local drug and alcohol rehab program.

Back in our car, on the way to Mikulov, a nearby city, Larry said, "You had it hard. I wasn't even in the army. I can't imagine living in a police state."

"Somehow it sounds more dramatic now, but we had fun too. A lot of fun. We had each other. Sometimes my grandma baked a duck. The best Sunday meal ever. There were smiles all around the table, mom, dad, my sister, my favorite aunt, my uncle, cousins... If there wasn't enough meat, we filled up on dumplings and sauerkraut. In America, once I baked a nice fat duck with that perfectly crisp, golden skin. The house smelled so good, but all I could see were the empty chairs around the table. There is nothing so sad as eating your favorite meal all by yourself."

For a few moments, we drove in silence. I marveled out loud, "America is filled with wonderful stuff, but there is a price to pay. I never laughed so hard in America like I did back home at jokes whispered about the Russian President

Brezhnev. And my first pair of jeans; I felt so hot walking down the street. In America, no one cared about my jeans."

"You were able to get jeans?" Larry asked, not moving his eyes off the narrow road.

"In Tuzex, a Communist-run shop. With special government printed coupons called bony."

Larry tossed me a questioning look.

"The Communist government needed Western currency, right? They knew that many Czechs got money from their relatives who had emigrated. So they created a store where Czechs could buy Western goods, sometimes even jeans, but you had to pay with coupons called bony. To get bony, you first had to cough up dollars from your rich American uncle."

"Wait," Larry said. "A Communist shop sold forbidden Western goods for some made-up government coupons?"

"I had a friend whose parents escaped to West Germany, hoping that Amnesty International would reunite the family in a year or two. In the meantime, the parents sent Deutsche marks, which my friend could legally exchange for bony, but bony were good only in Tuzex, which didn't sell milk and eggs. He needed Czech currency, so he exchanged his marks for bony, and then sold those to his friends for korunas. That's how he was able to survive, and I was able to buy my first pair of jeans. I waited forever in line in front of Tuzex when the word spread that they had jeans."

"Amazing," Larry said. "Buying my first pair of Levis was pretty uneventful. But then, they were shrink-to-fit!"

On the road, I watched trees as we passed, then I opened the museum brochure which the director handed me as we parted. It advertised a border patrol game. "We could catch ourselves a fugitive sneaking across the border." I chuckled, and then caught myself. It wasn't a game for those who died there. "And the public is welcome to spend the night in a dirty cell. I'm not kidding, it says so right here. Shoot! That could have solved our problem of where to spend the night."

58. The Border Town *Mikulov*

It's been said that the city of Mikulov owes its preservation to Gypsies. The town is unscarred by functionalist architecture and by industrial developers because the Communist government was reluctant to invest in a border town with a high Gypsy population. The government did try to mold the nomads-at-heart into marching socialists, but the free spirits just weren't the best candidates for carrying the Marxist torch.

"I feel the history right through my heels," I said excitedly as Larry and I strolled on the uneven cobblestones up the peaceful sunny street hemmed in by old, pastel-colored houses, some converted into boutique shops or charming hotels, red geraniums overflowing the window sills.

"I only feel my own ancient past through my barking knees," Larry groaned.

At the center of the old town, just by turning in a circle, we saw most of Mikulov's architectural jewels, from the copper onion towers to a Baroque drinking fountain, angels hanging off the column to commemorate the Black Plague. At the outskirts of the small town, between the twin towers of a massive crypt, we saw a curious hill. It looked like a child's drawing, a perfectly round half circle with a peculiar building at its top.

"Imagine the view from up there!" I said. But the strenuous hike wasn't what Larry had in mind. "Go ahead, if you want. I'll wait. I see everything I like right here," he said and aimed toward the patio restaurant where a couple of men drank beer.

Leaving Larry behind, I marched underneath an arcaded walkway around the plaza, stopping by the vegetable vendor to fill a brown paper bag with peas, among the first edible delights of spring. As I continued exploring, I snapped the green envelopes and picked the round, luscious candy of my childhood. Some things, like the crisp sweetness of young peas, don't change. What a shame it would be to cook them instead of crunching them raw. With happy thoughts, I continued in the direction of the hill, stopping to poke my head behind the gate of the Jewish cemetery. Abandoned tombstones stared back at me like multitudes of migrating ghosts. Tired, yet appearing strangely vigilant, some were leaning on their long journey through time. These ghosts used to be artisans, merchants, friends and neighbors in this town. They used to walk the same cobblestones as I did today, perhaps even with soaring spirits on a perfect spring afternoon, not a care in the world spoiling their simple pleasure, the joy of getting home, bringing their children the first sweet peas of the season.

When the Duke of Austria kicked the Jews out of Vienna in 1421, they settled here. With time, as more Jews from other places were ordered out of their homes, they too found refuge in this accepting city, building a thriving community. In its prime, in the first half of the 18th century, over 600 Jewish families lived here. When the rulers became more lenient, Jews could again move around freely, and their population in the city shrank. Out of Mikulov's 472 Jews, 327 didn't survive the Holocaust. All the Jewish people are gone now. Taking care of their cemetery is up to The Association of Friends of Jewish Culture. Their five centuries-old synagogue was converted into a Jewish museum.

After WWII, Mikulov's 8,000 German residents also disappeared. They were ordered to move out, their population reduced to zero.

In the 16th century, the Anabaptist preacher Balthasar Hubmaier and his followers were among those who found refuge in Mikulov. The radical newcomers believed in volunteer christening and communal living without private possessions. They refused to serve in the army. Even though they were seen as eccentrics, they were tolerated, at least for a while.

Eventually, Hubmaier was burned at the stake, and his devotees either converted to Catholicism or disbursed into the world. Today, about 50,000 Anabaptists live in self-sufficient colonies in South Dakota, Montana, and Western Canada. After I looked up their compound on the Internet, I was glad they didn't stick around. The Anabaptist architects' creativity matched that of the Communist functionalists. One could easily mistake their communal homes for state prisons. And that just wouldn't be a good look for Mikulov.

I began to climb the serpentine trail to the top of the round Holy Hill just like thousands of worshippers still do on their yearly pilgrimage. The path was lined by 14 white chapels. Inside some of them, statues and paintings depicted Jesus' Way to Calvary. A few chapels were vandalized, left with broken locks and bent wire rods. Today a person can sponsor and restore a chapel. I wondered if they were un-sanctified, and if there was such a thing. I imagined the holy water flying backward to the priest's aspergillum like in a rewound video. I would think the local artists would like to turn the tiny caves into mini galleries. On the very top of the hill stood the final, St. Sebastian Chapel, with a balloon-shaped roof. The high windows defended the chapel from vandals.

I turned my head, letting the soft wind dry my sweaty temples. The roundness of the hill provided wonderfully distorted views. It looked like I could reach out and embrace the chateau on the other side of town, or hop over the houses nestled beneath me. It was all very pretty, the crisp orange-colored roofs contrasting the white limestone I sat on. Towards the south, the colorful fields of Austria blended with the skies. It looked like a beautiful painted stage.

In my lifetime, a hike to the top of this hill meant an interrogation by the border police. Why were you looking towards Austria? Who were you sending signals to? Are you a spy? Are you planning to escape? The array of idiotic questions went on.

For hundreds of years, people sneaked, ran, marched or were forced from one side to the other. Thousands of homeless travelers migrated through here with great fears and even greater hopes. How many more are yet to set off on their journey? I would have never imagined I would be one of them.

Squinting, I searched for the road that led me into the world so many years ago. Once, in a store near the refugee camp, a shopkeeper, hearing my accent, scrutinized my every move, giving me a bitter taste of being the unwanted, suspicious outsider. I didn't find those distrusting eyes in America. How ecstatic I was to write to my parents that I got to try on my Japanese friend's kimono. And my Pakistani neighbor taught me to make pranta, the flat bread, and my yoga teacher was from Uganda. My multicultural experiences must have seemed outlandish to my family who didn't know what pizza was. They never tasted Chinese food, never saw a four-lane freeway or spoke to a black person. They were isolated from the world, and the world was isolated from them. How bizarre it seems today. Resettlement is the most common phenomenon in history. If not for immigration, the United States wouldn't exist. Its constitution helped evolve America's white Anglo-Saxon facade into a colorful, marvelous mural to which I was welcomed to contribute with my own tint.

I stood up, and with my fingers brushed the breeze into my hair. Someplace back there, over the mountains, deserts, and oceans is my new home. I smiled and began to walk down the hill. I wondered what my Ohio boy was up to.

59. Diggings in *Mikulčice*

North of Mikulov, in the midst of the flat landscape, arise gentle, round hills. They look like a napping giant stretching in a vast, green bed. His snow-white pajamas, the Jurastic limestone, peek underneath his green blanket. In the early spring, after the last snow melted, my parents used to take my sister and me to see Pavlov's Hills turning lavender. My sister and I called the rare and protected flowers the fuzzies. Their Latin name is *Pulsatilla grandis*. The velvety hairs, like angora shawls, protect their stalks from the cold. People come in large numbers to see Pavlov Hills adorned with this unique botanical wonder. But those weren't the only riches hidden in Pavlov's Hills. At its edge, in a small village, Dolní Věstonice, archaeologists discovered a real treasure: the oldest ceremonial grave in Czech territory — a skeleton of a woman dusted with reddish powder covered by two large mammoth scapula bones. In her hand, she clenched the teeth of a polar fox. The treasure also contained a few thousand tools like knives, saws, and screws. Among many ceramic pieces discovered in the area, the most valued is a world famous statue, the 25,000–29,000 year old Venus of Dolní Věstonice. It is the oldest piece of ceramic in the world. Its picture — a woman with broad hips and buttocks, breasts reaching below her waist line — always fascinated the fifth-grade boys in my ancient history class. Funny that in Communism, school children studied in detail the Paleolithic era, yet the curriculum skipped over the birth of their country.

Our Škoda took Larry and me northeast toward another famous heritage site, the Mikulčice Archeopark. Near a small village named Mikulčice, archaeologists unearthed the remnants of the oldest stone settlement in Czech territory. The remnants of an eight-meters-tall and almost eight-meters-thick wall that surrounded 12 churches and over 250 graves were filled with ceramics, swords, gilded bronze spurs, iron battle axes, knives, gold plated jewelry and buckles. This kind of discovery is the dream of every archaeologist. The findings were from around the year 800, the period of the Great Moravian Empire. The prosperous era emerged out of darkness. It lasted less than 100 years, and like a shooting star, disappeared into obscurity. The Great Moravian Empire was a European superpower, its borders surpassing pre-war Czechoslovakia, reaching to today's Germany, Austria, Poland,

Slovakia, Ukraine, Russia, and Hungary. The Mikulčice settlement was likely the headquarters of the Great Moravia Empire, the cradle of Slavic education and culture.

Larry and I stopped in Mikulčice for dinner. The small agricultural community looked like not much had happened there since the fall of Great Moravia. In the farmhouse converted into a restaurant we were the only customers, which should have been our warning sign. I asked the waitress with the dragon tattoo on her wrist, and a t-shirt with I Love LA, what was interesting in Mikulčice.

"Some diggings? I dunno."

From the kitchen I heard her telling the cook, "She wants to know what's in Mikulčice. Those things, those diggings, no?"

"I think I went there as a kid," said the cook.

Within walking distance from their village, archaeologists unearthed the most exciting evidence testifying to the greatness of their ancestors, and they didn't know for sure?

The waitress didn't come out of the kitchen for a long while. In the meantime, Larry went to the car to look for his cell phone.

"Still nothing?" he asked when he returned.

We left Mikulčice without seeing the dinner or the digging.

60. Mowing Contest in *Buchlovice*

From the moving car, Larry took a quick glance at the castle Buchlov peeking through the woodsy hill and declared, "Not enough towers." The bare, boxy fortress didn't look like the fairytale castles we had become accustomed to.

In the pension, a converted farm across from a yellow Baroque church, the owner reluctantly agreed to give us a discount. We were the only customers, so I figured we had some bargaining power. But he got us back. At dinner, he charged us the price from the deluxe menu even though we ordered from the regular menu. Too tired to argue, we paid, and in a way, we were happy for him.

Upstairs in our room, I took a shower, stepping on socks and underwear as I washed my body. Laundry done, I trimmed my bangs with nail clippers and went to bed.

One second we were deep in our dreams, the next we were upright, staring dumbly at each other. What happened? Did someone blast a leaf blower by our heads? A loudspeaker from the town's public address system, kind of a megaphone, pointing right at our window, gargled an announcement: *The librarian is on vacation, so the library will be closed; the butcher has ground pork on sale; all women are invited to a gym class, and the traveling fishmonger will be at the plaza between 8 a.m. and 1 p.m.* After the announcement, Karel Gott, the Czech pop star, sang how he'd show us the road to heaven, and then all was quiet again. Fully awake, we dressed and walked across town. At a little plaza, a group of housewives gathered around a blue trailer where lively trout and carp splashed their tails.

In the grocery store, the cashier asked us for a discount card, which we didn't have. She took a sip of coffee and hollered to people in the line behind us, "Who has a card?"

Larry and I sat on a bench and, with our rolls, scooped up the yogurt from the plastic cups. Together with the Virgin Mary who stood high on the Roman column, we watched the peaceful scenario as it played out, just like on various plazas all across other Czech towns; a few tourists with maps in hands checked out the square, moms pushed strollers, an old man walked his dog. Later, school children would invade the pastry shop, and couples would stroll along hand-in-hand holding ice cream cones.

We walked through the town in the direction of the castle, passing smartly remodeled houses. Lacy curtains with pink and white orchids decorated the windows.

In the book *Hidden Europe*, the author Francis Tapon tells us what the Czech Republic can teach us: *Beautify your town. The Czech Republic is one of the prettiest countries in the world partly because Czechs think about the outside of their buildings as much as the inside.*

He was right. The gardens were adorned with well-kept lawns, hybrid silver-needled conifers, red maples and massive wine-colored peonies. In the side gardens were weeded rows of green onions, garlic, lettuce, carrots, kohlrabi, radishes, potatoes, and strawberries. A plump woman in her 60s, wearing only a bikini, tended to a rose bush. In the corner of the property smoldered a pile of dry clippings. I told Larry the story about my Czech friend's relatives visiting California. "She was at work when her mother and aunt decided to clean up her front-yard. Not just did they both wear only bikinis, they set the raked debris on fire. Of course, neighbors called the fire department. The Czech ladies couldn't understand why the firemen rolled out their hoses and squirted their pile. The cultural shock went both ways. The firefighters probably didn't understand why the ladies weren't wearing more clothes."

With the last house behind us, we entered a forest, following the yellow tourist sign up toward the castle. The trail was steep and muddy, attracting swarms of tiny flies and mosquitos. It was only noon and already at least 90 degrees Fahrenheit. Against our better judgment, we pressed on, too exhausted to talk. At an opening of the trail, we came to a tramp's camp. Young men in army fatigues, some baking sausages on a stick over the campfire, some sleeping on mats in the shade, others just stared numbly as if recovering from a long night.

"Sorry for walking through your kitchen. Lunch time?" I said.

"Breakfast," One of them answered, and with a nod lifted his beer bottle.

We finally made the four kilometers up the hill to the castle. Under a plum tree by the parking lot, we collapsed, happy there weren't any bloodthirsty insects. In the outdoor restaurant sitting at the wooden tables, the thrifty Czechs dug into their lunch bags. They flushed down their schnitzels with Pilsner draft purchased from the open air bar, a strong incentive for Larry and me to get up. We drank our beer and then returned to lie in the grass under the tree. Neither one of us wanted to do anything, so we didn't. We would always refer to Buchlov castle as *the place that we didn't get to see.*

Down in the town, the bikini lady was now hanging laundry on the clothesline. At the village square, the school kids ambushed the pastry shop. The fish monger was gone.

In our pension room, we slumped on the bed and immediately fell asleep. Within minutes, we jerked into sitting positions. This time it was brass instruments playing a funeral march below our open window. A procession of mourners dressed in black followed the musicians out of the church, across the street and to the cemetery.

The cultural center in the remodeled barn by the church smelled of newness. Warm, yellow light spilled over glass showcases with painted pottery and embroidered dresses from surrounding villages. "Please help yourselves," the curator welcomed us with a sweet smile, two glasses of wine and two slices of rye bread spread with aromatic home-rendered lard. I liked this place.

"Our regional museum was funded by a grant from the European Union. Some locals, possibly in a hospoda over a beer, had an idea to send a letter of request. We still can't believe we got it. Now we have this beautiful place to show off our traditions, organize lectures and art shows. We do apple strudel and sauerkraut contests. We organize music evenings, puppet shows, and poetry readings."

The curator named more happenings that the center was involved in, like Night in the Castle, or the Garlic

Festival. I had never heard of The Celebration of Daybreak, the scythe-mowing contest. (Svátek ranního rozbřesku).

"It starts at 4:30 in the morning — "

"What!"

The lady handed me a pamphlet with the program.

4.30 am — grass cutters gathering and honing scythes
5.00 am — leaving for the meadow
5.00–6.00 am — scything meadows and singing
6.00–7.00 am — breakfast in the meadow
7.00–8.30 am — scything competition
9.00–9.30 am — announcing the winners

"Who wakes up that early?"

"We usually have about 250 grass cutters, at least a dozen folk music groups, all dressed in traditional clothing, and hundreds of spectators. It's my favorite celebration. You can't duplicate the atmosphere. Rows of men in white shirts with puffy sleeves simultaneously swing their long scythes, their strong shoulders twisting, each moving forward in the rhythm of a song. The scent of fresh grass is unforgettable."

"But why so early?"

"Because of the morning dew. The crisp, wet, knee-high grass doesn't stick to the blade. Later in the day, it's too hot. In feudal society, barons hired skilled cutters to clear their meadows. It was a hard job. Women walked after them, raking and turning the grass. The dry grass was used to feed animals and supply material for bedding.

"At six o'clock, girls with wildflower wreaths in their hair arrive in a horse-drawn wagon, bringing the men breakfast, traditional eggs scrambled in bacon fat, thick sliced bread, and jugs of cold buttermilk.

"Cutters are judged on speed and straight rows. The meadow can't look like a badly plucked chicken when they're done. It has to be nice and uniform."

I turned toward Larry, "Wouldn't you love to introduce scythes and rakes to our neighborhood in California? Imagine the world with no leaf blowers or lawn mowers. People would save money, get exercise, and most importantly — no one would wake up to the racket of motors."

"If the women would do the yard work in their bikinis, I'm all for it," Larry said, "They wouldn't even have to sing."

61. Grandparents' Farm in *Dambořice*

It was late morning, and our Škoda cheerfully followed the Southern Moravian country road toward Dambořice, the village where my dad's people still cultivate soil today.

As soon as I was old enough to take the bus alone, I spent my weekends in Dambořice with my grandparents, aunt, uncle, and later, three boy cousins. Coming to my grandparents' farm was always a treat. Holding a chick, a bunny or a piglet was a dream come true for a city girl growing up in a panelák. My grandma never asked how long I was staying; she just placed a bowl of steaming soup in front of me, asked if I pray and go to confession regularly, and then went back to her chores, leaving me to roam the farm on my own. I crawled into every corner, top to bottom.

Down in the musty-smelling root cellar, I admired the thick stone walls that had sheltered my grandparents and their four children against WWII bombs. The story once told by my dad haunted me. A four-year-old neighbor girl didn't make it to their family cellar on time. After the airstrike, her mom collected her remains into an apron. Dad heard her calling out the little girl's name, "Rosie, oh Rosie!"

That happened three days before WWII ended. Rosie's memory lived on in that cellar.

Underneath the steep tile roof, I built a fortress of hay where I lay daydreaming, savoring the space I had all to myself. Clusters of grapes drying into raisins hung on clotheslines between the wooden beams, providing me with wonderful sweet snacks. The hay fortress became my reading nook the year I discovered my aunt's book for newlyweds. It had pictures too. By the time I was eleven, I knew everything about sex. I learned that it's okay to have intercourse up to twice a week and that the man always initiates, ideally by rubbing the woman's earlobes. No one noticed my flushed cheeks on my descent from my reading hideaway.

In the basement food cellar, I scooped the bacon liver paté straight from a chipped ceramic bowl with my index finger. The flavor paired well with my grandpa's apricot and plum slivovitz, although the pungent fumes burned my eyes. I first took careful sips, and then full-mouth gulps. Again, no one noticed.

In my grandparents' bedroom, from their ancient armoire where grandma kept her long Sunday skirts and flowery scarfs, I unrolled embroidered ribbons, secretly cutting pieces for safekeeping while avoiding eye contact with the ever-vigilant Virgin Mary framed above my grandma's bed.

I don't know why my grandparents didn't kick my scrawny little ass out of there. Imagine a snoopy kid systematically going through all your stuff, drawer by drawer.

Larry slowed the car. The curve revealed the valley where red tile roofs crouched around a steepled church like chicks seeking protection from their mother hen. My throat closed and through misty eyes, I soaked in the loveliness and familiarity of it all. If Dad were in the car with us, his eyes would get shiny too. He would point to the row of houses and say, "My mom's sister lived in the second one from the end." Passing the stone cross on the side of the road, he would remind me, "It was built in memory of my cousin, František." I would let him retell the story.

"Outside was dark, and I was just leaving my aunt's house. The only light came from František's tractor. He was finishing work in the fields. Suddenly I saw the light blinking. That was his tractor toppling down the hill."

A few houses further Dad would point, his arm stretching in front of my face, "There! My mother was born right there."

Larry and I drove past my grandmother's birthplace. The house looked modern; newly painted, vinyl window frames, a nice car in the driveway.

I remember the village houses used to be single stories whitewashed with lime. The cobalt blue strip at the bottom discouraged chickens from pecking the calcium-rich stucco. The front of the houses had two small, deep, windows, a carved wooden door that no one ever locked, and a wide gate so horses could pull a hay wagon into the courtyard.

Not long after the 1989 revolution, I returned to Dambořice for the first time since I left the country. But the village didn't look the same. Strolling with my aunt, I was sad to see the one-story blue-striped houses had been replaced by modern homes. But there was something else missing. It hit me when an elderly lady in jeans and tennis shoes drove by us on a moped.

"Where are the grandmas in traditional clothing?"

"Auntie Maleňáková still wears the big skirts. But she is the last one," my aunt said. "The old people are dying off, and the young ones prefer jeans. Now, we only wear traditional clothes on holidays."

My aunt took me by Auntie Maleňáková's house. The old woman sat on a crude wooden bench in the shade of a tall pear tree, hands folded in her apron. With her flowery scarf, puffy-shouldered blouse with short embroidered torso, layers of skirts, black stockings and black shoes, she could have been my grandma. I wondered how it was to be the last of a species. I secretly took her photo.

Larry didn't turn right at the statue of Saint Florian toward my grandparents' house where my family awaited us. Instructed by my dad earlier, he turned toward the cemetery. Dad wouldn't let us leave without paying respect to my grandparents. Mom and Dad were already waiting by the gate, a wreath of yellow dahlias in Dad's arms.

My grandma died at age 78. Grandpa visited her grave every day. He sat on the cold stone, slowly rocking back and forth, "Stázi, Stázi..." he cried. My aunt brought him food. Grandpa brought it back home untouched. Three months later the stone mason added his name to hers. Now, Dad recited the Hail Mary while Mom, Larry and I stared at the ground. Afterwards, Dad, who doesn't like to part with cemeteries too fast, invited us for a walk. Colorful, fresh flowers decorated the immaculate plots, creating miniature gardens. Many headstones had photographs and short anecdotes revealing snippets about their loved one's departures. *Our beloved was taken from us way too soon,* or *Our dear son is covered by foreign soil far from his homeland ...* What happened? What happened? I always wanted to know. This time Dad was here, and he knew the stories. I stopped in front of the grave of Marie Maulerová who died in 1922. She was 22 years old. The plaque read: *Dearest, not for long you were granted to be a good wife and an honorable mother. God gave you heavens where pure joy doesn't end.*

"That was my father's sister," Dad said with reverence.

More dead relatives? That shouldn't have surprised me.

Marie died giving birth to twins. Strangely, Dad couldn't remember if the twins survived.

The inscription on the next stone read: *Why can't I be with you here? Why did I have to die when I wanted so much to live?*

"František was 17," Dad filled in. "He died of smoke inhalation while heating the room. His father was a miller. During the war he gave flour on credit to those who couldn't pay."

We slowly walked toward the corner where the botanical garden-like Christian resting place neighbored with the overgrown Jewish cemetery. There, hundreds of cracked and broken tombstones leaned in all directions.

"No one is left to take care of their graves," Dad said. "I was a kid when they came for them. They even took my friend Emil. He was nine, like me. In Auschwitz, less than a month later, they were gassed. All of them."

"How come no one hid them or something?" I cried out. My words came out angry, accusatory.

Dad stopped. At once, his piercing blue eyes pinned my ignorant righteous ass to a shame pole. "Do you think any of us could imagine what would happen to them? No one could! No one would believe it! Not even them." Dad had taken a few breaths and then his words came out soft again, "They were good neighbors. We all got along."

I let Dad, Mom and Larry stroll ahead. At the furthest corner of the cemetery I stepped over some bricks and remains of wire fence to the Jewish home of eternity. Accompanied by chirping birds, I walked through knee-high grass that hid tiny purple flowers. Thorny black locust trees shaded the sloping burial plots. Undisturbed by fancy flower arrangements, gold crosses and pious statues of angels, leaned the blackened sandstones. The Hebrew words were smoothed by rain. It was peaceful, a perfect place to absorb and contemplate. I would have liked to stay longer. On the way out I wanted to say something... something meaningful, but instead I just grabbed a handful of round pebbles, slipped one in my pocket, and the rest I balanced on a half-slab of the sacred pillar's broken, uneven top.

When I caught up with Dad, I didn't tell him that as kids we used to dare each other to run through the Jewish cemetery at night, and I didn't ask if he was among those boys who rummaged through their vacant houses.

"It was horrible," my dad said as if to himself, slowly moving along the cemetery wall, hands tucked behind his back.

"First Hitler declared marriages between Arians and Jews illegal. Nuremberg laws pushed them into isolation and poverty. Jews had to register, turn in their radios, jewelry, even their pets — " Dad began coughing, and Mom took over.

295

"New restrictions came out every week. Jews couldn't leave their houses after dark. In the cities, they couldn't use public transportation, cable cars, buses. Weren't allowed on some streets. Couldn't go to restaurants, theaters, libraries, even public swimming pools, and parks. In the village where I grew up, we had two Jewish families. They were marked by yellow stars sewn on their coats. I didn't understand, but I sensed it was something very bad and I froze every time they walked by. One of the families had a little girl. She always stared at me with big dark eyes. But we never spoke; she wasn't allowed in school."

"The Jewish kids couldn't go to school in Dambořice either," Dad nodded. "But there was a rumor that our Catholic teacher taught them in secrecy."

We walked in silence. Among the section of forgotten graves of newborns, where some ancient rusty metal crosses were peeling and leaning sideways, I spotted wild strawberries. They were almost red. "Would it be wrong to pick berries at the cemetery? Would you guys eat them?"

"That depends if they came with whipped cream," Larry joked. Mom and Dad said nothing.

When Dad finally spoke, he had a tired, faraway gaze. "Even soccer was against the law for Jews. I invited Emil to kick the ball, but he stopped coming. His family took the ordinances seriously and kept to themselves. Emil's dad had to turn in his fishing license, and could no longer raise pigeons. They weren't even allowed in the woods where they could trap a rabbit or pick some mushrooms."

Mom bowed her head, but the sniffles gave her away. "I can't imagine the hell they went through," she said in a small voice. "My poor mother had to lock the pantry from us kids so the food would last. One day my oldest brother broke the lock and ate everything in there. We didn't have enough, but compared to them — "

Mom tightened her lips and shook her head. Then she said, "Selling food to Jews, even a bony little chicken, was against the law."

I stated the obvious. "Hitler wanted to starve them."

"The worst came when they had to close their businesses," Dad said. Here, in Damborice, Christians were better farmers, but Jews were better businessmen. We needed each other. Although there wasn't much business to speak of, some second-hand clothes, thread, needles... A few times I sneaked around the back to buy some sewing stuff for Mom. I was scared, and I was glad when she didn't ask me any more."

"No wonder the Jews didn't rebel when they came for them," I said. "They were cornered."

The four of us drove by the school where the WWI and WWII memorial honored fallen neighbors. Some were gassed, some tortured to death, some died in combat. Others were killed by falling bombs.

We continued on to the park where a stone plaque reminded us of the once thriving community. Although the synagogue was long gone, many of the Jewish houses were standing. With new occupants, they looked bright and fresh.

"It's strange," I said. Such a small place had two communities, two cemeteries.

"Three," dad corrected me.

"What are you talking about?" Mom looked at him. "In Damborice there were always two cemeteries."

"There is also a Protestant cemetery," Dad said unperturbed. "Larry, turn here." He gestured up a small side street.

I was sure Dad was confused. Mom had lived here the first four years of her married life and had never heard of the Protestant cemetery either. Two minutes later, tucked past the last house on the hill, there it was, much smaller than the Catholic cemetery, but equally well kept. The gate was locked.

Protestants, Catholics, Jews. Three groups who believed in the same God, insisted on being separated, even in death.

Mom was reading familiar sounding last names off the tombstones, then she looked at her watch and said, "If we want to visit with some live people today, we better get going."

My aunt welcomed us in front of the house. *"Vítejte!"* She exclaimed, hugging her brother, my dad. I always loved watching them. Their hugs were complete and beautiful, as if they were the very first and the very last. They captured memories, and the joy of people whose lifetimes of struggles were lightened by each other's presence. The brother and sister. They remembered the thunder of falling bombs, and the animal instinct to reach the root cellar, the jolt of panic when someone screeched, where is the baby? Dad, the oldest brother, running from safety back to hell. His baby sister sat in the middle of the floor playing with the broken glass of shattered windows. Their hugs said: Oh, what a blessing to have you here with me!

My cousins with their wives and children now came out to greet us. So many kids! Who belongs to whom? I wouldn't even pretend to know all of their names; there were two new babies since the last visit. Hana, Leoš, Luboš and my nieces were also there, shouting, "Surprise!" Next, we were all squashed in the living room. My cousin Josef uncorked red wine from his cellar. Platters of koláče filled with farm cheese and raisins were passed from hand to hand. Hana and two of my cousins' wives helped in the kitchen. The little ones eyeballed Larry. My aunt's cheeks flushed when Larry complimented the crunchiness of their homemade sweet-and-sour pickles. She added open-face sandwiches to his plate. "Eat Lerrry, eat!" Soon the room became stuffy. It was wonderful, even though we had to endure the scolding for saving our visit to them for the last.

Everyone asked about Linda and Peter who were young teenagers when they spent their first summer in the Czech Republic. In my frequent phone calls during their stay Dad sounded miserable. "They touch everything in the stores," he complained. "Peter skateboards between the cable cars. They don't listen. We don't know what to do with them." One day, Dad answered the phone sounding uncommonly calm.

"How are you doing?" I asked cautiously.

"Great. They're gone," he said. "We sent them to Dambořice."

Now, years later, in this crowded living room, everyone had a story of my two untamed American children:

"Linda always carried around that red chicken. She even combed her feathers. We named it Linduška. Linduška never ended up in the soup," one of my cousins remembered.

Mom recalled her nightmare, "Peter's bed was empty one morning. He'd hitchhiked to Prague to see a skateboarding contest. A group of gypsies brought him back the next day. Without backpack, passport, and money."

"I took Linda and Peter to my English class," my cousin Josef said. "The teacher sat them in the front, facing the class. Kids raised hands, asking Linda and Peter what they thought of the Cold War, our hockey team and our Olympians. They never heard of any of those things."

The lively tones of polka quieted the laughter, and my aunt opened up the window to hear the loudspeaker broadcasting the village news. The voice sounding like an old crackling radio announced: *"Dear fellow townsman, I wish you a happy afternoon. Tomorrow in front of the school, from eight to three, you could have your umbrellas repaired. Also, bring your knives, scissors, and meat grinders to have them sharpened. The feather cleaner will be there to clean down comforters and pillows while you wait."*

When the broadcast ended, Dad said, "In my day, the village drummer made those announcements. With 40 or 50 stops throughout Dambořice, never had anything written down."

The younglings were amazed at that story, and begged Dad to tell them more from the olden days.

Dad began by unfolding his handkerchief, sweeping the crumbs off his lap. When the room quieted down, he pointed to the trays of powdered sugar koláče in front of him. "We didn't always have this much. During the war, we often went hungry. There weren't enough eggs. On the black market people paid up to 70 times the market value for basic food. One day, the German officials came to count our chickens. Every household had to turn in 60 eggs per chicken per year. We weren't allowed to decorate Easter eggs. Everybody had to give a portion of whatever they had: milk, meat, grain, butter. Of course, no one wanted to feed the occupiers, so people cheated. They hid their chickens. Some even managed to hide their pigs. My dad built a double roof in the chicken coop and hid a bag of grain there. One day the soldiers stormed in, turning the farm inside out. They found the secret stash and ordered my dad to turn himself in to the jail the next day." Here Dad paused, looked down at the table and fidgeted with his wine glass. My aunt stopped on the way to the kitchen, her concerned blue eyes pinned to dad's face. Dad took a deep breath and went on. "My parents talked it over and decided that Mom wasn't strong enough to keep up with the farm work and that it would have to be her who would serve the sentence."

Shocked, we all spoke at once:

"I have never heard that story!"

"Grandma was in jail?"

"Where was the jail?"

"For how long?"

"Some neighbors served up to two years. She stayed two or three months. I don't remember exactly. It was in the castle Ždánice."

"Ždánice? Our class went there on the school trip," my cousin's daughter exclaimed.

"Each time I went to see her, she sat in the kitchen visiting with the jailers, a Czech couple. In peace times they were castellans. And because the castle had a jail, the Germans made them the jail keepers during the war. They were good people, and let me stay as long as I wanted."

A story with a happy ending. Sort of. Only later I read in a village chronicle that a 34 year-old neighbor did not survive his imprisonment. Dad left that part out.

Even Mom managed to put a happy spin on her war story. "In those days, we weren't allowed to learn Czech history," she began. "We had to study German instead, and we hated it. One day, toward the end of the war, the teacher asked us to get out our German grammar books. 'Why do we have to?' We protested. Everyone knew Hitler was going to lose the war. 'Just do as I say,' she said, and, holding the book above her head, with one swish she ripped it in half. Within seconds, the classroom was white with flying pages."

We all clapped and cheered as if it had happened yesterday.

I got up, squeezing between the bodies, aiming toward the door. I wanted to see the farm before it got dark. My aunt and uncle walked out with me. I almost forgot how bad her limp was. In the hallway my aunt caught me looking at her leg. "Getting polio was a blessing, even though I didn't always think so," she said. "I entered my marriage full of gratitude. And the feeling of appreciation never left me. Couldn't believe that a good-looking, healthy man would marry me. I doubt I would have the same humble attitude if my body was perfect."

My uncle held the door for us. "We just celebrated our golden wedding anniversary," he said with a grin.

Outside, not much looked the same anymore. The farm was subdivided. A concrete wall ran through the property. A shiny black Harley Davidson was parked where the chicken coop used to be. The animal stalls were converted into tool sheds and workshops. Where the rabbits once were, stood a cage with yellow and blue canaries. "My new hobby," my uncle said.

How different things are now, I thought. My grandparents had pigs to feed, stalls to clean, fields to plow. Their hands were coarse, faces sunburned and wrinkly. Their only down time was Sunday mass.

"No one in the village has pigs anymore," my aunt said. "Not even chickens. It's easier to buy them frozen in the supermarket."

It was getting late, and Larry and I needed to get going. On the way to the car, my aunt thrust two jars of the pickles Larry liked into his arms. My cousin Josef brought four bottles of his wine for us to take. Hana and Leoš shoved a heavy bag on the back seat. "Something for Linda and Peter," they said.

We took pictures in front of the farmhouse, which wasn't a farmhouse anymore. The younglings promised they would study English diligently; we promised we would visit again soon. Dad and Mom, not hiding their tears, stood with arms around each other.

In the past, every time I waved good bye to my family, an image I saw once on some science show popped into my head, triggering the worst case of self pity: a single cell separating from a group swam alone into the darkness. This time, I wasn't feeling sorry for myself. I was smiling, happy to be a part of them.

"Watch out for the rental car people," Dad called out. "You can't trust them!"

Larry started the engine, and their freckly white arms sprang above their heads. I rolled down the window and waved back. After a few feet Larry checked the rear-view mirror, seeing them waving so vigorously he thought they were flagging us down.

"I think we forgot something," he said, slowing down the car.

"We didn't," I laughed, wiping my wet nose and cheeks with my hands. "That's just how they wave."

Epilogue

The next day Larry and I returned our Škoda to the rental place. I was glad to report to Dad that we got all our deposit back.

When our plane took of from the Prague airport, I pressed my forehead to the fogged up oval window, savoring the last glimpse of the forests, rivers, green fields, and clusters of red roofs. I squeezed the round pebble in my pocket and silently recited a verse from a Jaroslav Seifert poem:

> *Beautiful as on a jug a painted flower*
> *Is the land that bore you, gave you life,*
> *Beautiful as on a jug a painted flower,*
> *Sweeter than a loaf from fresh ground flour*
> *Into which you've deeply sunk your knife.*

I am who I am because I grew up in Czechoslovakia. What I love is rooted in the alluring little country nestled directly below my feet: hiking in the woods, foraging for mushrooms, telling stories around the camp fire, reading poetry, painting eggs, picking fruit from others' orchards (which Czechs don't call stealing), even relishing blood sausage, sauerkraut, and liverwurst.

I set out to find why my father was proud when he said he was Czechoslovakian. But what I really wanted to find was what it meant to be me, the Czech-American. I needed to grasp that baffling Czech part. I needed to fill that void.

The clouds obstructed my view and I leaned back in my seat. Larry was scanning through some of our photos. Together we visited over 60 Czech towns, retelling stories revealed by people, buildings, and landscapes. The stories were filled with horror, grotesque absurdity and triumph. We added our own tales. Still, there were many we didn't tell:

We didn't tell about the biggest statue of Stalin on this planet, raised on Letná Hill above Prague, and the Communist government's order to demolish it so no one would notice. The story would be almost funny if it didn't include the suicide of the sculptor and his wife.

We didn't write about the James Bond-like Czech paratroopers who, under the cover of darkness, descended into Hitler-occupied Czechoslovakia to assassinate Reinhard Heydrich, the Reich's top Security Officer and main architect of the Holocaust.

We didn't make it to Zlín, a Moravian city where Tomáš Bat'a, the son of a poor shoemaker, one of 12 uneducated children, became the single richest person in central Europe, with his global footwear enterprise.

How naive I was to think that seven weeks would be enough to see it all. But who would want to say that they'd seen it all anyway? It would be like finishing a fancy box of expensive chocolates.

I thought I would be melancholy for leaving my dear homeland, but I wasn't. Knowing what it meant to be Czech was like standing on a wider, sturdier base. My fresh new memories and discoveries replaced the stale cocktail of uncertainty and self-pity.

The question of who I was seemed no longer relevant. As before, I was still Czech-American, although now, when I said I was Czech to a lady who struck up a conversation with me at the airport, my voice quavered a bit. That's how pride tasted.

I stretched my feet and closed my eyes, suddenly realizing how much I looked forward to hearing the crashing waves of the Pacific Ocean. I was ready to wear a T-shirt, shorts, and Birkenstocks without worrying about the dress code. I wanted to exchange toothy grins with strangers, bite into a tall messy burger, drive my automatic Subaru station wagon among courteous drivers on roads with dividing lines, sleep in my own bed, see my kids. I was ready to return to my comfortable, familiar world.

My mission was over, and the gap was filled. The question of where I belong no longer troubles me. My home is where the soil feels good beneath my feet. Sometimes it is the soft mossy wooded trail behind my parents' house, other times the sun-beaten path along the Pacific Coast. There, among the whitewashed driftwood I'll find a smooth wide log and with my heart overflowing with gratitude, I'll recite a verse from a favorite poem. Sometimes from Jaroslav Seifert, other times from Robinson Jeffers:

> The storm-dances of gulls,
> the barking game of seals,
> Over and under the ocean
> Divinely superfluous beauty...

Glossary

Ahoj — Informal greeting meaning "Hi" and "Bye"

Ano — yes

Bramboráček — spicy, fried potato pancakes.

Becherovka — Czech secret recipe multi-herbal and spice liquor made since 1807.

Čtyři — the number "four"

Děkuji — thank you

Dobrou noc — good night

Domov — home

Fujara — Slovakian musical instrument originally for communication by shepherds.

Goulash— a type of beef stew, heavy on the paprika.

Halušky — potato pasta similar to gnocchi, often served with sheep cheese.

Hašlerky — hard candy with herb and menthol flavor.

Hody — regional cultural celebration, honoring the village patron saint.

Hospoda — pub, gathering place to drink beer.

Kofola — carbonated soft drink produced by the Czech company Kofola. It is the principal rival of Coca-Cola and Pepsi in the Czech Republic and Slovakia.

Koláče — sweet yeast dough pastries

Koruna — Czech currency

Kraslice — traditionally decorated eggshells, Czech folk art of egg decorating.

Kulak — independent farmer.

Májka — tall, skinned tree trunk decorated on top with a wreath and colorful ribbons, a part of the Hody celebration.

Mobile — cell phone

Naschledanou — goodbye

Odzemek — spirited traditional and cultural dance of S. Moravia. Registered with UNESCO organization.

Panelák — multilevel panel apartment building, mostly built during the Communist era.

Paternoster — a doorless, continuously moving elevator with numerous platforms or compartments that rise or descend on a moving chain.

Pension — a boardinghouse or small hotel, often in a private residence.

Pribináček — a popular creamy, yogurt-like snack.

Prosím — please

Rodina — family

Rohlíky — inexpensive, very popular baked rolls.

Škoda — Czech-made auto manufacturer founded in 1895, now part of the Volkswagen group.

Slivovice — plum or apricot brandy, often homemade. Very high in alcohol.

Sokol — the Czech word for falcon. An all-age gymnastic organization founded in Prague in 1862. Provided physical, moral, and intellectual training for the nation. The organization is still active worldwide.

Švec — shoemaker

Svíčková — traditional cream gravy, served with beef and dumplings.

Tvaroh — a popular cow's milk farm cheese

Tramp — outdoorsman, weekend camper, often sleeps under the stars. The Tramping movement is unique to Czechs and Slovaks.

Verbuňk — fast, traditional dance of S. Moravia, registered with UNESCO.

Vítejte — welcome

Vodník — the green fairy-tale character who steals souls.

Vůl — literal meaning — a castrated bull, but Czechs use it as a somewhat friendly cuss word or even a greeting.

Zmrzlina — ice cream

Acknowledgements

Many thanks to my Czech language teacher Jiřina Bartáková, who first gave me the idea to write a book.

To Patti Mortensen, who invited me to my first writer's group meeting, even though I couldn't spell.

To my Lafayette writers' group: Jack Champion, Christine Lavin, Gloria Lenhart, and Sandy Rogin.

To my English teachers writers' group: Diane Cookston, Paul Dalmas, and John Miller.

To Mike Krummes, Jackie Metzinger, Ksenija Olmer, Pavel Soltys, and Laura Vonnegut, who read a few chapters and asked for more.

To my mom Míla and dad Josef, who let me bombard them with questions and graciously answered them all.

To my long-time childhood friend Josef Kundla, who also answered my many questions graciously (most of the time).

Special thanks to DeAnne Musolf, Teresa Peters and Terry Sommerauer who were generous with their help.

Thanks to Michelle Davis and Renata Kobylík who inspired me with their stories.

To Jannie Dresser, Jarka Dušátko, Jiří Dužár, Luboš Groch, Susan Hueck, Jakub Kundla and Fiona Hughes who fell into my life from the heavens.

To my children for their inspiration: Linda Welch, for creating the title of this book, and Peter Polasek for propelling me forward with his — Mom, when you gonna be finished? I can't wait to read it!

Also, Ben Welch, who cautioned me against the usage of big words.

Above all, to my husband, Larry, who has always been my rock and my teddy bear.

About the Author

Lenka Glassner lives in Northern California with her husband Larry. From their house they see the top of Mt.Diablo, the sacred place where they were married.

Lenka is a well-known egg artist of the intricate folk art called Kraslice. She sells her eggs locally and gives lively educational lectures on this ancient Eastern European folk art.

You can see her work at *Egg Art by Lenka* on her Facebook page. She can be contacted via email: *Lenkashue@gmail.com*.